Rewind-Revive-Re-Live

With

The Karmic Rewind

Invoke Brahma – The Creator Within

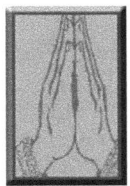

Author – Atam S. Dhillon

Live it as you Breathe for Life - Your Life will Change Forever

All materials contained in this book are the copyrighted property of Author Atam Dhillon. To reproduce, republish, upload, post, transmit, modify, distribute or publicly perform or display material from this book, you must first obtain written permission from the Author. We will enforce our copyrights to the fullest extent permissible under the laws of the United States, Australia, England, India, Canada, Europe, Africa, Asia and any treaties that may apply. Contact us for reprint or purchase of this article.

Edited by – Atam Dhillon (Author) & Neha Kumar (Student of Psychology)

Copyright © 2018 Atam Dhillon

Website: www.TheKarmicRewind.com

All rights reserved.

ISBN-10: 0987263838

ISBN-13: 978-09872638-3-4

Contact – For contacting the author in relation to this book, please contact via the below website

www.TheKarmicRewind.com

www.AtamDhillon.com

DEDICATIONS

'When you are faced with the possibility of an early death,

it makes you realise that life is worth living,

and that there are lots of things you want to do.'

– Stephen Hawking

This book is devoted to the person who saved my life when I drowned and was medically declared dead for 13 seconds on 26th January 1999

'No matter what you do, in no way you can pay back what you owe to your parents, as they are the reason You ARE, only if you think deeper.'

So a Special Regard to My Parents.

What this book is about

CREATE YOUR OWN PROPHECY

The best way to defeat your enemies is to learn about them thoroughly. This book is not a short or quick read solution, have they ever worked for anyone, when it comes to living the life you desire from your heart in all aspects. But I can promise you that once you get to the steps to start resolving and creating your desired life, this will be the book to get you there with quickest results. You will be learning about your life thoroughly and so you will implement thoroughly with a complete understanding and awareness of your life and its meaning and purpose in this creation. You will be mindful and create your own prophecy with awareness.

Most people are reading such books very late in life and only when they become extremely unhappy. Society is failing in this aspect of living happily for one reason or another. Such books and knowledge need to be part of school curriculums for building a strong and humane society. I have divided this book in four parts to make it easier for you to grasp the concept easily and understand the logic that exists in this universe. This book is an expression of my philosophy on aspects in life.

My philosophy as I call it

THE UNCOMMON COMMON SENSE

So you can start to exercise common sense.

Firstly, I have written about common sense, which I believe is not very common these days. No matter how hard we go about telling others how something is just common sense, when they don't act on something as we believe they should as a common practice, but they don't understand. And yet, we may be doing the same in our own lives. The only difference is that we do not like telling ourselves that we are not following common sense. Even more tragic is that we are acting in that manner for the really important instances and decisions of our lives. I will help you change that.

The second part of this book is to help you understand the circumstantial design of life and life in its own essence from a detailed and consequential point of view. How the decisions you make and actions you take or even how you react to certain circumstances, affect how the following moments will unfold in your life. The life is surrounded by the probabilities converting into realities based on your actions. Those probabilities form the sphere of life that unfolds into your reality.

I call it the FPS

FUTURE PROBABILITY SPHERE

The soul has travelled through the universe to enjoy Life, Happiness and Love on this planet. So, understand who you are, how things work in harmony with the universe. I am presenting to you a powerful tool that will help you Know Thy Self, understand your inner self, the law of Karma and apply the changes one needs to be able to live an abundant life. It will help you REWIND, REVIVE and RELIVE your life for what it was always meant to be. Live Life, Don't just Live By.

That powerful tool is

THE KARMIC REWIND

In the last part I will focus on

TIME FOR FOUR CHANGES

All we need to be able to achieve something different is to make a change somewhere, somehow. As a result we are sure to see some changes in the physical form. But, that is the biggest challenge we face - how to make a life changing change? I have given my best to help you in finding and implementing that change using baby steps and incrementally grow into big changes in life.

We are living in a trend of losing health for wealth and then losing wealth for health. We need to correct this problem and have our life back so we can live it as it was always meant to be.

> *'Money is the most envied, but the least enjoyed.*
>
> *Health is the most enjoyed, but the least envied.'*
>
> Charles Caleb Colton 1780-1832, British sportsman writer

I changed the way I looked at circumstances and situations in life and at life as a whole. I have always been a confident, positive and optimistic guy since my school days. My friends knew they could count on me and I knew that some of them were very reliable while others were the type who would run in a flash when trouble comes to you. Yet, did I ever take that as an offence n their part? No, because I was brought up in an environment where we were taught to be respectful and humble all the time. At a very young age I had already realised that it is not the people themselves who behave in that manner, it is the circumstances around them that have caused them to mould into the personalities they are today.

I will help you realise and understand what the root cause is for what we are today, the kind of life we live, the kind of habits and behaviours we have. It's all what is fed into our mind, our brains, directly or indirectly, consciously or subconsciously, intentionally or un-intentionally, and it all matters.

Read this book as importantly as you breathe air for life every day, the air as a whole is not what makes the important part of your breath; it is the Oxygen component of it. Ever wondered where that came from? Ever wondered we are not billed for it? Thus, I believe it is time to start showing gratitude towards whoever it may be that created us, and all the rest which was needed for our survival. Be thankful to God, and if you don't believe in God, then I am sure you can be thankful to all those circumstances, those people, those things that appeared out of nowhere at times to help you at some stage in life in some way. I am sure we all can relate to such instances, we just need to think deeper, think hard and realise.

Know that this book will Motivate you to achieve what you thought was impossible. But also know that –

Motivation is only Positive Fiction Until Practically Realised to become a Real Life Story.

So, *'Don't just read this book, live it.'*

I must insist – *Live it as you breathe for life, your life will change forever.* The tools that I will provide to you through this book are so powerful, all you need to do is read it with your true heart.

'Read it as you breathe for life every day

Take in the contents as you eat for living every day

Drink it as you drink water for dilution of concentrates inside you

So you stay healthy as you look after your body every day

Exercise it to look after your future circumstances the same way.'

This book shall invoke the creator within you. When Mystics say – 'God is within', then why not let's connect with him and invoke the creative powers through him, possibly just like God did in the very start of the creation. Let's Create with Mindfulness by understanding life in a logical manner.

Invoke Brahma - The Creator Within

As per Hindu Mythology, there are three powers at work in this Universe for the purpose of Creation, Preservation and Destruction. And these powers are the responsibilities or roles at the highest level given to each Deity (Gods with specific roles) by the supreme Lord as per Hinduism. Lord Brahma is the Creator, Lord Vishnu is the Preserver and Lord Mahesha (also known as Shiva) is the Destroyer. More so in the modern age, these deities are prayed to more in the temples than within. As God created Human in his own form, using the external mediums we were to realise the creation within the temple of this body. Those who realise that purpose have realised God than those looking for him outwards. Using the same concept, I want you all to use this book as the external mean to realise your Inner Core, your inner self.

Just Like God is within, so is Brahma being a part of God. To me his Three Faces signify one keeping an eye on the past, two, visualising the future and three based on those two, creating or living the present. So let's invoke Brahma within and consciously create a beautiful present. Let's Invoke the Creative Powers of Brahma within through the medium of Karma. Let's become the Creators in control rather than dealing with life out of our control and build a world of abundant happiness all around.

Table of Contents

GRATITUDE: A MUST 1

THE UN-COMMON COMMON-SENSE 13
- THINKING THE DIFFERENCE 16
- BRAIN CONDITIONING 21
- UNIQUE INDIVIDUALITY 25
- HUMAN GOOD AND BAD BEHAVIOURS 27
- ROLE OF HUMAN NATURE 30
- MATTER OF BELIEF 38
- PARENT'S ROLE AND EDUCATION 41
- EMPOWER YOUR WITHIN 44
- BE MORE THAN JUST BEING 52

FUTURE PROBABILITY SPHERE 59
- STANDING FIRM & TALL ON YOUR FEET 75
- DEFINE YOUR FPS 81
- THE LAWS OF THE UNIVERSE 82
- PUT THE LAWS TO WORK FOR SUCCESS 86
- UNDERSTAND SUCCESS – WHAT IT MEANS FOR YOU 89
- WALK YOUR THOUGHTS TECHNIQUE 92
- BELIEVE THY SELF 101
  - *Future Probability Sphere – For Daily Visualisation* 110

THE KARMIC REWIND 117

THE KARMIC THEORY 119
- CHAKRAS OF HUMAN BODY 129
- GOD – THE GREATEST EXPLORER 141
- THE RE-INCARNATION 145
- KARMIC BALANCE SHEET 150
- DESTINY WITH KARMA & MIGHTY NATURE 152
- TIME AND TECHNOLOGICAL BALANCE 156
- HUMANS: MORE THAN WHAT WE THINK WE ARE 162
- THE KARMIC REWIND 172

REALISING YOUR OWN SELF	174
HOLD YOURSELF ACCOUNTABLE	176
FAITHS, BELIEFS, FRIENDS AND SELF REALISATION	178
ART OF PURSUING YOUR GOAL	185
OVERVIEW OF THE KARMIC REWIND TOOL	194
BOOK OF YOUR LIFE - YOUR MAP	197
YOUR BOOK OF LIFE - YOUR MAP (WITH EXAMPLES)	214
Step 1 - Identify Existence of Your Self and Your Life	*214*
Step 2 – Identify and Plan for All Aspects of Your Life	*238*
ACT TO MANIFEST – REWIND, REVIVE, RE-LIVE	304
TRAIN THY BRAIN	306
TIME FOR FOUR CHANGES	**319**
THE FOUR FACTOR	324
REALISE THE POWER WITHIN & OUR TRUE ESSENCE	328
BEING POSITIVE	329
AUTOMATIC EFFECT	330
REWIND TO FAST FORWARD	332
TRIGGER & INITIATE CHANGE	334
CHANGE -1: GIVE YOURSELF TIME FOR YOURSELF	337
Step-1: Close All The Doors –	*339*
CHANGE -2: CREATE A LIST OF FOUR DESIRES TO FULFIL	346
CHANGE -3: DECISION MAKING WITH TRUE HEART	356
THE POWER OF MIND, LOVE AND HEART	364
CHANGE -4: TAKE ACTION IN STEPS	366

Acknowledgements

I am really grateful and thankful to the master I have followed ever since I was a young child. My life has always been guided by his teachings. It is him, who I respect and admire the most.

I really appreciate my parents and the efforts they have put in to develop me into what I am today, for setting the basics right, for building the foundation in me by which I can stand with humbleness for the rest of my life.

I am deeply thankful to the person who saved me from the troubled waters and revived me to re-live before the ambulances would have had to cope with another dead body. I thank deeply for my whole life to this messenger of God, my saviour angel.

My little daughter Vani, her smiles and cheeky ways, put a smile on our faces every day. I do regret taking time away at times when she wants to play with me. And I love my wife for being the soul mate I had once asked for from God and for all she has done to support me in setting things right for the right way of living life.

Thanks to Neha Kumar, who studied psychology at University of Canberra, for her help in editing of the book. I acknowledge her time spent on my book even during the exam times of her semester end.

Thanks to everyone else and everything else that has contributed towards my learnings in life, including all my teachers from school times till the days of the modern world of computers.

Thanks to all those great people who have helped the world through their valuable quotations. I have acknowledged them in this book, and my quotes in this book mostly do not display my name except in places needing **to distinguish from another quote.**

Gratitude makes sense of our past, brings peace for today, and creates a vision for tomorrow.

---Melody Beattie

Gratitude: A Must

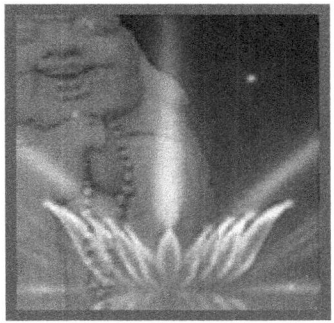

We don't need to look far to be thankful to someone; we just need to look with deeper thoughts. Just need to see clearly what we have, who we have around us, and how much our life is connected with them, the things we do, the people and possessions we have and the most precious - the life we have. We need to learn to appreciate them and show gratitude. My personal story below will somewhat help you on that path. I am thankful to be alive after being declared medically dead in 1999. The person who saved my life is unknown till date but he is the one who gets the credit for being the medium for me being alive today. Through this book I also hope to find that person.

Back in 1999 on Australia day 26th Jan, I went to the beach with some friends. We all had a really nice day having fun, playing with the waves. But let me tell you that I did not know swimming back then. I know a lot of you may be thinking 'ow owe.. This is going to be a tragic story!' Let me assure you, you are right, but do I have someone or the waves to blame? No, just my own lack of knowledge, skills and a bit of ignorance in not realising how dangerous the water could get.

However let me also assure you that I was no risk taker then and was known as a wise and sensible guy. So how could I have done something silly to be able to cause me such harm? So here we go, I was not entirely responsible for this; it was a tiny play up by the almighty nature through the medium of ocean, making sure that a destination set by destiny was reached.

We were playing in the waters and decided to call it a day. We all wanted to go and change clothes but with the amount of bags and other belongings we were carrying; it would have been a hard task to carry along to the change rooms and then to where we had parked. So, a friend Yogesh and I decided to stay there and keep an eye on the belongings until the others change and come back. We would then go and change. But while waiting, something triggered in our mind, we walked into the waters and started to play with a ball. The water was only about knee high then. Do you see any risk in it so far? I didn't, however there were some facts we were not aware of. Facts such as the beach we were at was a surfing beach, Life guards were gone and there were no flags for safe area after a certain time, the fact that at a surf beach, waves can rise really high all of a sudden. We did know that we both don't know swimming. Now you may have a bit of an idea what I may have gone through that day.

As we were both simply playing catching the ball in fairly safe waters in terms of depth, we were hit by a strong wave all of a sudden, and the water came up to our waists, we thought this was ok still but decided that we would start walking out. Just as we started to leave we were hit by another wave, raising the depth of water to our shoulders unexpectedly. 'Oh dear', we thought, 'this is going to be dangerous'. My friend Yogesh started to wave hands for help, I could still feel my toes touching the sand and I could manage to keep my face above the surface of water. I thought foolishly in my mind that 'Don't worry too much' and told the same to my friend while offering my fingertips to him. He seemed a bit behind me but I thought we could try to escape by relying on little jumps I could do on our toes. His face seemed a bit too worried, but not thinking another wave could strike, I had the feeling that we could manage to get out.

But then, another wave struck! This time what chance do you think we had? None really. With my only skill of swimming, that I could float, I decided to float with the next wave in hope that it would push me out towards shore, as that's what would happen in most case scenarios with normal waves. Then again, did I know they are not normal waves? Did I know that I am supposed to swim parallel to those waves to be able to escape? No. I surely do know that now and do know better swimming than back then but at that point in time I did not have the skills and knowledge about riptides. So, when I started to float with those riptides, guess what may have happened. If you know swimming then you may know what I went through. I was rolled in with the rip tide! Out of panic I could feel the water going inside me through the nose and mouth; I was not able to breathe. That horrific feeling which I had at that point in time was not easy to handle. The one and only thing I still remembered at that time was to be *thankful* to God. 'Why?' You may ask, thinking I wasn't having any amusement in going through that incident! But here is an example of how our brain works. I was born and developed with the teachings where we learned to be thankful to God for each and everything we have in life and what destiny brings to us.

So, at that moment of life, my friends, I realised something, something that was so powerful and so strong, which has changed my whole life since the incident. I realised I was going to DIE! And let me tell you one thing; that was probably the easiest moment in my life at that time. You may be thinking, what is wrong with this guy! But, why I say this is because, that was one moment in life that I did not have to choose something or decide on something compared to times when I would think in detail before taking any further step. Isn't it easy when you do not have to make a decision? Or so it seemed to me, a 19 year old, in that moment, compare to the hard decisions of life I was facing as a young migrant with no financial support, in a new country with a very different culture and no family around me.

'I simply knew I was it!'

I wonder how many of us have that sort of experience during our lifetime? Probably not many of us, however yes, there are some. I am not counting those who may have experienced it while crossing the road via a pedestrian crossing, when a car stopped just seconds away from them. The instant feeling/thought of death may have flashed before their eyes instead of thinking that 'I was almost hit by that car'. Hopefully you know what I am talking about. Not many of us go through that actual moment. We may think or we may wish at times that we could die, but fellows, that is not what life is about!

'Life is about living and giving it the best you can,

to get out of it the best you can.'

So there I was, about to die, as I was drowning with the waves. So, all I did then was to remember the spiritual master we followed in our life. I remembered him in my mind, visualised his face, and thanked him for his guidance in life and for helping me realise that there is a supreme power which controls the world in harmony from a higher region, which we as human beings fail to understand miserably. We learned all our life that if we tried to live our life following those principles, we would achieve what is referred to as Salvation of The Soul or Nirvana. So I remembered him and thanked him for everything and said these exact words - 'Thanks master for everything, it seems like all is done, OK then Bye'.

What do you think I meant by those words? I thanked him for everything I had in life and thanked him for my life being ended with contentment under his guidance. We have a famous saying by one of the great mystics of India, which means 'It is where your thoughts reside in the very last moment of life, that there you shall be born again'. This was an important quote that always lived in my mind and hence when I got to that moment in Life, this quote was so rigidly impressed in my brain that it automatically came on to the top when I realised that I was going to die. And this probably should also tell you about what I want out of life – to achieve Nirvana, to achieve salvation of the soul, but can you do it if you are thinking about only worldly things as we do every day?

Thinking materialistically is going to leave the last moment thought in our brain of something that we wanted or goals we never accomplished in life. We may have to be born into this world again to fulfil those desires. I have lived my life while believing in those teachings from the Mystics. You do not necessarily need to wait until you find the truth in those teachings as this can also be taken up as a way of life. And if, you choose to live your life the way you want, you just need to ensure this is helping you in gaining peace and happiness. If you are not achieving that peace and happiness, that means there are things you need to change.

Happiness brings success not vice versa.

So that is what happened when I went through that tragedy up until that moment of thanking God for everything. The next thing I knew was I was lying upside down on the beach, sand all over my body, the blurry view of ambulances in front of my eyes just across the beach on the street side. The ambulance officers rushed me on to the stretcher and started taking me towards the ambulance. In about 2-3 seconds, the first thing I uttered when I regained enough consciousness was 'where is my friend?' and straightaway the ambulance officer addressed my concern by telling me not to worry and that he (Yogesh) is all right and inside the ambulance. A nurse told me later that I was MEDICALLY DEAD FOR 13 SECONDS! Wow! What? Yes, I was medically dead for 13 seconds and was saved by some great soul who happened to be there as an off duty ambulance officer, as I was told. He had me out of waters and revived me to live the life I am living now, the second inning of life.

There were no lifeguards present at that time but this gentleman appeared from somewhere to save my life that day. I call him an angel sent by those protecting me from higher up in the spiritual regions. It is the fact that he was seen nowhere nearby after that incident and his resemblance, as explained to me, came close to some sort of holy man, which has made me believe in God and his angels even more. Taken from the beach, I was kept in the ICU for three days and survived that incident. Many of us may call this to be a horrible incident, but did I? No. Did I then become scared of waters and never go to a beach again? No. I ensured that all those scary thought provokers around me, who discouraged me to never go to the beach or deep waters again, didn't influence me.

I didn't listen to them. I held on to the way I thought about life and passed over it as just an accident, which was meant to happen but learned to be grateful of life. It was an incident that also happened somewhat because of our own partial knowledge, lack of skills and some missing information. I hope that this may help you in being grateful in our daily lives, towards the things that we generally take for-granted. The love, the affection, the air and water which are part of the absolute essentials in our life and yet, in some parts of the world, it is taken so much for-granted that we start to waste it. On the other hand we have places where people would walk miles to get some water, people would line up at the corner of their street while a water tank from the local municipal committee comes to deliver water, and it is of no surprise if the water is short of expectations in filling the buckets of all the people. You just need to look at some places in Africa or Asia and some deserts in some Middle Eastern countries.

The food is aplenty in the western world yet there are others who may be struggling to see food on their plates. I often read stories from different parts of the world where someone has sold their kidneys or certain other part of the body for money to ensure the survival of their family. I once read a news article in which the UN revealed the shocking news of 30,000 children dying in just one month - July 2011 in whole of Africa. Another painful story in Somalia where there were people dying of drought, they had been walking for days to flee their home towns and reach the camps set up by the United Nations for help. There are people who stay away from home almost every day to earn a salary just enough for their families to survive. They may not get to see each other very often yet their whole life is spent working hard for their family.

We just need to learn more about the people living on earth in its whole self rather than being central to our own demands and needs. As human beings we will never be short of our needs and wants. We just need to learn to be thankful for what we have and learn to live in harmony, peace and contentment. Once you have peace within, you will always be content and you can always achieve what you want.

If you've watched the movie series of Kung-Fu Panda, I really like the way they've added the idea of 'Finding the Inner Peace' so the great warrior could achieve the assumed 'impossible'. You can only be at peace when you learn the art of being content, have gratitude, align these with continuous efforts towards the purpose of your life and goals, and you have the recipe for a happy and peaceful life. You can achieve anything with those ingredients whether it is love, happiness, money or the enriched and empowered life of abundance.

To help you get started on thinking a little deeper into your life to pick few dots to connect to be mindful about what surrounds you in life, I will talk about few minor but impactful things in my life. Spend some time with the associations you have around you in your life and see what relevance you may be able to derive from them. Look for little things in life; many times in your life there will be things with which you may realise you have some peculiar association with. At other times it may just seem like a coincidence but by putting some emphasis on those you may find them to be your guiding force.

I would like to mention that I had this habit of scribbling. Now this is a habit a lot of people may have however, I did not scribble my signature, which is sometimes linked to not having found your true self yet or any other belief people may have. Instead, what I always did was that I made five dots and just repeated them in three different shapes – the letters M and W and a five-pointed star. Now I do not know at all how or from where that had come into my mind but I always had these unconscious repetitions – the repetition of scribbling letters M and W, the shape of a star, and also noticed that most people's names around me had the initials M and R.

I know for sure that these two initials have become very much associated with my life. M has become Mansha - my wife's name after marriage from her parental name which started with the initial R, and W has turned out to be the profession I had chosen which made me happy and something I would enjoy and love to do – Writing and the Web Entrepreneurship. I have been and will continue to put my 200% effort into making these goals a reality. I am fully determined to make those web businesses a success. Some projects are fully dedicated to serve the humanity for the better. I would encourage signing up on my website www.AtamDhillon.com so you may know and can participate in future programs which will encourage helping each other as a human race.

I am starting out with a community based website, touching on an idea globally, and I am sure we will learn some lessons from that before we launch into more commercialised ideas. It is a plan for my life and I want all of you to have one too. Just as you do not build a house without a house design and an architect plan, do not build your future without a plan. An unplanned life can take you anywhere spontaneously. Unexpected and unplanned things may still happen; be ready for them with an acceptance mindset; but a planned life will take you in the direction of the goals you want to achieve. The universe will embed destiny where it is meant to but if you plan well and follow up with your true heart, at the very least you won't have any regrets.

If you do not take charge and do not plan now, at some stage in life you'll be standing in front of the mirror and saying 'I wish I did that'. Just like the plans for a house are important because you have to rely on and work with others – the bricklayers, the labourers the carpenters, electricians and plumbers; you have to rely and depend on others; in the same way you'll have to deal with people of various kind in life. Some will solely bump into you to hinder you off your dreams and goals while others will help you to get there. Having a plan and a plan well set and clear in your mind will always keep you on track to build the life you want. So, think deeper and plan today for the life you want to live, the life you want to build.

Another association I realised with the letter R is that since I was born I have almost always been associated with this letter. R is the initial of something, which is very close to me in my spiritual life. It has guided me throughout my life. And then when I started to think more on this, almost every one close to me, my family and friends, all had either their or their partner's name starting with the letter R or M. My wife's maiden name had initial R; as it is sort of a tradition in our culture in which girls have their name informally changed with their consent to a name her in-laws may like. That is how I gave her the name Mansha beginning with the letter M. It was not intentional then, but now I realise how that may have come up from the back end of my mind somewhere.

Not just that, there are a lot of people who come and go in our lives, some of them play some important role which affects you and your life in some way; we should be thankful to them and show some gratitude towards them. In my life there definitely have been such people and most of them have been people whose names begin with the letter R. Though, am I now superstitious about the names starting with any particular letter? No, I am not. Yet it does have some significance in my life, when I think deeper and hard enough to realise. One just have to start looking. Even where we live, we have very close ties with four families which live nearby and each have one of the couple's name initial as R, and apart from them there are two other friends who we see on weekly basis and have their names starting with R as initial; my sports coach teacher Mrs Renu, who played a significant part in building the sportsman spirit.

Let me now also explain the philosophy taught by my Nana, I attach with the meaning of my name. The meaning is, Atam=Self, Jeet=Win (winner), Singh=Lion. This meaning, "Self Winning Lion", encoded the belief in my mind that I must match my character and personality with the meaning of my name. And as it turned out to be, my belief in that naming strategy kept growing and became strong. Because of those beliefs I had started to treat myself as a very self-independent kind of person. The sense and feel of responsibility always helped me develop a personality that is helpful to others around me in my full capacity.

However sometimes I felt very much unappreciated and made me feel as if I was taken for granted, but I always had believed in who I am and the theory of karma. I tried hard to not let myself develop into a volatile personality, and I could not afford to when looking at the challenges I had to face in my life.

At one stage though just a few months after the beach incident, I felt so lost in the battles of life and thought that suicide was the way out. I attempted to cut my right wrist vein as it seemed that I had lost a do or die situation in life. My whole life and family seemed to be dependent on that at the time. The opportunity that I was handheld into and then attempted a push out by the same person for the financial benefits. I still have stitch marks on my arm. But, a little later I realised that, it was all amateur thinking at the age of nineteen and did not think hard to realise that it would have caused even worse scenario. However at that point in time, I seemed to have bowed under the pressure of facing a failed life ahead, living with the fear of some serious loss. I survived with a friend's help, who took me to the doctors, got the stitches done and gave me some moral support that mattered to me the most at that moment of time.

Since then, I realised that we are much more than sometimes we think of ourselves under certain circumstances. I have turned out to be much more strengthened since then. That is what I kept telling me in those times when I felt I was taken advantage of and no appreciation. I still do that and say to myself - 'my teachings do not allow me to start hating someone just because they are not a person large hearted enough to appreciate my helping hand.'

I cannot stop extending my helping hand to others when they may need, as it may disadvantage a person who may be in real genuine need. And if I did not do something for them and later found out that my help could have gotten them out of troubled waters they are in now, I may not be able to forget that for the rest of my life. Yet, when it comes to me being taken for granted, I always align that with the Karmic theory. It must be a Karmic payback for me towards that person. And even if you do not believe in the theory of Karma, just imagine, what would you do except holding a grudge against that person and waste some of those moments of life that you could quite simply convert to some happy moments with your family.

You can just shift your attitude a little towards that thought that comes into one's mind after feeling betrayed or taken for granted. Just acknowledge but do not focus on the negative that has happened, rather create something positive, just think that it's better to know the truth about those people now than later. Turn to something that you love to do, and your mood will change, your mind will be taken off towards something better and positive. I am grateful to God to have me out of those shock waves in life and help me learn some important lessons very early in life. So be grateful and learn lessons to improve in life, don't surrender to the Riptides.

Now, lets talk about some common sense, or as I call it, 'The Uncommon Common-Sense'. There is a lot we do in daily routine that we may not want to do, or we even know we shouldn't do. But do we stop and make a conscious decision to do the right thing by ourselves? No. So let's read about the uncommon common sense. Although we know what it is, it has become a topic to preach but uncommon to be practically used. Hence it has become the **'Uncommon Common-Sense'**.

Part - I

The Un-Common Common-Sense

We know we should be caring more for nature; yet we do not.

We treat our lives No Different, Do we?

It's just COMMON SENSE.

Common Sense put to Practice

Old aunts used to come up to me at weddings, poking me in the ribs and cracking jokes, telling me, 'You're next.'

They stopped after I started doing the same thing to them at funerals.

The Un-Common Common-Sense

I believe it is not very commonly known to people that common sense is not very common these days. Isn't that true?

Let's just consider this; most of people are all living a life somewhat in the way they don't really want to. If not all, then one must admit that the vast majority of us are. It is a very common practice but not commonly admitted by our mind, our brains. Our heart does know this everyday practice of un-desired way of living, which has now become a habit of ours. Now just imagine, how powerful this would be to realise that within our body, there are two parts, which are highly functional all the time. We are highly driven by our emotions, our emotional heart, and our brain listens to all those emotions to perform actions towards fulfilling those heartily desires. With these two parts as a working mechanism for manifestation, it is only common sense to know and see clearly about what we want from our life, decide and follow up with our true heart. Then those heartily emotions will help our brain function towards achieving them. But there is one point we often see where our brain fails to listen to and act accordingly.

What is that point of life, point of decision? Do we all know? Don't we all know? It is the point, the turning point of our life where we need to take a **highly motivated step to create change** so we can get out of the undesired daily routines we are living in. We must act to change the routine that has kept us living in the same way for years, the routine, which has kept us working daily just to meet up our day-to-day expenses. Act to change the mindset, which has left us in the *Slavery of Survival*. It is that routine that we have to get rid of. We cannot blame our brain, for our brain it is only common sense to keep working the way it is and has been for years. Why? Because it has been trained that way. And it is only applying the rules that we have kind of hard coded or etched onto it, or trained it to follow whether consciously or unconsciously.

Another very interestingly common desire is that we all want to do something about it. Yet again it is tragically a very common practice that we don't do anything about this. Another common practice is that we keep pushing things further, the things that would change what we are doing now and move us towards what we want to do, or always wanted to do. In everyday life we know this as procrastination.

How true is that, another common practice, which is holding us back from our real potential. Even though we know our lives are not going to change if we don't change anything about these routines. This is common sense really, but is this something we apply as a common practice in life. Hence I say common sense not really common these days - *The Uncommon Common-Sense.*

Have we heard of the story of the highly regarded captain of Indian Cricket team; M. S. Dhoni? Would he have achieved his dream in cricket if he kept on with the job as a railway ticket checker? I wouldn't be writing this book and working on my entrepreneur dream if I kept on with norms. I could have kept my Government job in Australia! I could have kept on with it and live a so called normal life. But I did a Dhoni on that; left it all to follow my dream. You must watch a movie on Dhoni's life if you haven't yet "M. S. Dhoni – The Untold Story".

Thinking the Difference

We have all seen majority of us doing regular jobs, working for someone else while they make money. How do you think they are making money? They are making money because we are making money for them. Just imagine this - there is a soul who is running this business, selling some product. Now, just imagine the amount of money you get paid as a worker and you may think that is a reasonably good amount of earnings for your family to live on. But, you are still working very hard to prove yourself to be a good worker for that next year's pay rise, right?

Now next what I want you to think about is how many people like you are working in the same job, multiply your income with that many people and when you add up all that money, just imagine. The person running the show is selling something, making the profit, the profit that is paying hundreds of thousands of dollars in your wages, company and business expenses, product cost and still making thousands in their pocket and possibly millions and billions. And we as an employee are all part of generating that profit for them. Just because almost all of us are largely trained at schools to be able to find a better job, but not become someone who can experiment with things, invent or innovate things and create jobs.

What do you think those people leading the show are doing different than those working as employees? Have you ever been in a situation where you saw a senior worker doing something and said to yourself, 'I can do this better than him/her'? So, my point is that you should recognise those skills and abilities that come naturally to you, things you know you can do better. Apply the common sense of taking action to build upon those skills. You, as a worker, are working to provide someone else with huge profits, the difference is - they thought of things differently. This is what I call working for others to realise their dream and not one's own. It's probably okay for those who do not have any dreams in life, but I do not think there is anyone who does not have a dream to realise. So, what did those business pioneers do differently?

They used the **idea of leverage** and kept it as a secret. Now don't we all know what does leverage mean? YES, we do! It's using skills of others and putting them to work so one can generate multiple times of the revenue than they would if they worked alone. But, what do you think is stopping us from implementing the same idea?

Do we know the reason? YES, we do now! It is our brain, my friends. This brain is what is not letting us get through. This is what is not letting us get over that hurdle where we can start moving towards the life we want. It partners with scary thoughts the moment you want to move it out of its comfort zone. It will tell you all the reasons why you can't do it differently, scares you of all that could go wrong than what would it be if all went well. That is where the feed to our subconscious mind is playing its role.

A regular job may be a way of making money for those who are happy to do it that way, happy for their brain to work for others dreams and are not willing to realise their own potential. Or they don't feel they have a need for it or a need for those luxurious things in life including the luxury of being your own boss and luxury of having a lot of time and money on hands to spend with their family and kids.

It's perfectly okay for those who are just happy with someone telling them what to do and meet up their daily expenses. But, what about those who have recognised the better in them and are willing to do something about this situation, willing to come out of the rough rat race they are living in and living with for years. Our brains are quite visibly conditioned from the time of birth to what we are today. Coming over that hurdle by training our brain is our only hope. Our brain can do very well with some motivation and that push from some emotions and common sense but only if applied and acted upon.

Now, at this moment, you are reading this book. I believe you are reading it because you probably want to learn, and you want to know what's so commonly known as common sense but still not implemented by most of the human population. You want to learn about what is 'The Karmic Rewind', the Rewind-Revive-Relive message that I want to convey to people in this book. You may want to change your life for a happier life of abundance that we should be living or to simply add more fuel to your brain. Uncommon Common-Sense along with the rest of the content in this book will help the readers a lot in understanding our daily lives.

To be able to live an enriched life; one needs to learn from such people. But the problem is how do you get to accompany such people. I will tell you a little secret, a secret that not many accomplished people in the world would let you know; in fact would not want you to know. The secret to how they got to where they are, whether it was their inheritance or the hard earned success. Some are happy to share but do not have time and others just won't. Do you know why?

Could this be because, they know that they are no different to other not so rich people, they are same as majority of population, they are same as a common man; they are no different to the masses of humans out there; but the thing they did better than the common man was that they did successfully implement what we call 'Common-Sense'.

> *They made purposeful use of their Mind, Body and Brain*
> *and followed their Heart with true Love and Passion.*

It is the common sense to act upon the purpose of one's life that's not very common, and because it's not very common that's why a very small percentage of human population are living the life of fulfilment. They are very few of the common people who actually practically did implement Common Sense. And because they did implement it, they are out of the large and very common category of not so rich people. That other category of people is who understand what common sense is and what common sense is asking them to do BUT they don't quite successfully take action. They don't do the necessary, or they fail to completely notice and ignore the call of common-sense, or I should say that their brain power, their age old routines and habitual behaviour of brain successfully overrules the heartily desire. Overrules the desire to live that dream life, to achieve and reach out to the goals that will help them Live the Abundant Life and not Just Live The Life.

That's how most of the population behaves and that's why most of the population is not as happy and fulfilled as they wished they were. We all possibly hope for winning the lotto somehow or wishing inheritance from ancestors somehow but not make an effort towards what we can do with the abilities we have or can raise within us. It's one of those Chinese proverbs we need to implement in life –

> *'Give a man a fish, and you feed him for a day;*
> *teach the man how to fish you feed him for a lifetime'.*

We have a need to enable ourselves to be happy, rich and fulfilled. You can link it to being rich in money sense, rich in time sense, the sense of living an abundant life, a loving relationship or living an enriched spiritual and content life. Relate this richness to any instance of life but we must enrich and enable our own human selves.

Have you ever thought about a common perception in a lot of not so rich people, which is 'Rich people are mean, rich people don't treat everyone nicely; rich people always keep distance from not so rich people'. I had a lot of friends in the past and still do have some, who think the same way. But, do you know why? Have you ever asked yourself that question, or wondered about that question! Why? Have you ever tried working out why? Well let me try and explain why.

A large part of that is a perception and misinformation or lack of exposure to that life. But there is also another reason this rich category of people may be keeping their distance from other people and that is because they know, they very well know that the things they did are actually not so different but the way they did those things was different. They may not share their ideas, plans and actions with everyone. At times their behaviour of isolation is because they believe really strongly, highly, passionately and confidently in things they do and the goals they want to achieve that talking openly about their plans with others is what they try to skip. They do this because others may not have the same level of confidence and believe in what they actually believe in and want to achieve. By talking with such people, they may actually hurt their confidence, as often people may not even have the complete knowledge and full understanding of what they are trying to achieve. Those other people may simply make irrelevant comments according to their own perspective and with confidence, as they may believe that what they know is the best of knowledge about the topic that may be brought forward.

Using *Selective Isolation* is a technique that can be used to keep their confidence intact until they reach their goal. These identified as and may be not so liked rich people are always only open to discuss their minds and ideas with those who they think are at the same level of thoughts and intelligence or higher. They will speak to those who have achieved what they want to achieve and shown willingness to help. And that is because they know a secret, the secret of achieving anything with the self-belief and confidence along with their belief in laws of the Universe.

> *'They believe, they seek, they act and so they achieve what remains the secret to most for the lack of belief.'*

Going along with the quote I heard once and still have in my memory is that, *'Rich people don't do different things, they do things differently'*. And they know that any human being if keen to reach a goal they have achieved, can actually achieve it. If they have done it as a human being, any other human being can do the same too. You just have to get over that hurdle in your mind, get over that restricting mind frame. This again is only common sense to follow your heart and do the necessary. Why we don't apply this common sense is because the way our brain is conditioned.

Brain Conditioning

You are where you are because your brain was trained or conditioned to get you there; taking into account that you based your decisions upon how you were trained to act and react in life's circumstances. Whether your parents or teachers taught you those, whether some came from what you believed or whether some came from what your faith was or what your religion teaches. It all added up when you took the decisions, which got you where you are today.

It's similar to the way things used to happen in old days, when it was commonly believed that a butcher's kids will take up butchery as a trade, an engineer's kids will be engineers, a scientist, a baker, a farmer's kids were more prone to take over the same trades. In all sorts of trades and services it was a common belief and an expectation too to a certain extent, especially in the part of the world I grew up in - in India.

The reason behind it was that because those kids grew up in that environment, their brains were trained to do those kinds of works since childhood. They will more likely take up the family business as their means of living too. And in those days we did see that most likely that is what actually happened. The world was a little smaller in those days from an over all perspective of life. There were less other distractions and more interactions within families. This trend stayed till late ages until the technology exposed the world and brought the world closer.

However that may not seem to be the case in this century anymore. But that again is due to the same old reason my friends. The reason is how you train your brain or how it is conditioned automatically based on information it is digesting from whatever source it may be. If a farmer's kids did in-fact chose another career, that is also because they had access to information outside of their family's domain which they liked or they went into the surroundings or environment where they were influenced by some other happenings or circumstances taking place and their brain have adapted to liking those or may be something happened, which made them dislike the career option their parents inherited.

We are influenced beings and almost always operate under some influences. Even if we classify ourselves to be self driven, that will still need like minded influences to help us succeed. We do have the ability to apply controlled influence on ourselves though, which we should make use of.

Hence what is playing an important part in triggering the change that may guide them throughout their life; is the information that they receive in various shapes and forms, whether its looking, seeing or experiencing things in an environment they've been in; it all gets processed by the brain and stored in the Mind. Some goes to the subconscious mind and other remains active in the conscious mind. It is then the brain to the largest extent processing what has gone in the mind and being influenced by what one sees and experiences around them. It's their brain that has accepted to implement the choice made by their heart and mind during a particular stage of life under the influence of surroundings it encountered; while being comforted with familiarisation to the different view of life, being guided by what gets stored in the mind. And it has started functioning towards that direction towards achieving the choice made. And in the end they have turned out to become what they chose and made a decision about in their mind through that influence of an environment.

The irony of most people today though is that they've completely sidelined their heart from this decision. Their heart is what tells them about what they love and their heart is what may be the divine signal to their life and yet their heart is actually what gets completely overpowered by the influences and the way our brain works. It is a tragedy because when you look at all those people who are successful, accomplished, achieved and happy in their lives; they are those who have followed their heart and forced their mind and brain to work with their heart and passion. That is why I say –

> *Your Mind, Love & Heart, Together they are Smart*
> *Together if they Live, Together they will grow;*
> *Not just Your Life, but Let the Whole Galaxy Glow*

Your Mind will acquire all the knowledge that is required; whether on purpose or not and your heart is what will guide you towards your purpose in life. It is when you put your Love into it, that's when it gets that energy that electricity; the power going into it that will light up your life. These three together has the power to steer your brain to start acting towards and achieve that purpose of your life, the goals of your life. When they all work in synchronisation, there is nothing that will stand in your way; nothing remains a secret to your success. It is only common-sense that once you start exploring, that is when all the secrets vanish. **What remain unexplored remains unknown; what remains unknown is what becomes the secret**. By taking action powered by your mind, love and heart, your brain will help you undo the secret. You'll know how to light up your life. And when your life lights up, you'll not just glow your life but glow the life of all those around you. You will have the power and energy that can light up the whole galaxy around you.

If we were to compare our mind and brain to that of a computer; then our mind is the memory, which has a conscious mind as a RAM (Random Access

Memory) and the subconscious mind for everything that gets stored. Our brain would then be the CPU to process what exists within its own program as needed to run this body and to access what exists in the memory with the commands given for our needs or by our heart & soul.

The whole recipe also works very well and very closely with the laws of the Universe, something that's very commonly known as "The Law of Attraction". People who have worked with these laws in their life; also know how the brain works and how to manipulate it for their own benefit. They know the influence of everything around them, so they only want and selectively choose the influence that will help them succeed in what they believe in and want to achieve.

And these are the reasons why I have implemented same strategies in my life. I will explain the strategies throughout this book for you to be able to understand how to add more to the life, to add whatever it is that you may want. **Selective isolation** and the way to use the power of the brain by being in sync with their heart and mind are the techniques what the accomplished people want to keep intact and keep working on, hence they maintain distance from most others who may be at a different stage of mindset and create an image of being mean for themselves.

Another reason why some enriched people may not want all to know there techniques and keep them a secret from most is probably because they don't want to lose the power of leverage. If all became their own boss, then who would work for them. Who would they compare themselves to or probably show off to, who would they compare their richness to? It is again a common sense for them to keep it as a secret and they use it, they practice it for what they want to achieve. And they do that quite successfully by maintaining a distance. I wouldn't really want to learn from that greedy breed of people. But there could also be a genuine case of just not having time while being busy in following their dreams and making the world a better place. One thing we all must know and respect is that everybody is unique and should make the most of their unique yet powerful self-being; do it for the better of humanity and you can never go wrong. Let's try and understand a bit about uniqueness within the humanity while the creator is the same power.

Unique Individuality

It is common sense also to use our discriminatory sense to realise our unique individuality; use this powerful sense of discrimination that God has gifted us. If all became the same then the world would be a much different place, a place I believe humans are not made for. We are given this brain and its function is to keep us running, to keep creating, to exercise the sense of discrimination and hence it creates a world, a life, and a universe differently for everyone. We need to follow our heart to realise our own unique self, our purpose in life and act according to who we are rather than reacting to situations. The moment we react and how we react creates our upcoming future. Not only that, alongside it also creates the good and bad for us, and for people around us.

Pay attention and realise the common fact we see around us every moment but fail to realise its significance. The fact is that life for each and every living being is different and unique. It may be walking on the same road but we all have our own space on that road which is different to others and that is important for our survival too. We do know what happens when two physical particles try to occupy one physical location at the same time, it never happens. Either one gets hurt or shattered but can never occupy another's place. That's how unique everything is and still capable of achieving higher states of their unique individuality. And we not only physically or geographically stay in situations, locations, and positions until we like it or feel comfortable in, at or with them but also psychologically we only stay in a mind-frame if its giving comfort to our brain. That is where they bring NLP (Neuro-linguistic Programming) in play to push the boundaries of our brain to break through such comfort zones that may be restricting our actual abilities and potential to fulfil our desired goals.

So it's not just our physical presence; the same happens with our minds. If it doesn't like a thought or gets bored it switches to something else. The moment our mind does not feel comfortable in, at or with a particular situation, location or position, what do you think it does? Our mind commands our brain to get out of there. Now just imagine the scene, a particular location we were at and shared with someone, the position, or place we were in at any point of time. Some people may find those absolutely lovable moments while others would absolutely hate it if an accident occurred or the love story did not go well probably for those lovebirds. The brain works with the memories we have, it is influenced by those experiences that form our mind. What goes in our mind then determines what action is taken onwards. Based on past experiences and memories, the commands are indirectly coming from our mind and followed by the brain to act and start the process of manifestation in the physical form.

Even in general, we as human beings do not and cannot stay hooked in just one moment of time, looking at just one piece of existence. Why? It's because of our mind. Unless you are a Buddhist monk or a yogi, our brain was never trained to remain still in any sort of scenarios for long time, and that is why it does not like it either, it becomes its nature. If you are someone who is a bit 'lost in own world', then you may be ok with spending a lot of time in just one location or place, but most people are not. And that again is because of how you may have been trained in your past, which influenced your behaviours in present age. The mind is constantly in action and it is very hard to hold it on for long in one state. And hence has refused to stay in one situation for long. Yet, that is what it needs to realise the unique you, to find that inner peace and contentment, the inner happiness – this is why people find it hard to sit in meditation.

That is why meditation is used for self-healing, because it is so powerful to be able to still the mind and train the brain and use its power in the way it can benefit our body and us as a soul. Hence my point is that **it's the brain which will take you places and get you out of places** – whether they are physical, spiritual or career gains/achievements in life. You just need to find your unique self and make that important decision to train your brain and you will be living the life you actually really want. Because after training hard enough your brain will start behaving well to move in that direction of achieving goals which make up your dreams, your true higher self. It will start giving up the unwanted or bad and start taking up the good and nourish it. All this slowly starts to mould our behaviour as well and how we carry ourselves in the world. Our behaviours will reflect our mindset and we also have to start being a bit careful about our associations and practice selective isolation. Let's take a quick look at good and bad human behaviour to gain a little understanding about behaviours.

Human Good and Bad Behaviours

It is true that we all have good and bad within us. Whatever the reason may be, people with good and bad personalities do exist out there. It is a fact, which we know and must acknowledge about human beings. Though we must also admit there is some degree of good in everyone no matter how bad their projection in the world is. It all depends on how one interacts with other people. After all, those known as bad people are good towards the people they do love, so there must be a reason they have in their mind based on their experiences since their birth for why they do hate.

The extremism of the bad combined with personal greed and sheer disrespect for others rights is what then gives birth to crime. If the balance in the world is not struck, things start to get out of hand; good starts to hate bad, bad hates good, rich hates poor and the poor hates rich. The towns and cities get divided into rich and poor areas rather and then good and bad areas. Could the good and bad behaviours be linked to one's wealthy or poor socio economic background, I am not sure; I have seen good in poor and bad in rich and the vice versa. So, there must be other reasons.

Whatever the reasons may be, there are good and bad behaviours in people out there. Let's try and understand somewhat the cause of such behaviour to some extent. Let's take a look from the point of view of how some people's brains may act or react towards others according to the way the wealthy people are looked upon, in terms of the comparison of good and bad behaviours by such people.

When one is poor he or she may see wealthy people with hatred if they are not a nice, humble personality themselves. Their behaviour could either be because they have been treated badly by someone; or they could be influenced and inured to behave that way because they've mostly seen people around them being bad to others. One's behaviour gets determined by the experiences and associations one may have had in their life. The same exists for rich people whether or not they are a nice personality because of the same reasons mentioned above or whether a goodwill gesture by them was taken advantage of and caused them to make their mind up to dislike and isolate certain kind of people. It's also a level of give and take as well as what goes around comes around.

How many people would give high regard to all the rich people if they became rich themselves. I do agree that they will to some of them – those who did nice things for others, donated to charities, worked hard and put up with a lot in life, etc. But it is human nature to have such feelings of love, like or hatred towards others based on our interactions and experiences with them.

This emphasizes the fact that the brain will be influenced by the circumstances, situations and experiences in life. Based on those experiences it may develop habits or behaviours to start acting in a manner that will turn the person into 'good' or 'bad'. Another reason for dislike towards the rich in some parts of world could be the law and order system. For instance in India, the law and order system is a bit different on the ground levels than what is its purpose. The rich one is always right and poor one has to bow down and mainly due to the corruption, bribery and the power money brings with it. Though it is improving with time, it may still take some years, why? Because of the same reasons, the way in which the brain works; people are used to a certain way things have been going on for a while and it will take a while before the change will penetrate and make its place. This may not be an issue in western world countries but is in the developing parts of the world.

Then again, this somewhat helps in understanding the influence of the circumstances and situations in determining human behaviour. The brain and the mind are reacting according to the circumstances that surround us, in every aspect of our existence on this planet. We need to train them to act and not as much react to mould our behaviour in a given way. We must create useful influences with awareness of what we need to achieve what we want in life.

How many times have we heard the stories of some psychopaths, and stories of people classified as mentally sick, or even people with split personalities? What kind of mental situation do you think they are in or how do you think their brain is behaving while they are behaving or living as psychopaths or dealing with their split personality? It is again the brain, which triggers those effects. To them, at that point of time, in that vision of scene, according to their life and circumstances, what they are doing is right and the absolute correct action for them to take. Certain malfunctions, as we call them in medical science, are insisting on performing those actions in the brain and they are turning those thoughts or those reactions in mind into reality. A different way of explaining the power of brain my friends but my idea is to help you understand as deeply as possible the power of brain and how to use it in the positive manner and in the manner you want to live your life in.

So if those people with split personalities or psychological disorders have certain malfunctions which are causing their brains to be pushed to such levels in which those thoughts are pictured as real scenarios in their brains and turned into reality for them because they treat those thoughts as real happenings, then my dear friends, it is also a proven fact that the power of positive thoughts are hundred times more powerful than negative thoughts. What makes you think that you cannot dream of a time and money rich abundant life, travelling around the world and happily enjoying the life on planet Earth? I believe that is what we are made for and that is what planet Earth is made for. So where have all these worries and miseries and pains of life come from? If anything, I must say we brought it upon us by the way of our thinking. We thought our way through to them and brought them upon us by accumulation of Karmas, the actions taken by us under the influence of good or bad behaviours we let prosper within our self while ignoring the power of discrimination to stick to the good.

In similar way my dear friends we can think our way to positive attitude and lead on to live a prosperous and abundant life. Let the bad die and let the good prosper and grow. Every now and then, as we have often seen and know that proven examples exists for miracle medicines and meditational healing techniques. We have one way or another seen those examples in life. So I insist that you train your brain and start creating those energies around you, which will help you to succeed in the motto you put in front of your brain. That motive may be the spirituality, may be the relationships, the business, the job, the health, or money.

Role of Human Nature

Let's try and analyse more into how the circumstances that we live in and experience affect our thinking and unconsciously mould our nature, our brain towards living the life we are living now. The fact is that you and I will have different experiences in life. They may be good, bad, excellent, fantastic, terrible, worse or horrific or marvellous, whatever it could be. Directly or indirectly they do affect how people may behave in the circumstances they face in the future. And because of the way they behave in their current circumstances, they actually pave the path to their future life.

I've always heard some little stories here and there about certain people became what they were because of the action they took under certain circumstances, and when they look back at that time they realise if only they had thought a bit differently. Their lives would have been much better and they themselves would have been different to what they are today or better than they are today. Now, let me share an example with you.

My dad, in his younger days, never got to finish his schooling. He was so brilliant with maths and numbers and calculations in general life that he was better than all his brothers and sisters. He wanted to study and find a white-collar profession because it was considered to be a position of authority and respect. He obviously may have had such influence from someone. But due to certain things, which happened in those days - the partition of India and certain losses in family, his dad, my grandfather, made certain decisions, which he felt was the best he could do under those circumstances. They started a business of horse farming, trading and selling – so my grandfather needed a helping hand with the business and obviously domestic help was what he could look at first sight. He made a decision that he would let my uncle continue with his studies as he was elder and was close to finishing school earlier than my dad. Just by that thought crossing his mind that the one who will finish school sooner will gain employment sooner, he pulled my dad out of school, not because he may have been intelligent compared to my uncle, but because he did not see him as an income provider any sooner.

Now, that caused an intelligent man the heavy loss of a successful career. My dad was a helping hand to my grandfather so, as a matter of fact, he became an income earner much sooner than my uncle, but into a bracket where he could never get out of the daily hard work, and will be tired at the end of the day to use his brain towards anything brilliant. Hence he got into a schedule of life where he can only learn about and work at a horse farm and to keep doing that for the whole life. Now my uncle finished his high school and started working as a clerk at a government department.

Why they ended up that way was a result of the way my grandfather thought at that particular stage of his life, and why he thought like that is because he could only think as far as getting a helping hand within the house. Had he thought a bit differently, it may have been the elder brother in the circumstances of my dad and my dad in the circumstances of my uncle. Had my grandfather thought a bit more smartly, or may be had thought more intelligently, he could have got someone else who was willing to do that job and pay them their share of labour and got my dad to study further as well. It would have cost him money, meaning not much profit in hand, but the circumstances would have been better in the long run in the future.

I want all of you to give a bit deeper thought to this story and try and imagine the circumstances that may have forced my grandfather to take that decision. It could have been the need of money, it could have been that they lost a lot of their money and land due to partition of the country at that time, or it could have been lack of intelligent advice - that intelligent advice of far thinking could have benefitted him much more and in a larger extent than what he did just because of his decision at that point in time.

We all know the story of the Colorado gold mine where Mr. Darby and his uncle lost faith just 3 feet away and sold all machinery to this guy who was smart enough to get professional help. And when the mine was scanned, the new owner just had to start digging again and find gold only about three feet away.

Hence, I say, Mr. Darby's brain was trained and developed to only think as far as he did at that time and so was my grandfather's. So, see how the circumstances played the part in deciding his own life and what trade he would take up for years in coming after losing all their wealth during partition of India and how that affected the lives of two of his sons in two completely different manners. And perhaps you should go on and think a step further to how does that affect the lives of the family tree further down the years.

But let me tell you, my dear friends, my dad worked hard and then it may have been stuck in his mind the loss of education in his life so he decided to ensure that his kids did not suffer the same. He changed businesses for what he thought would be better. And here I am, my friends; far away from horse farming and life is in a different direction for better. Why that has happened is because of the decisions made under certain circumstances faced by my parents and furthermore the opportunities which I recognised and wanted to pursue as to my likings while fulfilling my responsibilities towards my family who did their best to support me.

This is why I will say; don't be stressed when you are required to take an important decision. Always relax and you will realise that your mind works much better in natural state. The decisions, which you will make, you will never regret. You know why? Because you have used your mind, your brain and knowledge to the best you can. The result may be positive or negative but you at least know that you gave it your best shot while thinking right. And that is what I want to convey, give it your best shot, seek expert advice if you think the need be, it is only common sense to do so. Build this calmness and relaxed use of assets into your nature.

Once when I was looking for a job change; I went for the interview at the second largest telecommunications company in Australia. As we went through the interview, I was very calm and confident, but not over-confident and over-smart. I answered all the questions with confidence. When the interviewer escorted me back to the reception, in the lift he asked me this question, 'Didn't you feel nervous at all?' I answered the same as I told you above, I said, 'Being nervous will only make one lose control over their nerves and they may perform worse than they would otherwise. So, why be nervous if one wants to perform their best?'

'One should learn to control their mind rather than be completely influenced by it.'

This is only common sense, so put it to practice. Common sense is all around us; we know what we should do; yet we don't do it slowly it has become our nature. Why we don't do it is very commonly known to us but remains unnoticed. It is because we don't act on those necessary actions, which will help us achieve what we want. Why we don't act is because our mindset, our brain doesn't allow us to. It is sitting too comfortably in its safe and comfort zone. We are never trained to be risk takers but to stay safe. It is only common sense to train your brain to be able to take those actions, take certain risks for benefits by large. You may start doing that by little actions in your daily life. It could be a simple step as to getting your mind to wake you up with the first alarm bell rather than hitting the snooze button. It could be waking up with the rising sun, it brings tremendous amount of positive energy with it. Do it. You may not want to do it for one or another reason to satisfy the lazy corner in your mind, but I recommend and insist you do it. Then it will not be long before it becomes a habit and you will embrace this positive change in life, in fact you will love it.

Think hard and you will find little things like that to start training your brain on. And believe me, after little time your brain will be ready to take further exercises and changes. It will ask you 'OK, I have done that and it has become my nature, my routine habit now. What's next?' Then you will suddenly realise your potential and will be talking to yourself. What I mean to say is that you will be telling yourself things like - 'Oh, I never thought I could do that. I never thought I will be able to get rid of this habit of mine or adapt to that good habit, I never thought I could feel this good after just changing little things in life and I did. OK, now I am ready for more. I am ready for next step.'

You will start looking for ways to improve your life and guess what, you will find ways and you will start paving that path to success. More importantly you will start living a happier and prosperous life. You will start asking questions rather than just shying away from things. You will start learning, and as you start learning you will begin to mould your brain, your mind unconsciously with those happy thoughts, with those happy learnings and improvements. You will start creating those energies around you. And then, as they say about the law of attraction, you will start attracting the life you want to live. And it will come to you only if you do yourself the favour and apply the COMMON SENSE.

Common sense to understand your life, common sense to know the actions you have to take, common sense to take action on those actions, don't just think about them and let the life roll. Tell yourself to take action, to be accountable for yourself and your life and indirectly for the life of those around you, the effects it has on the people who are looking up to and counting on you. Act to make their lives better - your partner, your children, and may be your parents as well, for some it might even be there pets.

So dear friends, take charge, tell yourself that you will start doing at least one thing different from today. Then in no time you will train your brain to adapt to change for the better. We always see the examples of how our brain behaves and develops into whatever circumstances we put it in. We have all heard of the story Tarzan, or the Jungle Book, right? Some may be saying that it was just a story, but we only need to go to the trained hunters and talk to them about how well they know to make those sounds which help them convey their message across to the animals.

So, what does those stories tell us? It's a story of a human who is talking to and interacting with animals. Why and how? Because he lived with them and he only learnt their way of interacting but then some humans get in contact and teach him about his reality being the human race. And he starts behaving and interacting like humans. A best living example, similar to Tarzan's story, is the Buddhist temple in Saiyok district of Kanchanaburi province of Thailand. The temple is known as Tiger Temple or (Wat Pha Luang Ta Bua) in the local language. They have tigers as their pets and they are nothing like the tigers, which roam around in jungles and eat any big animal they can find as food. They roam around with monks and visitors can have photos taken with them at no risk really but only if you can fight the fear within you. I still remember the photos brought back by one of my managers in my past job. I thought how cool it would be and was amazed by the fact that these big cats were only fed a diet that did not involve the killing of larger animals. We know that Buddhism promotes vegetarianism so we can imagine what they would feed them. I was told that one of the caretakers, who was born in the year of the tiger, was responsible for feeding them, nursing them and also training them. Also being a Buddhist monk, he believes in reincarnation and believes that in his past lives, these animals might have been his friends, enemies, or even father or mother.

So it's the brain the ultimate power my friends, it is the mighty powerful part of human being. Learn to train it. I always say, 'Train your Brain' and you will become what you want depending on how you train it. *Again it's just common sense, but how widely common is it that we don't apply it. It's just sad.*

Now, I am not sure of all but I believe a lot of readers would have heard of the famous scientist Stephen Hawking. Please read below extract from Wikipedia and a News.com.au article about him and do some more research on him over the Internet and you will be amazed.

****

Britain's most eminent scientist Stephen Hawking said that he did not learn to read until he was eight years old and was academically idle until he was diagnosed with a form of motor neuron disease.

UK scientist who admitted in 2010 that he could not read until the age of 8 years. Was nicknamed Einstein and lead the research into Black Holes and the Big Bang theory. I don't mean to say you should believe in what his beliefs are because he believes that the universe is not created by God, and we all have our own personal beliefs in that regard. But this should teach a lesson that it is the determination he had after he found out at the age of 21 that he will only live for few more years. Hawking has a neuro-muscular dystrophy that is related to amyotrophic lateral sclerosis (ALS), a condition that has progressed over the years and has left him almost completely paralysed. He became the first quadriplegic to float in zero gravity. This was the first time in forty years that he moved freely, without his wheelchair. The fee is normally US$3,750 for 10–15 plunges, but Hawking was not required to pay the fee.

Hawking's illness is markedly different from typical ALS in that his form of ALS would make for the most protracted case ever documented. A survival for more than ten years after its diagnosis is uncommon for

ALS; the longest documented durations are thirty-two and thirty-nine years and these cases were termed benign because of the lack of the typical progressive course.

When he was young, he enjoyed riding horses and playing with other children. At Oxford, he coxed a rowing team, which, he stated, helped relieve his immense boredom at the university. Symptoms of the disorder first appeared while he was enrolled at University of Cambridge; he lost his balance and fell down a flight of stairs, hitting his head. Worried that he would lose his genius, he took the Mensa test to verify that his intellectual abilities were intact. The diagnosis of motor neurone disease came when Hawking was 21, shortly before his first marriage, and doctors said he would not survive more than two or three years. Hawking gradually lost the use of his arms, legs, and voice, and as of 2009 has been almost completely paralysed.

In Hawking's many media appearances, he appears to speak fluently through his synthesizer, but in reality, it is a tedious drawn-out process. Hawking's setup uses a predictive text entry system, which requires only the first few characters in order to auto-complete the word, but as he is only able to use his cheek for data entry, constructing complete sentences takes time. His speeches are prepared in advance, but having a live conversation with him provides insight as to the complexity and work involved.

During a Technology, Entertainment, & Design Conference talk, it took him seven minutes to answer a question. In 2009 he won the Highest US civilian award Presidential Medal of Freedom: He has also achieved success with works of popular science in which he discusses his own theories and cosmology in general; these include the runaway best seller A Brief History of Time, which stayed on the British Sunday Times bestsellers list for a record-breaking 237 weeks. Read this article.

Hawking says his sister was smarter, But he was nicknamed 'Einstein', Tells of lazy days while at university.

Hawking, who gave a rare public lecture at the Royal Albert Hall in London, said, 'My sister Philippa could read by the age of four ... but then, she was definitely brighter than me.' He added that he was never more than about halfway up the class at school.

'My classwork was very untidy, and my handwriting was the despair of my teachers,' he said. 'But my classmates gave me the nickname Einstein, so presumably they saw signs of something better.'

Learning he was facing the possibility of an early death was the catalyst for his most prolific period as a scientist, which led to his discoveries on the big bang and black holes. 'When you are faced with the possibility of an early death, it makes you realise that life is worth living, and that there are lots of things you want to do,' he said.

Although he gained a first-class degree at Oxford University, he said that he scraped that result and worked for an average of only an hour a day during his time there.

'You were supposed to be brilliant without effort or to accept your limitations and get a fourth-class degree. I'm not proud of this lack of work. I'm just describing my attitude at the time, which I shared with most of my fellow students: an attitude of complete boredom and feeling that nothing was worth making an effort for,' he said. However, being told at the age of 21 that he would not live for more than a few years galvanised him into intense productivity.

****

How amazing! A very inspiring story, just imagine, all you have to do is decide with your true heart on making life a positive outcome and be inspired from such stories around you. Now, as I mentioned earlier, it is one's mind frame that gets them where they got to in life. I am going to relate this power of mindset to a bit of the religious sides now as well as some cultural beliefs.

In Christianity as well we believe in becoming one with God. I used to go to a church once in a while during my school days. I really felt calm and peaceful every time I went there. I had some friends who are and were Christians during my life thus far. We often discussed the Christian beliefs and the knowledge I had as per my followings, which is a way of life and not a religion. One thing we always agreed on was to believe in God and becoming one with God as a soul.

Now let's look at the ways and see how we talk about becoming one with God. They teach you to pray, to meditate, and to remember God in as many ways or as you can in your own way. You live by and behave according to the ways you are taught and they say that if you do it with enough devotion you will realise the eternal world and will become one with God. Now there is a huge lesson to be learnt here.

What is it that gets you to that level? It's what we are taught about and if we follow it we train our brain and if we want to achieve that then it is only common sense that we follow all that we are taught to do, we train our brain to that tune. And again it is only common sense that if we want to achieve that target, we need to follow those rules. And when will we follow those rules, only when we will have the heartily desire guiding the mindset that we want to achieve that goal. So it is the brain, the mindset if we set to a certain task we must believe in it completely, follow it from the heart and then act accordingly. And then we will progress towards that goal and achieve it.

Matter of Belief

Now here is an example where I will try and help you understand again another nature of brain and the power of belief system, believing in what we see. Just imagine this scenario.

A man walked past a wall that had an old wall clock hanging on it. He sees the time and it is 6 pm on the clock. Now another colleague of his walks by the same minute and he looked at the clock. The clock showed 6:30 on it, as the minute leg of clock actually fell loose in the moment just after the previous person looked at the clock and is still standing there. Now this colleague who just walked in and looked at the clock just murmured that its 6:30 pm. The first person heard him and went off at his colleague saying – 'no buddy, its only 6 pm', but the way he spoke it made his colleague a bit offended and he started arguing with him how could he say its 6 when he had just seen the clock and it's 6:30. They both have started an argument now without bothering to take another look at the clock. Both of them were so confident about what they saw on the clock. One probably did not want his colleague to go home early or something, who knows. So, they have both started arguing with pride on their self-belief and what they had just seen. And obviously in their minds what they noticed was truth and they stood by their witnessed moments of time.

Now they are both strong personalities and both not willing to give up and cross confirm whether the clock was correct or malfunctioning. But they both had seen the clock showing the time they saw, the clock is supposed to be working fine all the time and has never showed wrong time for years, they both trust and believe in themselves, on their eyes and brain, and words coming out of their mouth as an effect of what they saw on the clock. Now, none of the two is really incorrect in their own ways, because how could half an hour have gone forward or backward in that tiny fraction of time between when they looked at the clock. And they both are trying to convince each other of as to what they saw is correct.

So, what I insist here is that we need to use that power of our brain where once we believe in something, we are fully devoted to prove it regardless of others beliefs on a same scenario or concept. And I don't say to do so to prove someone else that they are wrong, but to prove it to your brain that what it has been unconsciously holding you from doing has not worked towards giving you the solution for the life you want, so you need to change and start believing in the actual potential you have within yourself. Believe in that big dream in your mind that you've only shown little light to. Use the degree of belief in that dream similar to what was shown by those two men who looked at the clock once and worked hard in convincing of what time it is. Both talking with confidence (obviously common sense, but the argument could have benefitted with the cross check technique) about what time they know it is.

And one technique you will learn from this book is that, there can be different points of view to the same scenario; you must pick up the positive views only to help yourself grow more. Life and experiences come in all kind of packages, when they come to you grab what you need, use your skills similar to when you eat a fruit, an orange, for example, we do not eat the seeds inside or the skin it has on that orange but just the juicy stuff. So learn and pick up the good from anything and anywhere you can and think about how you may be able to use that to grow yourself more into an able, skilful and successful person you want to be, so you can achieve the life you want to live.

When it comes to looking for a role model, or people who we may look towards to learn more from, you need to first look at what you may want to achieve. I have used examples from some movies at times in this book, but do not follow the actor who played a particular character that you liked, instead follow the role played by the actor and find a real life achiever of the same kind. Following an actor will only help you become a better actor but not the actual character you want to be - it will motivate you, that is the good part, but to find the real achievement in becoming what you want, look to someone who has achieved in real life.

Just imagine if you have gone to attend a seminar or conference on something of your interest. You get two presenters on the stage. They both spoke about the related topics. One presenter was really passionate and full of enthusiasm when he spoke about the topics he was to cover, and then there was another presenter, who looked really dull, and had no enthusiasm while trying to convince you about his words. Who do you believe in more? The person who was really passionate about what you went to learn or discover, or the person who was dull in presentation, did not seem like he believed his own words. You have gone there with full enthusiasm, and you need someone who is at higher levels of belief than where you are at to make an impact on your belief system. That is the person you will believe in, the one you should believe in as that is the person who can lead you with enthusiasm in the direction you want to travel, on the path that will help you achieve the desired goal. Find someone who you may be able to learn from and then practice what you have learnt more and more to become an expert on that. That is nothing new-

'Practice makes a man perfect', I will add *'A woman too.'*

Parent's Role and Education

Repetition of things will help you achieve things practically and perfectly. Slowly it all starts to add confidence to your belief system and you become what you believe in. Just imagine, as a child who is just born knows nothing about this world. It is believed in some cultures that even after birth, the child is still connected with the astral world in their subconscious. That is why you would sometimes see them smiling and happy during sleep and at times getting scared all of a sudden and start crying without any physical reason that you may try to find. And then slowly and more frequently he or she starts to see the world around them more and more, and becomes accustomed to the life we live on this planet. Now it's the repetition of things around the child that are taking his/her attention and is starting to get the child to attach the feelings with them, whether it's people or toys.

As a little baby, how do you know your name? Just imagine, how a little kid responds to their name being called out from a distance once they know their name. They start to respond because they have heard it enough repeatedly from their parents, they begin to recognise the voice too. If a child doesn't see or have much interaction with their father because he was away for months for business or job reasons, the little kid won't recognise and start to cry when sees him. It may be a while before he gets used to seeing his dad around for a while and becomes comfortable and friendly towards him. So, from a very early age it shows how much of a social animal we are and we mould according to our surrounding situations and people who influence them.

Think about the basic theory of learning at school. Why you were sent to school, there is a lot your parents thought of the basics as to why you need to go to school. There is an awful lot around the world who did not go to or finish school, some who just did not get a chance to go to school in certain parts of the world. Now just imagine if you did go to school but you got in the company of those who didn't want to go to school, but attended the class because they were forced to after going through terrible detentions and punishments from their parents; What idea would they have to give you about going to school? Not much of an encouragement to do what your parents sent you to school for. But your parents knew what would help you succeed so they tried their best to keep you to stay out of that company and continue school. Maybe they enrolled you into a lot of other activities outside school hours, so you were tired enough at the end of the day to not even think about indulging into certain bad habits. Common sense isn't it? They knew the basics and applied common sense. So the point is, if you want to succeed in a direction it is highly important that you accompany the ones who are on the same road or going in the same direction. It does matter big time that who do you accompany.

There is a common saying in Indian culture, and I am sure in others too, which implies 'Empty mind is a shelter for the Satan'. There must be enough evidence for them to believe in that saying. That is why you need to be educated and because the brain works at an enormous pace and potential during those teenage years of life. It is very important to keep on the right track or more importantly on the track, which leads you to the goal that is set by parents during those early schooling years until you are at the stage of deciding for yourself. And I think a good parent's view should always be respected, as good parents most of the time would have put in a lot of effort in deciding that goal for you, because they do know you as a child very well. They have been monitoring each and every activity we perform or undertake as a child, and it is during those years when we act with the best of our natural mind and according to what we have been fed in the mind until any given stage.

That is why it should be very easy for our parents to know and work out, what may be best suited to our nature and skills, which we show from an early age. And that goal gets reassessed when we have grown up to the stage where we can understand the basics of life better. By that stage one would have gained enough skills to recognise how the world operates and how one can align it all together very well to make a better life. I do not mean to say that going to school is the only way of education, but it's a best place to start the learning process. And once you are out of the teenage years, you are wise enough to make your decisions about life. At that point in time any spoiler company would not matter much if you have wisely made up your mind about life.

But, only if all that was done and happened perfectly and ideally, we would all have been happy and content already, but of course there is much more to life than what is currently taught at schools. And that is where the education systems need to change to make children better equipped with real life skills as well. There needs to be much more emphasis on developing the leaders who can innovate and nurture the world to lead into a better future for all existence on this planet. Not just the better future for themselves. Everyone should be trained to be a leader. Most people are educating their kids just so they can get good jobs for their better but safe future. Why not support to educate them to be the owners of the new ideas they may be able to bring to the world, the entrepreneur world that is emerging now in some parts of the planet. And there should be more offers for mentoring students, so they can learn from the real people in the area of their interest, what they love, the area of interest they would be happy to spend their life working in and working with.

That way they will accompany the like-minded people and learn and develop more than just a qualified employee. What you associate with is more likely to have an impact on who you become. We humans are social animals. We need to start associating with the ones who can nourish us further to achieve the goal we have decided to achieve in life. Same applies to great athletes, scientists, engineers, architects and magicians. And again the 'greats' are those who chose the direction and looked at no deviations, distractions and disturbances, which came along the way. And to some of those achievers, it did not come easy. You only need to talk to their family members or partners and they will tell you how much time they spent away from them to achieve those goals. But they did it for the love of it and of course the family members at times may regret not spending much time with them at early stages, but they also would rather support them during those early stages of achieving success.

It is again the full support from every aspect that helps to achieve success. Again, common sense isn't it. If you want to achieve something that must be your prime goal then isn't that right to say that you should do everything in your power to create the supportive and helping conditions. That is why accompanying the right kind of people and empowering your self with all the knowledge and abilities you need to achieve that goal is so important. And that is why you should just do it, cut off all the distractions one way or another for the sake of achieving the ultimate goal of your life.

Often I speak to some young people who has just finished school and started going to university for higher studies, but they also often are distracted with all the buzz about college or university life and the feel of freedom often tends to divert them towards certain unhealthy habits, not the habits that may do them physical harm but also things which can affect their life with such an impact, that they may suffer with it psychologically for the rest of the life. They often tend to do things, which may cause them to be expelled or suspended from their institutes of study. And yes, I do hear a lot about them falling in love with someone and then wanting to die when they break-up. It is the belief system at work again and such thinking shows it's a very short-sighted belief system in action. But I always tell them this is not the end of the world and advise them to concentrate on their studies first.

Their belief must be changed to believe that there is much more to life. If they can achieve that goal well and keep away from such distractions they will have plenty of time and opportunities for all those love stories and what not. They will also have more success in those areas once they have succeeded their goal of building the career they want. When I see the same people walking around with another partner few days later after they almost wanted to die because of the last break up, I just give them a little smile, and they give a tiny one back. Life goes on.

Empower your Within

And because life goes on, it is only common sense that we understand better that very fact and build a better life for us to live, not that of misery or pain. We do have the potential but we just need to start seeing ourselves in a clear mirror and recognise our true potential. We are living as if we were given a blurry mirror to see ourselves every day. We have taken that as a true identity of our self. We are much better than how we see ourselves in that mirror, in that sight of ourselves. Clean the mirror of your life, clear out the blur or fog of negativity and then one can start seeing the positive reality and one will start behaving that way too. Make that person to be you.

Just imagine, one day if you see yourself in mirror and you don't look your best. You don't have much time to spend to look better as well, how do you then feel for the rest of the day? Pretty low in morale, isn't it? The same applies on the day when you spent a bit more time getting ready and looking the best of you, not only do you look great but you have marvellous confidence all day along as well. If any rubbish comes your way it doesn't affect you because your positive attitude is so high. Why? Just because your confidence is very high, and why that happened is just because you know you look and feel really good, and that is what you love, you love to look and be the best you can all the time. You have great personality and you behave that way for the rest of the day as well. That is why it is so very important to see yourself the way you want to be. Then you start behaving in that manner and you become that personality. And why not be what you really are always and all the time? You will become contagious with that kind of personality and start influencing the surrounding atmosphere. That is how we want to live; we all want to live in happiness and a peaceful environment.

Never allow any circumstances to disturb your peace of mind. We do have the power within us to be able to overcome any situation and if you do not believe so, then try this quick technique to change your belief in that regard. Realise the importance of power within. We as small kids often played with little cups or drink glasses. We would often put them on our ears and some stormy noises were heard. We then often moved the cups closing and opening some gap between the skin and surface of the glass to hear different effects. But what is amazing is that how come there were such noises of kind of a storm, when there is complete silence in that empty zone created by the cups when its edges completely touched our skin. If anything there may be its some air only, but not a stormy wind. Later we were told that that is just the hollow noise, someone probably thought we were too young to understand much on that topic. But try that and then try what I have below, and that should help you realise what lies within this mortal body, realise the depth.

Close your ears and after few seconds you will start hearing a sound. The sound of a storm, the sound of being in an underwater vessel, a plane or whatever you may associate it with. Now realise that sound. Where is it coming from? There are no deep seas we are travelling in, no planes, or no storms we are in. Some may even relate it to something like what you may hear from those high electric voltage lines or transformer grids, the sound of the current that is unseen. That sound is coming from within this body, the ears- how many people have realised that only today- when I say realise, I mean the origin of this noise, I don't mean 'oh yeah I've heard it before', I want you to realise that the origin of that sound, origin of the energy of life for this very mortal body to physically exist starts from within. And hence the chain reaction takes place to result into us starting to act in the outer world making this body the reason for things which are happening around us and things we do around us. So realise the depth of the energies and power within. And how it is controlled, the mind the brain and the heart are the powerful drivers of us into the future of life.

So learn to train your brain if it starts thinking it's powerful. It will become powerful. How many times do we see people around us – people who may think they are perfect or they are the expert at everything, regardless of how much of what they say could be held true? And at times you may not agree with the personality they are trying to wear on to themselves because you have seen that person too often to realise their true identity, and they do not adhere to the 'practice what you preach' statement. Nonetheless, take the good and leave the bad. Learn the good from anyone who may help you in developing your own mind and brain. From such person, take the quality of confidence and practice it with methods of increasing your knowledge within to become perfect at your own gig.

How do you know if someone is perfect at something that you see them doing? That is by looking at them doing it so perfectly, right. But how do you know someone is practicing something really well; when you see them doing the same thing in a perfect manner all the time and consistently. It's due to the practice they do that particular task so effortlessly and precisely while others may struggle? And it is by one's actions in real life, which help you determine how much they put their **heart in to practice**. We need to follow the desires and dreams every moment of life with practical actions if we want to see them come true. Only with actions if we follow through on dreams that we have, we would very well achieve those as goals and they will become reality. The dreams and desires, which were once said as words will be manifested to realisation with practical action and by practicing the skill to achieve them.

Those successful people achieve perfection by practicing over and over again. You can do it too; only if you change the attitude from telling yourself 'I can't do it' to 'I can/will do it'. Imagine the feeling you get, when you say to yourself, over a task you have gained expertise in by doing it several times, 'this is nothing, I can do it!' Just imagine that feeling for anything you want to do, even if you do not succeed the first time, you are bound to do better the next time you get on to the same task. Make that task the dream of your life - the dream to LIVE the life, not Just living it.

And with the exercise above, the brain will start to act in that powerful manner within, which it realises by covering both your ears for few seconds. Practice that often and you will feel so empowered. You will start putting in that strength you realised within you, into your daily life and efforts. Hence your life all around will become empowered. However, you need to ensure there are no contradicting behaviours. You cannot start thinking you are powerful and capable of doing a task and at the same time start to doubt it as well. That is why you need to practice as often as you can to believe in yourself.

Also think about the human **reaction mode**. How our brain and body reacts to the input we feed or allow by the medium of listening, feeling, smelling and seeing etc. Just imagine the day you just walked out of home to go to work and someone you bumped into gave you a nice compliment. You will feel nice; you will feel happy and be in a happy mood all day. This may sound weird to some but who do you think the first person you regularly see is? The person you see before you start the day into the world after being asleep throughout the night and you have no idea where your conscious has been all night after you declared sleep time; but that person is the person who sees you every morning while ensuring you look the best you can for the day - it is your own very self and yet it takes an outsider to give us that compliment to make our day and make us feel happy. Why not give that compliment to yourself every day and start the day with that beautiful feel? Then the rest of the day and events will follow your flavour. We must take charge ourselves.

I hope you have understood what I am intending to say here. It is your own self, it is you who can empower you from within and initiate that process from the start of the day and what does it cost you? Only the effort in developing that self-confidence in your self and may be some time to be devoted towards dressing up to get that personality of you out of your skin. Believe in yourself. And if you don't think you have those capabilities at this stage then you need to stop and wipe out that thought from your brain right away and start working towards achieving that personality, achieve that confidence. Do whatever it takes to implement that good change.

If you haven't done that even yet, then do so now. It is only common sense, not to procrastinate anymore. Just click your finger and say good-bye to that thought of not being able to do what you want to do. Do it as soon as you can, find ways to do it, if you can't find a way then MAKE a way. It is your need to improve your self-confidence, and need is the mother of inventions. Adapting to the idea of change is what becomes the first hurdle to overcome within us for starting on the better path for life. This book is going to help you invent a lot out of you and help you get rid of what is not working for you to make your life what you want it to be.

'Our body as a whole is created as a beautiful biological gadget and what a master piece it is. It's a sophisticated piece of equipment created by its engineer, with the best operating system capabilities. Let's upload the useful programs and data so we can use it with the useful programs and applications to get the best performance and results.'

Let me explain a recent research that somewhat helps us understand the kind of intelligent operating system our body has, and how the hardware of the brain, **'Neuroware'** as I call it, works as a sophisticated piece of equipment within this body system. The study was published in the Neuron Journal and research that was conducted by US's leading researcher Christina Zelano.

The research used functional MRI techniques and cutting edge pattern based analysis to identify the existence of predictive coding in the olfactory cortex of the brain, where the sense of smell is deposited; explains that 'It is likely that our brain is already preparing our sensory system for the familiar smells, in this instance; familiar floral smells before we even 'Stop and smell the roses'. This research from North-western Medicine offers strong evidence that the brain uses **predictive coding to generate 'Predictive Templates'** of specific smells, setting up a mental expectation of scent before it hits your nostrils. Research reports that predictive coding is important because it provides animals and in this case us with a behavioural advantage, in that they can react more quickly and more accurately to stimuli in the surrounding environment.

Christina also suggested that People often overlook the power of the sense of smell. She used an example of a bottle of rotten milk smell. She said it is hard to determine by just looking at the bottle but if the brain can successfully form a template of a rotten milk smell, it is more likely then that one can more accurately determine the rotten milk and save yourself from getting sick.

Some may think that one really have to be real dumb, that they are not able to determine whether milk one is drinking is rotten or not. Well, my point is to help you understand the actual fact about how the brain operates. In this case the study clarifies the fact about where the sense of smell houses in our body and helps to understand that the brain has already started to work towards what you are going to smell. As you see the roses your brain has started to prepare you for smelling the roses and hence causing that action in your brain which directs you to stop and smell the roses and then of course a template is formed either based on previous experiences or new if its your first time smelling roses. And further based on that template you determine whether the smell is good, fresh, or a bad smell where the flowers may be old and withered. Ever noticed someone smelling a few times before they'll determine if the food is off or not compare to someone who knows it in one go, that's the difference we are pointing towards with the above study. It proves that brain can develop templates and helps you become smarter and quicker at certain tasks, which can also be linked to "practice makes you perfect".

So realise the potential, realise the dynamic operating system and hardware equipment, which are provided and fitted within this body, and each operating system in this world has its own unique identity – proven by genetic coding and unique DNA. Not all of us have exactly same features in the way we live; we all have something uniquely different. At the same time we are not exactly machines like computers where we can get rid of any viruses or malware in minutes and upload all those new programs and applications which give us amusement and pleasure or great feeling. Though, similar is the way the body can work if we can realise and understand the sophisticated piece of biological gadget that we are. We can definitely reprogram it by reformatting or eliminating and deleting what we don't benefit from and keeping what we can benefit from. Just as we defragment the memories of computers, we can defragment our memory too, this can be hard work for some, but we know with love and effort it can be done. We just need to ensure that we create and keep the supporting environment of friends and family around us. This can help us greatly in achieving something positive even quicker.

There is no actual computer chip of some kind that can simply be plugged into us to make the change, at least, not yet. We are not in the movie 'Matrix' just yet. Scientists are working on that though. But, what we do need to do is that we need to realise the potential, which we have, the ability to be able to overwrite what has gone into the brain with a systematic way of manipulation and training. That way we can get ourselves to reach goals, which we want to achieve, quickly. The efforts we need to make towards those goals will be supplemented with those new additions - the corrections in our memory. Those corrections whether in the subconscious or conscious mind, whether in our thoughts and/or the beliefs, will all play a supportive part to ensure success in achieving all that we want.

I did that, and I am seeing what I wanted to do in physical existence. When I would think about what I wanted to do, it was always something which would give me the freedom of life, more importantly I always wanted to have the luxury of being able to work from home so I can give all the time that I can to my family while enjoying what I would love to do. And I saw that the thoughts and desire of wanting to work from home had started bringing about the opportunities which were very much in line with what I always wanted to do. The opportunities were the ones, which would have helped me achieve the 'work from home' goal.

I was thinking about such a lifestyle all the time, I would have loved to work from home and wanted to use the best of my brain in intelligent manner. I was always thinking about setting up an office at home. I got the opportunity to work from home as an assessor, where I would work few hours a week outside and then come back home to do the rest of the work. I guess this can be aligned with the power of thoughts and the law of attraction and also with the grace of God, who is the creator of all those laws and forces. With this work I started to get time to be able to think hard on identifying my natural skills and abilities, the opportunity that I could adapt as a profession for the rest of my life. First I tried few options that seemed financially rewarding but would have involved a lot of time away from home, travelling eventually defeating the whole purpose of achieving a well-balanced life. My love for working from home showed up the opportunity to work in the world of Internet, the recent revolution of the world and I now enjoy being an IT guy as well as being an author.

The results are so obvious and visible that I cannot ignore the power of thoughts and efforts, the power of doing something with love, the power to do something with passion and above all the power of the universe, the God, the energy that designed the Universe in such manner that one who can realise their own self, will realise the power which created the whole creation. You may call it God or energy. We would have all commonly heard this quote *'Self-realisation before God realisation'*. We need to realise who we are in reality, it is only common sense to do so as it plays a very important part in creating the future we want to live. Everything exists for us to exist. God created everything for us on this planet. We have all heard "God created man in his own image." Hence, all we see around us is eventually created by us. And the action to create is what Karma is, which further influences our life and then our future lives. For those who do not believe in God or Karma, do read below scientific support from a famous German Physicist, Max Planck -

> **'All matter originates and exists only by virtue of a force which brings the particles of an atom to vibration which holds the atom together. We must assume behind this force is the existence of a conscious and intelligent mind. This mind is the matrix of all matter.'**

Be More than just Being

So, all that simply explains that the composition of the Universe or everything that exists, the existence of us as human beings at any given time is because of our consciousness and thoughts that help direct that consciousness towards a direction, the direction in which we see our future. And if you believe in science and not god, then science also tells you as per the Quantum theory that, to change your current reality at any given time in future, one needs to work on their thoughts and tune them towards where you want to see yourself in future. There are a lot of people who have changed their lives with that belief and they have realised that there is much more to life than simply making money and living rich. They have not been able to find that inner peace and happiness that they wanted. This simply implies that for one to be really happy in life in all aspects, Money alone is not going to help. However it may give you the ability to gain happiness by spreading happiness further with the money you may have been blessed with.

One of the many success stories I admire is that of an Australian self-made millionaire John Fitzgerald. He made his fortune in the property investment market. John is living a successful life and not only he made his life a success story but he also does a lot to help other kids as well from what I have read and learned about him, tells me that he started with $200/- in his pocket. The timing was that of a property boom. He sold his first property for $100K at the age of 17.

What he does apart from his property ventures is sponsoring this school named Toogoolawa, in a heritage listed Queenslander home on a horse paddock at Ormeau in south of Brisbane, Australia. This school looks after no more than 20 students at any time. And these kids are troubled kids, the ones in special need, and special need of care. I guess that is why it is named as Toogoolawa, which in native language of aboriginal Australians means ' a place in the heart '. John has a dream to fund 50 Toogoolawa schools across Australia. He spends about $800,000/- per year on these schools. He has been doing this since he was 26 and now he is 46-47 years young, still going strong in his motives.

The students at school recite the school's affirmation in unison: 'We start the day with love, we fill the day with love, we end the day with love. This is the way we live.' There are about 500 or more students that have passed through these schools, doing their two years program. Dr Ron Farmer is a clinical psychologist and pioneer in behavioural therapy in Australia. He devised the Educare system, which drives this school as well. He designed Educare based on the notion 'The behaviours are learned and can be un-learned'. They use the five human values of Love, Truth, Peace, Right Conduct and Non-Violence. He believes in building a troubled student's character and their thirst for knowledge will grow with it.

John had earned and made enough money that he wanted to and retired at 26 years of age. One day he was having dinner with a friend. They often discussed the idea and meanings of life. His friend mentioned to him that if you are standing still, you are going backwards; then, how are you going to leave your legacy. And this was probably the thought that triggered these schools idea in his mind. He does not mention about this great act of his on the stages when he is giving seminars about properties. But he does this with a great heart.

He was almost a troubled kid at 15 years of age, but it was his Mother's words which carried him through such times. He mentions 'I never had a conversation with my mum in which she didn't tell me she loved me. On the phone; in person; every time. That's the difference I had. That's what got me through'. So the message here is of love, love has the power to change, you just need to develop that love for your life and the way you want your life. What we do what we see, what we have around us does and has an impact in and on our lives somewhere somehow. As John explained in one of the stories of two kids who stole about two hundred dollars from the petty cash box. One of them steals all the time as per John. 'The kids will fail, but the thing is, we can't expel them because where will they go then? I say, 'You've stolen from me, how can I help you?' Now I am saying that to a 13 year old kid. I realise there is a part of his brain saying, 'This guy's kidding himself' But I also know that if I am honestly saying that I care for him and his future, then that's going somewhere as well. I will get through to this kid eventually.'

We need to be more than just being on this planet. We need to be able to do more than what we currently are, apply this common sense for our own sake as well as for the sake of the whole universe and the world we live in. And, to be able to do that, we need to become more than what we are, more than what we think we are, as what we are is only limited by the thoughts and hurdles we create within our mind. Being more can be achieved simply with the help of thoughts, create positive thoughts they will act 100 times powerful in achieving your goals than what the negative thought helps you achieve. It does work really well, right?! You know you do not do something once you have a negative thought about that something. The thought is successful right there and then in stopping you from doing that particular task. Then why and what makes you think that a positive thought will not work? Just check on that strength of "Belief" behind that thought and you'll know what I am talking about. Power of thoughts is so miraculous, realise it, put your belief behind them and make use of it to your advantage.

What is painful is that we do not do it to make a positive impact. Yet we want more and more things that will give us comfort in this world, but we would go about them in the painful way rather than the way it should have been. The way it should have been from the day one. We, as humans, started doing things we were not supposed to and now we are in such a karmic mess on this planet, that rather than enjoying what we were given as a natural habitat, we created more out of what was given to us. We thought what is given was not enough for us, and out of greed we started creating and committing such karmas that we are incapable and unable to reap the rewards of those karmas with happiness. We need to start moving and start manipulating that ability of taking actions or creating karmas towards the positive to be able to neutralise the negative effects and then we will push through to see the positive outcomes. As the positive thoughts are and have hundred times stronger effects, it does not take too long to see those effects. One just needs to decide with the true heart, and then follow with full love and devotion.

What hurts me more is that while there are people like John, there are large amounts of people out there, who have been working hard to attain things they love to attain and achieve, and tend to forget the true meaning and purpose of life. A really touchy story I received in my email, which touched me at a very deep level. It raised the urge in me to try and spread the word about the real meaning of life and love and how we exist emotionally with others that make part of our life.

The story explained; there was a gentleman who worked hard to make some money. He had bought a car he really loved and always wanted to. On a nice weekend before taking the kids and his wife for a ride, he washed the car and was giving a quick tightening to the tyre screws after putting the new wheel caps he wanted. While he was doing that he saw his son walking in front of the car and few seconds later he realised the son had started to scratch the car's front panel. All of a sudden his temper rose to the highest level and he went on to give his son a smack on the back of his hand, while looking into his eyes ensuring the kid understood well what his dad was trying to give him the beating for. He loved his car so much and hated the act by his son so much that he did not even realise under the influence of anger that he was hitting his son not with his hand but the spanner he was holding. The poor kid was hurt badly and his fingers were full of blood and badly damaged. What happened next was the rush to the hospital. His hand was so badly damaged that doctors advised; he might not recover the strength in his hand ever again.

Dad realised what he had done. And when he walked to the car to see the scratches made by his son; the scratches read 'Love you Dad'. The story continued to tell that he committed suicide the next day as he felt so hurt and ashamed of his act when the kid asked 'Dad, when would my fingers be all right?' It's so sad the way the love for things in the world can overtake our actions towards the people in our life, the ones we love and care for. We need to spread more love. We need to create more love, more for the people and then for anything else. The individuals, who have identified the law of love, are abiding by it and hence receiving more of it too.

So, all that I mentioned above are some of the natural and scientifically proven facts recognised and used by people who understand the theory of life more deeply. They know how life is affected and also how it can be knowingly and deliberately impacted to bring the desired change. You just need to understand more and decide to take that first step, to implement the change that is necessary to bring about the change that is needed. This is Only Common Sense to make that change, but we all know how uncommon it is that people will apply that in their lives. That is why I called it 'The Uncommon Common Sense'.

I always had a fair amount of interest in astral physics and how the basics of physics worked. It always was one of my strong subjects during my school studies. And the kind of spiritual and religious beliefs I have lived by and grew up in, have always hinted towards what science actually uncovered as the mysteries that we know today about the universe. In a way the knowledge already had existed in religious ancient books.

One of the mystics was of a fairly well known religion which originated from India known as Sikhism (Sikhs, these people are considered as the bravest and warrior tribe of India and wear turbans on their long grown hair and also have long grown beards. Not to be confused with Muslim people who may also wear a turban with long beards. In the ancient history of India, a mystic of the Sikh religion, respectably known as Guru Nanak Dev Ji (15 April 1469 – 22 September 1539), had always preached about the purpose of human life. He always preached the message of love, peace and harmony and he gave an insight into the eternal truth of life. He had already made his followers aware of the hundreds of thousands of galaxies, planets and moons - ones that scientists are still finding more of them day by day. Quote – 'lakh akashan akash, lakh paatalan pataal', which testifies this, can be found in the Sikh religious book – Sri Guru Granth Sahib Ji.

His preaching suggested that hundreds of thousands of planets and galaxies exists out there, and so would have been the message by some other saints and mystics around the world. He had told that during his lifetime in late 14th and early fifteenth century. He had followers from both the Hindu and Muslim religions, as you may be aware that India has the second largest Muslim population in the world even today. When Guru Nanak Ji passed away, his followers as normal human beings had a dispute over how to go about his cremation. Muslims wanted to bury his body in the earth and Hindus wanted to burn the body as per their tradition. But, when they lifted the sheet off where his body was, it is noted that they only found flowers and divided them amid each other.

When he had divine enlightenment, it is said that he expressed to the world, 'There are neither Hindus nor Muslims, then whose path shall I follow? I shall follow God's path'. So from that point onwards he had declared that religions do not matter and God created all that exists. So we should all follow the path of the creator, widely known as God. You may call it whatever you want, but the supreme idea is that of love, peace and harmony among all that exists. Based on the way the world operates and what science explains about life, and all those mystical beliefs and teachings they have provided to the world, in different languages, different religions, different tribes in different parts of world, it is no surprise to conclude that God must exist or that supreme power or source of energy must exist which is making the world go round. Even the actions in the form of Karma adhere to **'what goes around comes around'**. It is that ability of us human beings, being able to create those Karmas that also help us understand that we can plan our destinations in life.

With all the above my friends! Please exercise the Common-Sense and take action for the good of your soul. There is a vast amount and number of possibilities as to where we could be at any point in time depending on the actions that we take in this world. Your actions and the direction can only and only be tamed by destiny at its best, but many have proven to change the destiny based on their strong will and actions behind a greater cause. With the cause of taking action in mind, let me introduce you to what I call Future Probability Sphere (FPS) in the next chapter to help you equip yourself better on your journey.

'Only if we spotted our destination and be there with a dare

we could realise our direction, where our future is giving us a stare.

Without the clear vision; we could have been here or even somewhere there.'

Part - II

Future Probability Sphere

*'There are some people who live in a dream world,
and there are some who face reality;
and then there are those who turn one into the other.'*

-Douglas Everett

While gravity is pulling to the core of Earth,
Time is something running away from us.
That movement of time is the force, movement into future force.
Give it the destination to follow a direction.

Future Probability Sphere

Future Probability Sphere - What do I mean by that? I base my theory of life on a sphere, which is what the earth and other planets or stars are like in the closest sense of shape. All these planets and stars are revolving around like a sphere, still maintaining its balance at the core of it. They are all cruising along nicely in harmony at such a scale in this universe while maintaining the balance at their centre. And similarly, we should maintain the balance at the core, our mind our brain and we should keep resonating in this universe with harmony. We are also made of the Atoms, generally known as the small tiny spheres of energy maintaining us in the shape and form we are in. And while we maintain that balance of our physical existence we are always constantly facing and dealing with what we are surrounded with not just in physical form but also mentally. And as part of evolving with time we have the capability to place our vision at any desired probable possibility of our existence and realise it in the atmosphere around us, in the universe we live in.

As everything that exists can be viewed in a 360 degrees perspective, and depending on at what angle you see it from, it will have a unique view, as it appears to you in a physical and geographical shape. And that is where the quantum physics conveys that you can visualise what you want to be in life on this planet. Visualise it to be whatever you want as all the variable views are possible. There on just focus on achieving that targeted view, the outcome or goal. Quantum Physics is continuing further researches with some more theories in similar relation.

The Universe as we know it through our eyes is three, four, or even five dimensional, as explained by the physicists. **Fourth dimension** to our existence as three-dimensional human beings is the **time or age** we can say in easy to understand words. It is when you try and understand the fifth dimension, you'll know that what you set your eyes on is really truly possible with your mind totally set to it. **What you actually become** as a person as time passes is what your **fifth dimension** is. The physical creation of who you are as a person based on your qualities is the fifth dimension in other words. If you wanted to become a doctor but became a nurse instead, being a nurse is your fifth dimension. However it happened but it is still possible for you to become a doctor but not at a point back in time, but surely in future if you set that to be your target. It is explained that there are multitude of paths we can branch out to at any moment in time or in life. And that branching out is influenced by our own actions, or otherwise by chance, influence or actions of others around us.

As per Michio Kaku, based on his String Theory, the concept of multiple universes, the Multiverse is eleven dimensional. He further explains that within this eleven dimensional hyperspace we can have many universes. He referred to universes as bubbles, also known as membranes, which can be three, four, five or up to eleven dimensional, it collapses down if we go beyond eleven and settles back to eleven. These membranes for short are also called brains in his theory, and these brains can exist in different levels of dimensions. He further explains on what Einstein also investigated and wrote about during the last thirty years of his life – 'The Mind of God'. He explained that the mind of God in this picture would be a cosmic vibrational music, generated by these membranes or the brains resonating through our eleven dimensional hyperspace.

Some people may be asking about how did this dimensional thing, the mind of God, the cosmic musical vibration buzz started all together. The moment we are able to understand that, we'll know we are all one with the universe with some serious capabilities as human beings. We are what we are because of the frequency we are vibrating at. Let me talk to you about the Sound of OM; the sound that relates to the Hindu philosophy. OM is the cosmic vibrational music of the universe and as explained, OM is made of three sounds combined – the Aaa, the Ooo and the Mmm. And would you believe these are the only three sounds of letters that humans can make without the use of their tongue. OM is probably the most used and repeated word in all the enchanted mantras and also for meditation.

OM is considered to be the sound of inner silence, the supreme consciousness of the soul and therefore all that exists.

Scientists have also recorded the vibrational energy from sun or so called the sound of the sun. And because its very deep and exist at a much different frequency to what we can understand, they compressed it so we could understand and the sound is clearly defined to resemble with the sound of OM as enchanted by Sadhus and Yogis ever since. Somehow it does relate with what has been said above by the scientists Michio Kaku about the cosmic vibrational music. In the theory of "Music of the Spheres" even Pythagorus proposed that all planets, Sun and the moon all make their own unique hum (orbital resonance) depending on their orbital revolution.

The cosmic music hidden in OM has always been used in Yoga and is a belief related to the Hindu tradition, as is Karma. And if you learn more about Hinduism, the yoga and meditation you will learn that all those achieved people in history had used the knowledge of meditation and karma to achieve their goals, whether in spiritual life or the worldly life. All those who recognised this ability and prayed to the almighty God the ultimate power or the supreme source of energy, have been able to awaken the mystical force within. If they used the force for the purpose and prosperity of Love, Peace and Harmony, they would always prosper. If they used it for the benefit of all in conjunction with the laws of the universe, they would benefit themselves and also all the others around them.

So, if science and the mystic community are in the almost same belief and practices at the core level, then I don't have to disagree with any of them and just believe in what lies beneath as the basic composition of those concepts. The concept is that of the belief in that superior cosmic power. And I am happy to call it God and live by the laws, which regulate the universe and spread the message. In ancient Hindu stories as well as in Christianity and Muslim religions as well, they all believed and still believe in miracles. We all know that miracles happen. Most of the time their occurrence is due to a deeper level of prayers, love and belief, which is shown in a particular saint or a mystic. It is that truthful heart and sincerity, which becomes the reason to receive or experience those miracles by those mystical identities, whether seen or unseen, a saint or a mystic.

If the miracle does happen through some sort of a medium then how can that medium, whether a saint or their statue, have the power to perform a miracle. One should be thinking little deeper about how did those saints, mystics or holy men or women get those powers, after all for those powers to exist there must be a creator of those powers. If them, being born as humans, could achieve that certain level of miracle performing capabilities with a certain level of powers by the medium of love and devotion towards that supreme power, the supreme creator who I refer to as God, then you can too. You need to believe in yourself, that supreme Creator and show love and devotion towards Him or Her or that energy to receive the magical touch. With that magical touch you can start realising the deeper meaning in your life. The results will be visible as long as the respect is there, the gratitude is there, and love and harmonious intentions are present within your heart and mind.

And that is why you can become whatever you want to be, only if you put a sincere heart and mind to materialise that fifth dimension of yours, to be what you want to be. You need to recognise that sphere of possibilities around you, consider this as the future you are heading towards and once you have decided on a goal and place where you want to land then a designated path of projection is clearly visible to you, your full attention will be there, on that goal and you will get there. The Future Probability Sphere travels with you all the time being centrally attached at the origin, your brain, your mind being the central core of it. That centre of the brain is also recognised by the science as an area of brain where the memory of our brains resides as well. The FPS exists around you all the time. You just need to recognise it and find the place and pinpoint where you want to be on your FPS.

Once you have set the goal, that goal, the fifth dimension becomes stationery as is explained by the quantum physics. Quantum physics explained by Einstein stated that as soon as the attention is placed on a particle; it becomes stationery and exists as a stationery particle. His theory explains that any particle exists like a static particle sometimes and at other times it exists like a wave. The position and momentum of particles cannot exist simultaneously. Then there is the String theory, which explains the same in its own way. The very well respected scientist, Professor Michio Kaku says –

> *'All the subatomic particles they found from the hydrogen collider were nothing but musical notes. Physics is nothing but the laws of harmony. Chemistry is nothing but the melodies you can play on the musical instruments when they bump into each other. Universe is the symphony of strings.'*

He also explains the freewill as 'In some sense we do have some kind of a free will, no one can determine your future events given your past history, there is always a wild card.' He also defines the Mind of God as that the 'Mind of God would be cosmic music, resonating through 11 dimensions of space.' He also confirms 'When we look at us in a mirror, we are looking at us in a billionth of a second in the past, in history.'

In other words there were two mainstream theories provided one by Einstein, which explains and suggested that when you concentrate on a particle it becomes a stationery particle and exists like a stationery particle. The other theory by Neil Bohr suggested that the particle is a wave and not a stationery particle. Now we have a number of other theories such as Bohmian mechanics pilot wave theory, Many Worlds theory, Quantum De-Coherence theory and there is the String theory that claims to go beyond the other theories as they break when reaching the centre of the universe or the centre of a black hole. Though I am not a Quantum Physics expert, I do believe in the basics of the theories, which is widely known as 'the Copenhagen Interpretation of Quantum Physics'.

I strongly believe that everything exists the way you look at something. As per science the moment you are concentrating completely on something it becomes a stationery particle target. And while you are looking at it without concentration, you are still looking for other possibilities and hence you will find it as a wave particle because you are looking at it with a mind frame that is still probating the existence of something. That only scientifically explains why seeing a goal clearly as if it is in actual existence is so important.

As a non-scientific human being, we can put aside all experts' arguments. The important thing is that you exist and you must exist in your fifth dimension either by choice or by chance! You would rather make it by choice, the only exception being when destiny strongly interferes. But, know that destinies may be changed with a strong will. And if your will lets you down or destiny works for better, accept that as a positive in this karmic world in the overall scheme of things and put together the new plan and destination point in your newly formed Future Probability Sphere.

To set up the clear view and goals you need to recognise the Future Probability Sphere around you. Learn about all the probabilities and possibilities that can exist, and set the destination by seeing it clearly in your mind. That is when you will see something in existence and realise that it is possible to travel and reach that goal. You are keeping and moving that FPS around you all the time, be aware of it. Then once you have achieved the goal you decided, reached your destination, from that point you can recognise and set a new goal or projection point in the FPS as it exists around you at that point in time. You can even reassess a goal that had come into your mind in the past but had to slip down the priority list. It may have either become much easier to accomplish now than before or somewhat even harder. The way you will see a goal from one position in your FPS will differ from another position.

We know this as a matter of fact that the closer you reach towards a goal, you look at it as easier and easier to achieve. Conversely if you do not work towards achieving it, it becomes harder and harder because the fourth and fifth dimensions keep moving and keep creating the present you. Time is slipping and you are becoming what you become by not doing what you want to as per the identified and desired goal. As they say – "If you are standing still, you are going backwards". Similar will apply if you temporarily changed your goal to achieve another. The way you looked at your original goal before will now differ depending on the situation you are in when you have achieved the new shifted goal.

While you are on the journey towards your goal whatever exists in between also has its own tiny attraction and that is why it can also be dangerous if you are not focused and clear about what you want to achieve. As you move along everything else along the way will present and introduce new distracting opportunities within your FPS. As you make progress, every moment acts like a settled sphere in its own self-existence as well as they project a different view, a new trajectory at every move you make forward into your future. Those new momentarily settled spheres do look lucrative and achieved, so you can also achieve whatever comes in your way while you are on the way to a final goal. But you must concentrate and focus not to deviate from the actual path that you are traveling on, and not change your goal. If you wish to be agile to improvise and do recognise a new point of projection, a new goal that you want to reach you can well and duly do so, and that will just become your new destination in FPS. You must be careful that you assess any improvised goal with due diligence to the purpose you have determined for your life, otherwise you may never reach a milestone destination and only keep traveling in between a lot of them. So decide those goals carefully with your true heart and you will see the results.

> 'Quality is never an accident, it is always the result of high intention, sincere effort, intelligent direction and skilful execution; it represents the wise choice of many alternatives.'
>
> - William A Foster

Let's now have a walk in the real life and talk about the technique used in sports by the people who play athletics and are probably participating in discus throw, shot-put throw, hammer throw or any such sport. Just imagine what difference it makes to where their throw may land by deciding the strength and angle with timing of when to throw. So that not only their throw is the best but also they remain qualified or do that act of sport in a particular manner so they don't violate the rules of the game. Only that determines their success in that sport altogether. How about the karate champions we see, breaking few stacks of concrete slabs or ice or wood just with bare hands, while a normal human being otherwise may still have to have a number of attempts with some hammer to break them, and even then some may not be successful.

So, what do you believe it has taken them to be successful in achieving those goals in their life? It is the direction they decided to take on at a certain stage of life, followed it with their heart, followed their passion and started practicing hard on making the attempts. They did it over and over again. Did they succeed the first time around, were they the champions on the very first day? No. They achieved it by continuous devotion and practice, by doing whatever it took them to achieve their goal. Take anyone who has been successful in sports, in business, in life, in spirituality in any mode of life you can talk about. It is the people who have made up their mind with true heart and decided on what they were going to do for the rest of their life. And as that is what they wanted to do, they have pressed hard on those ideas, those motives, they have taken every action they could to succeed in their motive, they decided with their true heart and followed up with love and devotion.

What about some of the famous love stories? For example, Romeo & Juliet or any other such love stories you may have read about. They all suggest one thing in common; love has no bars, no borders, and no hurdles. If the love is true, it is bound to succeed no matter what and how many hurdles may be thrown in the way. Similar should be the story of our life, and the way we live our life. We should all love our life. Even if you don't right now for whatever your past life may hold, you should decide to change that and love your life for the fact that you have decided to implement change for good. And then depending on what decision we take at times, we determine where our life will be, be it a day, a week, a month, a year or a decade after. It all starts from the tiny first step. And the direction you will take that step in.

Just like a discus thrown at the speed of 10 km/hour at an angle of 10 degree will not end up at a same place as a similar disc thrown at a little different speed and angle. Just like a shot-put throw will be affected in the same way, and as would be the hammer throw. Similar will apply to your life, depending on the precision and effort you put behind the goals you may want to achieve.

All you need to do is take examples from life, from around you, from the people who have succeeded, also from people who have failed and failed numerous times before they succeeded. What do you think would have happened if they decided to give up when they failed the first time around? They would have been stuck with the life living the way they didn't really want to. But they had decided with their full heart as to what they wanted to do, this became a little like their love story to achieve that goal. The goal became their beloved so they had to achieve it. How can you let your beloved be lost when you know you can win it with the true devotion and action.

> *'Success in life is a matter not so much of talent, as of concentration and perseverance.'*
> — C. W. Wendte

You should understand the importance of deciding with your true heart and giving yourself, your real potential a fair go. Do not die with all your wishes buried within your heart. Get them out, let them come to being and flourish, let them become alive and let life vibrantly prosper. Live the life with full happiness as it is meant to be and as everyone should be living it, full of love, happiness and joy.

So, live life, don't just live by. Decide and take action today, what you act upon is surely to bring some sort of changed results in your life. Since you would have decided with full and sincere heart and in the direction of what you want; the action you follow up with can only be in that same direction and will help you proceed further. Do not let the hurdles, failures or de-motivational comments by others put you off from your goals. The actions you take will matter a lot. Your achievement is entirely dependent on you and the action you will take. Your **love for your goal** is what will determine your success at that point in time and when you may be feeling down. That is why and that is when you need to make sure, what the atmosphere around you is like; the places you go to, the company you are in, the people you associate with. It all matters in achieving the goal that matters the most to you.

Where you would land up in the FPS of your life really depends not so much on the present point of placement you are at but, how you launch from there onwards. And we all know that when you throw a stone in some direction it only goes as far as the direction given and strength used to throw it. It may be the maximum strength you could use, or half strength if you did not do it with a full heart and devotion. It is also about empowering your self. How empowered are you to make that throw, in this case of FPS, how prepared and equipped are you with the resources you may need to travel in a particular direction, the direction and trajectory of your goal.

If you are to shoot a bullet and you use your hands to throw, you may need to reach up to it few times to throw it again to get it to the target you may want it hit. You still won't kill with that bullet. And instead if you have a gun to shoot that bullet in a direction, it is equipped with the technology to make it go precisely in the direction you want to shoot and it also travels longer distance with faster speed too. With your focus, it will hit the bull's eye. You know what I am getting at.

So, one should work on the need to equip themselves better, become equipped with clear knowledge of your goals in your life. Become knowledgeable with all that you may need to pursue the journey towards your desired achievement. Seeing the goals clearly and equipping yourself with knowledge or required training will turn you into a person with a gun not a hand thrower. And obviously you will achieve more and land more towards the goal you set compare to a hand thrower person. That is what will get you towards your goal sooner. That is why you need to assess more of yourself, and then address the needs to better equip yourself. This is also just common sense, isn't it?

That reminds me of a T-Shirt I use to wear, a black t-shirt with grey painted writing on it, which said 'Fully Equipped'. That did tickle few nerves in my mind to ensure I tried to equip myself with any knowledge and concept that I could. So I strongly recommend becoming fully equipped with whatever you may need to take that life changing action. You will be amazed with the person you will become and then, when you are shooting towards the goal, you will be much focused, much sharper and you will achieve your goal with much more efficiency. That is the way you can define your landing in the FPS. How much concentrated effort you put in, being well equipped with tools and mental strength, will determine your landing in the future. So prepare well, this is the mission for the life you want to live, the achievements you want out of your life. Prepare well and then take your shot, make it the best shot. Use the present that is at your hands, use it well, and use it wisely.

'The art of living lies less in eliminating our troubles than in growing with them'
-Baruch

Struggle as it may seem, it is part of living the life on this planet for most people. But it does not have to be that way. We as human beings do have the capabilities of changing things to the way we like. We do it quite often and do it quite successfully as well. We are doing it really well in convincing ourselves when we are telling us what we are actually incapable of. We do not use it successfully in telling us what we are actually capable of. If we did use the same effort in telling us about the things that we are capable of, then imagine the things one can achieve.

One may say that you can't be good at everything, but what I am trying to say here is that practice makes a man perfect, and women too. And if you recognise what comes as natural abilities and talents to you, it is going to help you enjoy the journey of life and it is like making use of the assets you have. Yet you are able to achieve anything in life with practicing more and more, and by practicing it again and again you are bound to succeed.

There may be initial struggle on the way but eventually you will make the cut. An interesting story we were always told at schools in relation to this was that of a piece of rope and the stone-wall around the water wells. Now we all know that a piece of rope made from plastic or coconut shells can no-way be stronger than the huge piece of stone. And yet, when the rope is rubbed against that stone again and again for pulling the water out of the well with tied buckets; it does damage the stone. The stone is actually cut through; it wears off with the weaker rope, just because it runs over it again and again. So is the impact of practicing again and again. That is what a lot of well-known and successful personalities have proven. We have a lot of those examples in sports also.

'I think and think for months, for years. Ninety-nine times the conclusion is false. The hundredth time I am right.'

---Albert Einstein

Albert Einstein knew that persistence is the key in achieving something new, something different. The answer did not just drop out of nowhere. He tried hard, and used elimination of errors technique with applying a variance to get things working. Did you know that he did not speak until he was four years old and did not read until he was seven? His parents thought he was 'sub-normal,' and one of his teachers described him as mentally slow, unsociable, and adrift forever in foolish dreams. He was expelled from school and was refused admittance to the Zurich Polytechnic School. He did eventually learn to speak and read. And we all know what he achieved.

> *'That is why I say Do not let the past take control of your future if you are not happy with it. It will happen by default if you do not instruct otherwise.'*

It is very important to realise the present and make the most of it. There was a show we went to watch, something that was said by the presenter has unconsciously had added to the way I looked at our life and our existence in this world. In this show they used a dome made with modern technology, which created a round cover over us. The light effects were so great and combined with this specially designed dome; it made us feel as if we were looking at the real sky at night. But the one thing he explained in some context was that 'we are all living in the past, we are all seeing each other as an effect of energy that occurred the tiniest fraction of a second ago, a billionth of a second'.

Now, those words struck my mind straight away, we all talk about the past, the present and the future but never before I had heard it in this context. From that day I started to see the world in a different perspective. What he said was so very true. And accordingly, our present is really just that fractional short-term memory. So why not start creating the memories for the way we would like to see our future at any distant future's present moment, which maybe 5, 10, 20 years away. And we actually can do that. We do have the capabilities. We just need to realise it.

All those personalities that we know as great achievers in this world also encountered some sort of failure before they succeeded. But they succeeded because they loved what they wanted to do and they persisted. Here next are some of the statements from all those people in History, who made their mark in creating the History.

Some old and gold quotations

'Many of life's failures are people who did not realise how close they were to success when they gave up.'

A statement of 1877, as quoted in From Telegraph to Light Bulb with Thomas Edison (2007) by Deborah Hedstrom,

'Only those who dare to fail greatly can achieve greatly.'
- Robert F. Kennedy

And when you look into sports personalities. Michael Jordan and Bob Cousy were rejected from their high school basketball teams. Jordan once conveyed,

'I've failed over and over again in my life. That is why I succeed.'

Stan Smith was *rejected as a ball boy for a Davis Cup tennis match because he was 'too awkward and clumsy.' He went on to clumsily win Wimbledon and the U. S. Open. And he also won eight Davis Cups.*

The first time **Jerry Seinfeld** walked on-stage at a comedy club as a professional comic, *he looked out at the audience, froze, and forgot the English language. He stumbled through 'a minute-and a half' of material and was jeered offstage. He returned the following night and closed his set to wild applause.*

In 1944, **Emmeline Snively,** director of the Blue Book Modelling Agency, told modelling hopeful *Norma Jean Baker, 'You'd better learn secretarial work or else get married.' We all know that Norma Jean was Marilyn Monroe.*

After **Fred Astaire's** had his first screen test, the testing director of MGM, commented in 1933, 'Can't act. Can't sing. Slightly bald. Can dance a little.' He kept that memo over the fire place in his Beverly Hills home.

Astaire once said that *'when you're experimenting, you have to try so many things before you choose what you want, that you may go days getting nothing but exhaustion.'* And here is the reward for perseverance: *'The higher up you go, the more mistakes you are allowed. Right at the top, if you make enough of them, it's considered to be your style.'*

Charles Schultz had every cartoon he submitted *rejected by his high school yearbook staff. And he went on to make Peanuts, a show that ran for 50 years successfully.*

A Paris art dealer refused shelter to **Picasso** when he asked if he could bring in his paintings from out of the rain. *We know what Picasso achieved and that the art dealer eventually went broke.*

John Milton *wrote Paradise Lost 16 years after losing his eyesight.*

I hope these exemplary quotes will help you understand what is possible with the full heart and devotion; if you put it to work behind something that you love to do, love to achieve. Sometimes I get this argument that not everyone can be like them. But I need you to understand that, they were like everybody else, they applied the common sense that was needed to succeed; and they also devoted completely to what they wanted to do, their whole heart, their whole effort, and their whole life. Do it yourself and see the results, but make sure that you clearly decide your destination in your FPS. Do it with your full heart, with love and full devotion.

Standing Firm & Tall on your Feet

'Flops are a part of life's menu
and I've never been a girl to miss out on any of the courses.'
~ Rosalind Russell

Flops are a part of life's menu. And as I said, struggle may be part of life and actually it is from the day we are born. There is struggle in learning to walk; learning to talk, and we were naturally blessed with our instincts on how to get feed. It is a natural occurring for a baby to take the breast feed from his/her mother. And even that is a struggle at start as it is a learning process for both, the mother and the baby. And from there on there is always a struggle before we tend to deem ourselves as experts in some things as kids and teens. Our parents very well knew that there is a lot we lack even at that stage, as they have seen the life past those stages, the life, which is more likely coming up in front of those kids.

If more life handling techniques were taught at school, in helping the kids develop on their natural talents by recognising them. The purpose of education should be to nurture natural talent. The world will not be struggling; going to work on Mondays and coming back home happy on Fridays just to enjoy the two-day weekend. Only if we all loved, what we do. And that is what we all need to achieve, 'Do what we would love to do.'

If you believe that you are long way through your life. Let me tell you that there is no stage that is too late. You just need to assess your own self. And if you are happy with what you are and what you have, I am happy for you. But as long as you have recognised that you didn't give up on your dreams or you did not unhappily accepted to be happy with what you are today and what you have achieved or what you are working towards achieving.

I realised that at the age of 32, and I now look back and realise that, this is what I always wanted to be apart from not being able to become a pilot. I loved creativity, I loved proposing creativity, I loved suggesting ideas that were efficient and whenever I spoke to someone about them, I was always discouraged as my ideas always walked across 200% positive attitude and 100% efficiency. And perhaps I realised that I was talking to the wrong people. I started looking for people who were doing what I wanted to do - those who were living the life as to what life is meant to be.

One thing I realised was that the way I wanted to put my ideas and creativity to work was hard for others to understand. The very problem I encountered was with the first social website I wanted to launch. I had outsourced the work and more than 10 months later I was struggling to get the things done the way I wanted to. And the launch came to a pause for a while. Finally I decided that I would turn my love towards technology into a skill for me to be able to implement what I wanted to do. And that's when I realised my FPS and my destination on it. This helped me in seeing my goal even clearer.

I realised that because I found it hard for others to understand what I wanted to put across in terms of making something creative. It could have also been that I simply got stuck with someone who wasn't really keen on doing that work or the way I wanted to have things done. Most of the work, which was common sense and logical to me and all my friends, just did not seem that way for him. For example, I had asked for a single form with relevant links and flow of options hidden or presented based on if the user was an individual or a business. Instead what I got was a single form that will register individual members as well as businesses, that made DOB and Sex options mandatory for all, for businesses which were to be registered on the same form and giving no option to have the business name entered on the form. Now that is real uncommon-sense I gathered.

I loved the idea of the Internet and the Digital Revolution the world is going through. And I thought computer's languages are what we can control the best way to bring out the desired result. If others are not giving me what I wanted, then I can build upon my interest and experience and why not get involved and empower myself. This was a change in my fifth dimension and a deviation for the final goal I wanted to achieve. But I weighed the options of this change in the FPS. This was part of becoming well equipped to achieve my final goal. I had actually signed up for a domain and hosting account about a year and a half before this incident occurred. I played around with things for a while and then I was busy doing other things as normal hard-work. I saw it even clearly, what I wanted to do after this incident. I started playing with the software in my hosting account that I had signed up for. I published few pages that looked a bit basic at the start and then slowly I played around and developed a perfect looking website from there on I started to come up with more and more ideas.

As the ideas came by, I started putting all of them on paper whenever something struck my mind. I will pull aside if I was driving to take note, even if I was about to drive the car to go somewhere, I did not move the car until I had it written down just so, I do not let that fly away without further consideration. A big thanks to technology as paper and pen are not always handy, I used note-taking facilities on my phone.

Then I started looking for all those nice and intuitive, self-explanatory domain names that could make some impact just by the name alone. I will be putting them out to the world of Internet, slowly as I develop them. But for me to realise my dreams the way I wanted to. I knew I had to learn more and equip myself with the knowledge and skills that will help me succeed in that stream. Hence, I took up studying web development. Even if that was going to cause some pressure in life for some time, I still made that decision. I just had to; as I could not see myself to go on for the rest of my life struggling every day to go to work that I did not really enjoy. I decided my destination in my Future Probability Sphere and the projection of path I would take in that direction became more clear and easier to follow.

Starting times are always a bit rough, but I was happy to deal with that. Its all part of becoming more of you, being more capable and live life as more of being a complete and enriched human being with a more depth and weight in life. I'll get through a lot on depth in life a few pages later but for now imagine the times when you started driving a car, or started learning anything for the first time. We tend to go in a particular flow. A lot of previous studies have used the examples in a different way but let's take a look again.

At first we all '**don't know that we don't know**' something until we feel the need to know it. Then when we are made conscious of something that we don't know, or as in case of learning to drive, when the need arises or the time comes that we want to learn to drive; we all know that we don't know how to drive. This is the next stage of learning '**we know that we don't know**'. Then we start to learn things, we learn about it slowly, about the mechanism and how all the accelerator, the breaks, the steering wheel and engine raving works. Now we come to the stage where we '**know that we know about driving**' or whatever else it is that we are learning.

As we progress and gain more experience in driving, the whole mechanism of not only the car but your body movements also start to work without you even knowing. We all know the state while we started to learn driving, during those initial stages when we asked friends sitting by our side or a family member to tell us whether we should change the lane or not. You tend to avoid looking in the side or back mirrors at times just to ensure that you stay in your lane, and not turn the steering wheel in the direction of the mirror you are looking in to. And once you are experienced you don't even know and your eyeballs move so quickly to note the traffic around you through all your side and rear view mirrors. So we all know it, it becomes so much of a natural reaction and we are finally at the stage of '**we don't know that we know**'. So, practice is a must, and you are bound to succeed if you persist and try hard enough.

Practice hard on what you want to achieve and you will succeed. The best example of following the heart and mind with passion is no other than the CEO of the last decade gone by. Steve Jobs who was the CEO of Apple and a master of some great innovations of this century thus far. That is how I regard him. It was 5th of October 2011 in the USA and we learned that Steve is not with us anymore, I pay a special tribute to him for his work and urge the readers to learn whatever you can from his life stories and books that followed after his death to reinvent the innovation in your life. An amazing guy who innovated the world we live in today. And even that was done during the times of a financial crisis that has hit the world and economies are still suffering and trying hard to recover. What better could be the timing to innovate your life and plan to live happily without getting affected by such circumstances ever again? Some experts are still expecting another dip around 2019-20. I read about the same issue of finding a better solution for work and life all the time. This is the issue for majority of the population in our world. This book is my attempt to help you all in finding that balance, recognising the FPS around you, to help you find your destination and by understanding the deeper meaning in your life. Read an article from news.com.au as below.

****

'OUR working lives are at a crossroads - to find the way forward, we need to hear from you. Economists and business leaders, including the head of the Reserve Bank, are warning us about the threats to the economy of our stagnant productivity levels. Meanwhile employees are expecting our salaries and our job satisfaction levels to grow at ever-higher rates.

According to a UK survey, three in four people think workplace flexibility would boost the economy. But in this country, only one in three workers has a flexible working arrangement. Something has to give. That's why News.com.au's New Work Project is looking at ways to promote or create better ways of working, for employees and bosses alike. It's a conversation taking place in boardrooms and break rooms across the nation - but now it's time for a national approach.'

****

I also remember that there was a debate about government and there strategies on the same news site sometime in late 2010 or early 2011. I posted a comment saying the same. What I said was is in the similar contrast and suggested that If the next government; whoever wants to come into power want an agenda to win the elections; then this is what it needs to be; support everyone in retraining themselves to do their dream jobs, the jobs they love to do, the work they want to do as their passion.

A clear proof and indication from the above article for a need to work in the field you love. Of course the productivity is going to be hurt if you are forced to do something or forcefully doing something. We need to develop that change within, a change that will make us daring enough to face this truth and for a lot of people it may have taken the pain felt from the global financial crisis, and some still may have been in the hope alone for things getting better. I urge people to take the step forward. Make the change happen develop that strong will and you will be forced by that will to take those actions that are necessary to turn your wish into reality, the reality which you can see and live. As said by George Bernard Shaw:

'Imagination is the beginning of creation.
You imagine what you desire; you will what you imagine;
and at last you create what you will.'

As with Apple; the personal computer revolution started in June 1977, The Apple II designed by Steve Wozniak had a built-in keyboard, colour graphics, audio, a floppy drive and of course a screen. And we just need to look around how far that start has arrived. A New York Times columnist Thomas Friedman asked Ex-President Obama to **create more Jobs- Steve Jobs.** His idea is clearly about creating a mechanism that fully supports the innovation and creativity to develop in the young generation in the manner that they should be all successful. And that can only come, if one is following their heart and loving what they do with full devotion, not just because they need a job to be able to pay for their mortgage or bills. No, that is not a way of life and that is not how it should be.

So, it's never too late. Just give yourself the best shot; the shot for life, at the least you would have achieved satisfaction of at least giving yourself a fair go. Sometimes I wonder if that is what did not happen with those people who are classified as terrorists in the present world. I wonder if it were the circumstances that pushed them into those acts. And I also wonder whether there is a set of power hungry people who have used the secret of influencing others in the name of religion and taken advantage of innocent people by offering them money along with the urge for serving their religion. They used these *young and not only restless but best-less minds*. The young people, who were probably depressed because they were not getting to do the right thing by themselves, had no direction and guidance to become their best self but someone came and took advantage of them for their benefit.

But no religion teaches hatred, as they all teach about Loving God and we know Love is God, God is Love. That is what I know, and believe in. Humanity is the only religion. If one can't be a better human being, then they can't be better religious person or practitioners. All are made of similar flesh and bones and blood.

The creator would not have created humans to kill each other, which is why there is something called natural death.

And even if there is no creator, even in general, we need to give respect to receive respect. And how can we not do that to the ones that are similar to us. We behave like animals over having a bigger share of something that may be available for grabs. We need to promote peace and harmony among all of us regardless of country, religion, colour, race, age or sex. And only then the problems as they seem in the world today can be overcome. I am talking about all that to be able to think deeper, so you know we are much more as human beings than just to get by life. There's a lot more to contribute to the world that we can but we must build capability within ourselves first to be able to help the world. So let's get to defining our own FPS so we can gain clarity and find ourselves our landing base, the fifth dimension we want to build in coming future.

Define Your FPS

'Time is moving; we are bound to move into change regardless of its scale. Give it the direction; there is a good chance you will progress in the direction you choose.'

We all know and it is medically proven that for each one of us to be born, we all had to struggle as a sperm with millions of sperms among us to reach the goal ahead of us; to land in our intended place and receive that special care within our mother's body before being born. We succeeded and once we are born into this world, just like a mother, the Father Universe and Mother Nature provides all that we need to grow into being for our purpose in life. The reason we suffer is because we deviate without realising the purpose of our life and get influenced with our surroundings, which are also in the same mess for centuries. The atmosphere around us is discretely influencing the life we are living. Just as the sperm cannot develop into the human being without the proper environment it needs, such is the way our life gets affected. The surrounding atmosphere around us, the energies we have around us, moulds and affects our lives. So again, very importantly the logic of love and care to manifest and nourish energy in physical form flows through out the universe and from infinity of past time till the infinite future.

Our surrounding atmosphere and behaviours play an important role in our life. And similar is the effect of what is created around by the laws of universe. This is an important factor that you must also realise; there are certain laws that govern the Universe. We may not have been aware of them as yet, but that is OK as we were never told much about them at school, at least not all of them. But it has always been known to a certain number of successful people in the world, let's now raise that awareness within you as we have this opportunity now.

You will find understanding these laws of the Universe useful in helping you understand more about your universal existence and how you can work in harmony with these laws to create a better form of your life and better define your future self in your FPS. You must clearly define your FPS and your landing point, the destination goal to where you want to be in that FPS. See your goals and visualise them clearly so you can take action with clear mind. Before you define your FPS though, let's equip you with some wisdom and techniques.

THE LAWS OF THE UNIVERSE

The Law of Attraction or Vibration states that; everything vibrates and nothing rests. Vibrations of the same frequency resonate with each other.

That is why like attracts like or similar energy. Everything that exists in this universe is energy in one form or another. It even includes our thoughts that come into our mind. Consistently focusing on a particular thought or idea attracts its matching frequency vibrations. (This is very much in line with the outcomes of Quantum Physics, and Reticular Activation System as proved by modern science.)

The Law of Polarity states that; everything has an opposite. For a hot measurement there is a cold measurement, for a distant (far) measurement there is nearby (close by) measurement, if there is darkness there also exists light, There is an up placement and there is also a down placement, there is good in the world and there is also bad in the world.

We know that even on our planet earth, there are coldest ends of Antarctica and then there is an equator line with the warmest regions around it. And in the similar way as we exist as energy particles, we know the particles have positive (proton) and negative (electron) elements to it, as is proven by science, the electrons and protons are negative and positive charges, this can mean that we too have two extremes of such behaviours within us. At the same time there is also a neutron particle, which is a neutral particle, does not have a negative or positive impact, but the positive is also stuck to the neutron all the time. Could this also mean that the nucleus can be interpreted as the centre of the universe and only positive thinkers and neutral minds can come close or achieve assumed oneness with the core or God as per religious practices. This argument does have some weight though.

But to make use of this knowledge of polarity in our lives, we just need to assess people around us a little and we will understand there are negative behaviours as well as positive thinkers around us. We also have some who are fairly neutral most of the time causing no troubles with or for someone. It is all about logic of the values. All you need to do is bring yourself in harmony with the law of attraction and you will see yourself as a person moving towards the behaviour you want to achieve in yourself and will start to attract similar people and environments. We know people can change, it just depends what it takes to trigger that change. You need to decide and take action. Start seeing and concentrating on more positive you will attract and shift your polarity in line with what you want to achieve. It is only common sense to do so as I explained earlier in the book.

The Law of Relativity states that; nothing is what it is until you relate it to something. Point of view is determined by what the observer is relating to. The nature, value, or quality of something can only be measured in relation to another object.

We know that in life or even some problem solving at school or work trainings, not everyone had same way of dealing with same problem. It's about how everyone relates himself or herself with a given situation; that is how we understand the situation or problem or any other task within our brain, and accordingly we react. So, start seeing yourself in place of the person before you say anything that may affect them in certain way, how will the words out of your mouth or your action towards them affect them. Your voice has the energy, a vibration to affect someone; I call that **VOICEBRATION**, use it to spread the positive in the world. You must present yourself to others in the manner you would like to be treated. It's about respecting others views and relating with them to allow for modifications in your own views for good.

The Law of Cause and Effect states that; for every action, there is an equal and opposite reaction. I call it the **Law of Karma** with the factor of intentions.

Newton's third law would have been studied by most of us in schools, to every action there is an equal and opposite reaction. And we know that if you cause something to happen, an effect will definitely follow. With every move of us, there is something happening which is affecting the universe as a whole. We move there is air around us that is moving. We breathe, that is affecting the whole body system to keep functioning. Close your mouth and close the nose completely now, and soon you will realise something very important - the movement of oxygen in air and deep within our body. Try to move to a closed chamber and do not let the airflow in. Soon you will run out of oxygen and I will let you imagine the consequences. The flow of everything, as it is meant to be is very important, this is the natural law. If energy flows well in our body, no sicknesses will be the benefit we'll avail. So I believe if we let the nature flow the way it was meant to be; there may never be floods or such disasters. We have caused something to see those effects. Forgiving behaviour may bring lots of benefits. Continuously think about positives and you will cause something positive to see some positive effects.

The Law of Rhythm states that; everything has a natural cycle.

The night follows day, and life regenerates in rhythm with the conditions that are made for it. We all know the seasons follow one after another to give us change that is necessary to stimulate us living beings, and so they affect the forms of life on earth, the food farms, crops, fruits that grow with the relative seasons to give us the food which we need to live. We all have good times and bad times, but nothing stays the same. Change is constant and meant to happen. So are the good times and bad times. Good times can affect the change towards bad future and that is seen to be the effect after indulging into bad behaviours and losing the love and harmonious behaviour - which means you are concentrating on the negative and hence bringing negative towards you. If you are reaping the benefits of your good practices as a human being, and if you continue to maintain those values and respect towards everything that surrounds us, you will maintain the life at the positive pole of your Future Probability Sphere. Maintain love, maintain peace, maintain harmony and you will maintain the rhythm of life the way it was meant to be.

The Law of Gestation states that; everything takes time to manifest. All things have a beginning and grow into form as more energy is added to it.

That is how life evolves, as a human, an animal, or as plantation. We did not start running from the day one of our birth, it took us that time to have enough food in our body to be able to grow and develop our muscles and a proper diet which ensured our brain grew equally well by learning from what we saw and what we were presented with in our surrounding. Stay focused and while you are maintaining your rhythm with everything around you the way it is supposed to, as per the laws of nature, you will have the goals coming your way. You will see them as reality which once started up as a thought as a seed in your mind, you will manifest it with your actions, and as you keep adding all the energy that a thought needs to flourish, it will be seen as grown one day, and you will realise your dreams.

The Law of Transmutation states that; energy moves in and out of one physical form to another.

Our thoughts are creative energy; they are creating something at a smaller level within us. The more we focus on our thoughts the more energy of our mental strength starts to be transferred towards that thought, the more energy it receives the more it grows and develops into us taking action. That action then manifests it in the form we want to see it in, the physical form.

The more you concentrate your creative energy on to that thought, more it grows and will transmute its form from mind to the physical world. The Universe around you will reshape itself to accommodate that thought and with more energy devoted, it will take the form you finally wanted it to be. Put all your energy and efforts into your thoughts, it will work with other laws of universe and actions will start to follow. And you will see yourself doing things once you thought were impossible for you.

Put the Laws to Work for Success

Now that you understand these laws of universe a bit more and physics has proved them too. You just need to make yourself more aware of these and start spending some time on working with these laws. You will see the difference, you will feel the difference, you will notice the difference, and you will not only create a difference in your life but will make a difference in other people's lives around you as well.

Find that place for you in your Future Probability Sphere and take that shot at life, make it the best target you want to hit. Aim for success and do not measure your success by what others may define it. Find and recognise what success means to you. Is it the love, money, business, career, relationships, the spiritual life. Whatever it could be, any single one out of these alone will never give you happiness though, yet any of those if missing, may cause you a bit of pain. So define it carefully just as a lot of people who have ever been seeking spirituality, will always advise you; aim for happiness being detached from materialistic gains. I haven't still read that book, but have heard and like the title, 'The Monk who sold his Ferrari'. Does that name ring a bell, if not; it does not matter as I am only trying to convey the message that 'Only Spirituality can bring you the life of completeness, abundance, and contentment'. Everything else will give you the worldly pleasures, and those pleasures may still fall short at times as it did for the monk in that book and probably many others who always resorted to charity to fulfil that void. Define your own success but personally.

'Success is to be measured not by wealth, power, or fame, but by the ratio between what a man is and what he might be.'

H.G. Wells 1866-1946, British-born American author

A quick note on the Great Alexander's success and end of war when he met The Indian resistance - he was considered to be great and still is for his great victories. He achieved a lot for his lifetime and his bravery, but I heard in my history lessons and heard it fair bit in a lesson about what goes with us after death is this - *'When we leave the world we do not take anything with us, all that we gain materially stays here, only the deeds live ever after'.* It is said that Alexander had asked for his both hands to be kept uncovered and lying outwards open as a sign that even with all the great achievements, he died taking none with him. But it's his legacy that lives. Whether you think it was worth all the bloodsheds now that humanity is back to being divided into multiple countries! I'll leave that to you. Such stories only help us dig deeper into the quest of "**know thy self**".

But that is really a deep message and what we do need to recognise is that, we should live life with happiness, enjoy it and also there is no harm in making the material gains, we just need to be grateful and achieve those with respectable and honourable ethics and not cause the harm to anyone else for our personal gains. And the way the laws of universe works, we can achieve a lot in any aspect of life, while abiding by those laws and working with them. So discover, what success means to you and follow it with your heart to achieve it, keep your intentions in check.

***Success** – Hold tight to your aims and accomplish what you set out to achieve. You will be regarded as a capable person. Success comes only if you persistently work at a task and remain totally focused.*

- 17th Buddhist Gyalwang Karmapa – Ogyen Trinley Dorje

Whatever your definition of success may be; there is one thing I would recommend to help you in the journey - **'Learn from Experiences of Others'**. If you want to cover more distance, want to achieve more in life, then rather than relying on personal only experience, you should learn from credible people who share the same vision as yours and learn from their experiences. We all have heard often about- why reinvent the wheel. This may not apply to each and everything but I suggest that you use it the way selective hearing is applied at times. If there is no need to experience something before you can apply it in your life, then the choice is yours whether you want to learn or not. Only make sure that whatever and whoever you decide to learn the experience from, you must believe with your full heart. Don't forget your own will power and belief, you may achieve better than who you learn from because you had the edge of a role model, which they probably did not.

I did that in terms of spirituality. I trusted what my parents taught me in relation to spirituality. I also trusted a lot of other people who told me their own experiences about how all of a sudden they realised the help of someone from somewhere, practically out of nowhere, and that help got them out of the deep holes of trouble in life. They always refer to those helpful moments as God-sent Angels.

This is a bit like the story you may have heard often. When this person had this vision when god said he is always with him. One day he had a vision again in his dream that he was walking on the beach. While leaving his footprints on the wet sand, the trail of life he looked back at it as the journey of his life. He noticed that for every step he had walked, there was another set of footmarks alongside. But he thought at first that there was no other person walking beside him. In a very short while he realised that it must be God who said he would be with him all the time. But then he realised that there were parts of the path where there was only one set of footprints.

And then he stood their facing towards the sky and said, 'God, You said you will be with me all the time, then how come you were not present at those certain times of journey. Those were the times probably when I was feeling so down and troubled, and had to make it through on my own'. Then there is a reply from the sky, advising the person that, 'You are right, you were really in troubled moments then, and it was at that time that I was carrying you in my arms, hence you see the single set of foot prints'. The person felt so amazing afterwards and never asked such a question ever again in life.

I also did the same; I trusted the experiences of others, I felt very comfortable with those lessons and happy that I got to learn from them. Having such a feeling of knowing that there is certain supreme power looking after us all the time is just amazing. This faith becomes even more evident and even stronger in our feelings as we see the physical bodies around us, unable to help us in some way when we are in need. And just as in business competition world, we see some people out there are busy and putting their full heart and soul towards ensuring ways of disaster for someone else just so they may succeed. The tragedy is, such intentions do exist in most of human beings for various reasons and accordingly with a degree of variance. Depending on what circumstances we are surrounded with.

> *'The trouble comes when we try to fashion our success to the outside world's specifications even though these are not the specifications drawn up in our own hearts. For whom are we succeeding, for ourselves or for somebody else? Success, if it is to be meaningful, must be a personal thing.'*
>
> --- Howard Whitman

To live a successful life does not mean success in terms of money alone. Success means in any term - trade, love, work, business, peace of mind, content mind, relationships or spirituality. Whatever it could be for you, you need to decide with your clear heart and see the goal very clearly and treat it with love. Success has a very personal meaning to everyone individually so don't create your success definition based on someone else's. You just need to be brave to accept the journey associated with the change you want to bring about in your life and take action.

You must not be only interested but fully committed.

Understand Success – What it means for you

Something somewhere in our life has gone really well and we are so happy. We feel like we are on the moon that day. We all love that feeling, and to have that feeling every day, one may need to change few things. After all happiness is primarily what we are all looking for, just the money alone can't give you happiness. There is a whole lot more to living life happily than having plenty of money, achieving the business success; the balance in life is very important.

Once I was having a chat with one of my close friends and while discussing few things about life and the way things have been going over past few years. He said; I understand that money is not everything, but money does bring a lot of happiness in your life, which just does not seem to be there even in the relationships, if one doesn't have money.

I did not say much to him at that stage, as I myself had started to feel the same in my family to certain extent. But I thought if we were giving our best to the situations we encountered, then the family should also understand you. The money should not be their first concern; otherwise let them take some weight and see if they can fix what they think you are not able to. They should be supporting you while you are doing the best you can for your family. Of-course the essentials of survival are to be taken care of but while looking after those needs, keeping the bigger picture in vision should also always be part of everyday living. Maslow's hierarchy of Needs is good expression of how we address our life and needs.

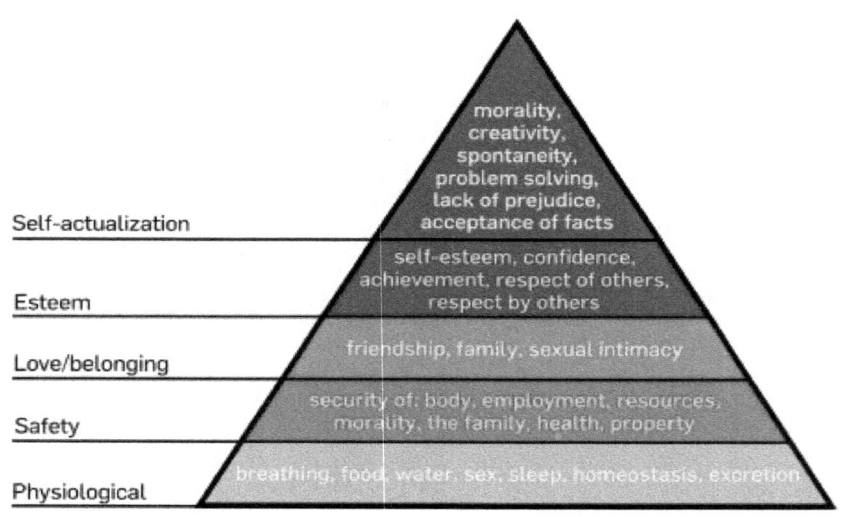

MASLOW'S HIERARCHY OF NEEDS – from Wikipedia

In such scenarios of family dissatisfaction, I believe Communication is a must. A lot of misunderstanding can happen once communication, especially clear communication stops. Even though you may have huge plans to make something big for the benefit of all, if you have not clearly communicated to them, their interpretation might be different; their understanding may be different. One needs to clarify that regularly. You will be amazed with how this can help you create a supportive atmosphere for you and eventually the whole family. Whereas, if you did not clearly and frequently communicated with them, that may instead add some stress when you actually need the most peaceful time and support to accomplish goals in the best manner possible.

So, think hard, make a decision, see the life you want to live very clearly and start taking action with passion. That is the way to achieve success. Build up your ultimate success with smaller success goals in place. If you are not able to even start the journey towards the goal you want to achieve in your life, then that itself for now is what success should be for you. If you can successfully start on the journey for change, everything else will follow. That ultimate success is not to be just about the Money. It has to be the best possible balance of everything in life, whether it is money, love, relationships, business, career, spirituality, or peace.

That balanced and happy life is much more than an achievement in business, a job position, a large house and the best car alone, it's about having everything in the balance to achieve happiness. Success should be living happily, while making the best effort at achieving the best of what you want. Only then you will be able to have happiness and may be contentment in life long journey; only then you will be able to make others around you happy, and also teach them a better way to live life.

Enjoying life with happiness is what you should want to achieve, everything else becomes the part of it and joins in. As you start sowing the seeds of positivity and happiness, you will only reap what you sow. With time you will start to feel the positive things happen in your life. **Start Living, not Just Living By**, decide with your heart truthfully. Let's now take a look at a technique that will help you visualise in more **practically emphasised** manner and help you in making decisions. Everything starts with a thought; we will take those thoughts for a walk a bit further to see how they may grow out.

Walk your Thoughts Technique

'Always take your thoughts for a walk on a probable scenario.'

That goal you wish to achieve is your future reality and when you are capable of comprehensively imagining everything else that's connected with achieving your goal and how it will appear once that goal is realised, you can even refer to that final stage of your FPS as FRS your Future Reality Sphere while working towards it. The more comprehensively you imagine, more you will be in synchronisation with your future reality. Sometimes I wonder if only long term thinkers are the ones who get frustrated for not getting desired results sooner because you know it's not helping in getting to their goal sooner, compare to others who keep moving from one thing to another without keeping long term outcomes in mind and end up living life that way forever. Some people may use this to their benefit but in that case, they know they must know what they may be discovering out of being that grasshopper. So, developing long-term thinking is an essential and important skill, so let's try and develop that.

We have all heard of simulations. It is generally a technique to mock-up or create almost real like experience of something we may be trying to create or achieve practically, just as aeroplane pilots do a lot of flying on flight simulators before flying a real plane so they have a fair idea of what it will be like in reality. All you need to do is master this technique to take your thoughts on a simulated walk. This will help you develop the abilities of better thinking, and better decision-making and also develop your thinking sphere for creating better future for yourself. Before I go into more details on this technique, what I would suggest is that even though you will develop this technique to make better decisions, there is a large degree of your faith and beliefs that are set in your brain, which will direct this simulation as a director of a movie. We will practice to modify them in The Karmic Rewind tool based on needs. For now it is fairly important that you understand these basics of human nature, the way you behave and how the beliefs, the circumstances and situations have always influenced in the outcome of life you are living now.

This is important as this will also help you recognise the corrections you may need in your beliefs, faiths, behaviour and actions, as you will simulate the scenario with the best directives from your inner self. Once you have mastered this technique, what you will simulate in your brain will guide you in making a well thought out decision; this will help you assess your reaction to a certain situation in life moving forward. **Your reactions will be more informed, well thought out, so they won't really be reactions but you taking control and taking action.** Reactions are mostly impulsive and emotional rather with less thought process gone into them. And once the reaction takes place, the journey has begun further. Sometimes you may, and other times you may not be able to step backwards on a path to make any correction, certainly not in time; Time travels not backwards. Sometimes you may have to live with it for the rest of your life, and other times you may just get away with saying- "OK, that time or opportunity could have been utilised better by taking a bit more informed or thoughtful decision".

It all depends on the degree of the importance or severity of the task that you need to decide on. Sometimes your attitude, other times your ego and at times, your lack of knowledge and capabilities could have caused a certain reaction from you. **You must tame your reactions and empower your actions to lead your journey**. That is why equipping yourselves better will help you a great deal. It all matters, and how you will be guided on the journey ahead after taking a decision in your own mind will highly depend on beliefs and faiths that you have within. The brain is going to simulate the advice to play the future within your mind by visualising it and help you decide what's best for you. So, if you can learn this art of simulating the possible scenarios to understand and assess quickly about what decisions to take, it is the best way you will help yourself to move towards your destination in your FPS.

Not very often you would simply rely on advise from others on your personal life matters. You may seek help for legal or medical matters, but when it comes to your very own personal life, you always do what feels right to you within your heart and mind or otherwise things happen the way they happen with your mind in indecisive state. So you are the one responsible for everything that happens around you. The decisions you take based on what feels right to you will mould the future path of your life. If you take command and take an action, a reaction is bound to occur to materialise the outcome. If you don't take command in any current situation, the after-effects of or momentum created by any past action that relate to this situation will decide for you and make things happen. So you must take command to play an active part in building your future self, your fifth dimension.

So here is how you can simulate the future in your brain and decide on various decisions that may need to be taken. And I do encourage that you make different variations based on available or workable options you may see, while you are creating this movie of your future within your mind. It will give you an emphasised practical insight into your options before making a decision to follow through. I am going to give an example that will hopefully make it easier for everyone to understand the concept.

Lets talk about defining and deciding on the personality you want to wear, the personality you would love to be in line with your natural aura. Just imagine that you have a photo taken of yourself. It may be with an awesome cute smile on your face, or with a crying face, in a jumping pose, or with a sad face, in an eating mode with mouthful of cheesy pizza or drinking a beautiful cocktail or in any other possible scenario. The question to be asked is - if you were to display that picture on a wall for people to see but more importantly you would want to see it every day of your life! Which photo would you prefer? Similar applies to life; there are a several ways you can think of living your life, and the decision you may be able to make right now does have the capability of changing your life to a more desirable life full of love and happiness or contentment.

The hardest thing that I have seen in people's life or happens in most people's lives is that it is so much **easier** for them to believe in and take an action quickly that keeps them in **negative zone**, may land them in some sort of trouble but when it comes to taking some noble, some **positive decisions** to pull them up in life which they know they must take! All of a sudden it becomes the **hardest thing ever** to decide upon and act upon. If you were to decide on becoming a bad person or a thief or thug, you know it's so easy to do that, right? Quite easily you can walk down the street and give someone some sort of trouble and there you go, a perfect recipe on the start of path to that journey of troubled life.

Yet, if we were to act in a noble manner and walk down the street to help someone and lend a hand that may benefit them someway, even without costing us much effort or anything at all, a lot of us just hesitate so badly that the first thing may come to our mind is - either **someone else will** always help them, or **Why should I** take the trouble out of my time. But we all tend to forget that it all matters in one way or another. I will explain that further in the Karmic theory but it all does matter, every tiny thing that happens or action you do, whether positive or negative. A painful instance I heard on news was that of a young girl in China who was lying dead on the side of a busy street for over a day, but no one bothered to check if she was OK.

There is a famous saying which implies that – the Heavens and Hells do all exist right here. You do good deeds, it comes to you, *what goes around comes around* is a famous verse in the whole world. So do keep it in mind all the time.

Lets take a little longer walk of thoughts now. Just imagine if you wish to paint a drawing on a canvas, there are surely lots of variations you can think of painting, it could be any object that you want to draw. There you go! The first question here has already poised a multipath scenario. As they say, **every decision you make, causes a split in the universe**. We start up with selecting a canvas to paint on – which has a decision to be made about its size, which wall and where you may hang the painting. Then next just imagine about the decision you need to take about what to paint on that canvas.

What you want to draw will and is going to design the rest of the actions you will take to complete that drawing – this will also add an impact on your life until the painting is complete. I hope you get the message about importance of making a decision. For the sake of understanding, the goal to '**paint a specific image on canvas**' is your specific, clear **goal point on your Future Probability Sphere**. But, right now we are probing the scenario so let's seek further clarity.

So continuing on, let's say I like flowers rather than a human portrait or an animal, I may like little kids playing in a field and having fun, I may also like a peacock painting and some scenic views as well, but there is a question poised of what I may want to draw. Which wall the painting will be hung on may impact what size canvas I may need or what I may want to paint. If I decided to draw a peacock then this decision will straightaway start the further thinking process. I will be thinking into different paintings of peacocks that I may have seen ever in my life. Also I may think about going to a zoo where they have a peacock so I can take a photo and start my painting from that. I may also start searching on the Internet for a nice photo that may have been uploaded by someone who has already gone through the trouble of taking a nice photo and uploaded to the Internet. The time and effort it may have taken them to do so will not generally come into most people's mind, but hey, someone has in fact happily made that effort and we most likely don't even know them, yet we are happy to have found what we like and are going to benefit by their effort and work.

Spreading happiness, beyond boundaries – a similar concept applies if you decide to paint a scenic view or flowers. The actions you may need to take will or may differ from what and how you may think if you decide to paint a scenic view, a flower, or a peacock. This decision will determine further actions. It will cause you to look at what kind of canvas you may need, what size you may need, and then further on to what colours you would prefer. Now again when choosing the canvas you will be thinking about whether to draw a single flower or multiple, or even a single beautiful big peacock or a few of them in a nature park. Whereas drawing a scene will be slightly different, whether you want a sunset, or sunrise, just a beautiful rain forest, or a beach view, it all matters in paving the journey ahead and the actions you will take to accomplish that task. Your personal likings and beliefs will play there part as to whether you should be at a scene to paint it live while being there or copy someone else's picture that may be available on the Internet. Or you may even take a picture of a live view and print it to then further paint it at home.

Let's take our thoughts further now. How you choose these things is different for different people. It is largely driven by the degree of your likes and dislikes, which in turns are influenced by the beliefs and thoughts and scenarios that have influenced your life ever since you were born till today. Your conscious and subconscious mind will play their part in going through the memory banks to get you to make your decisions. For instance you may have been visiting outdoors a lot as a child with your grandma and seen someone painting a canvas outdoor and you loved the idea. Your conscious mind may not remember but your subconscious mind will dig that out and influence you to go and paint your canvas outdoor. Things may seem small in daily routine, but it all matters and it influences your decision-making and as an end result the life you may live. Let's now move forward to start painting the picture.

Now that you have decided on what you may want to paint, you need to come down to buying the colours and canvas that you wanted. The day and time you would take out to buy those things needed for painting will also depend on how much you would love to paint that picture and how you prioritise it in your life. For a painter, it would be their heart and soul, so they would be kicking themselves out of the home straightaway and not return until they have found what they needed. The time to be spent here is the result of the decision made to paint something on a canvas.

So, what you need to understand is that a decision made has already paved the path for the day that did not exist at the time before making a decision. It would have been different if you decided to give up on the idea of painting altogether and decided on going just for a walk to the beach or play a sport or decide to buy a readymade painting, or whatever else that could have been. That decision there would have been followed by related events to bring that decision into the reality. Painting is a very light weighted example but it's all about learning how action and reaction theory works based on decisions we make. Once you learn the art you could simulate the scenario with any decision you face in life. That is the idea and purpose of this technique. Practicing is what one will need to master their simulation ability for being able to think all the possibilities as soon as they can to make an important decision.

> *'Life is a Decisions based actualisation of time so make informed, well thought out decisions with awareness and actualise what you want your life to be.'*

Just think of the world chess champions (*Rank-1. Magnus Carlsen, Vladimir Kramnik, Viswanathan Anand*), that is sort of what I am trying to get you at, in the sport of making decisions in your life. So, getting back to the painting scenario; for someone who paints just out of hobby, they will be telling themselves at times that - 'yes I want to paint that picture, and I need to take time to go shopping for all the stuff I need to paint'. If you are not passionate about it, you may be leaving it till you find absolute time for doing nothing else and say - 'OK I got nothing else to do, so why not get the things I need for the paining, I did once thought of painting my own picture'. If you are really passionate about making this painting, you may even skip lunch during your lunch break that day and make a point of shopping and the first thing you want to do when you get home is use that awesome skill of painting.

At the same time, there may also be someone who does not like painting at all but have to do it for the sake of work or students who have to do it for their compulsory subject or assignments, etc. so their approach would be different. So you see that there is a degree of all the feels, beliefs, circumstances, priorities, that come into play and is influenced by each other to a certain extent. But largely, what plays the role in designing the future is the decisions that are made and has been acted upon. There is a lot that start to happen once a decision is made and action is taken.

So simulate in your brain about what would happen if you decide to take a certain path, or if you decide to take that different path or another one with another option and variation. Then you would be able to visualise well the circumstances you are in or you will be in, while acting upon a decision. Start including the relevant people in that scenario in your imagination, people who may play a larger role to support you in reaching your goal. While you are visualising taking a certain path to reach that goal, introducing people will help you in deciding on your selective isolation of people so you stay focused to achieve the goal. You will need to see clearly the end results that you want to achieve when you are acting upon your decision. After all that friend at work or college who always praise you for everything you do may be a help in motivating you in accomplishing the task, while not the one who will always nudge at wrong time and poke your feelings, push you into negativity and make you feel down for the rest of the day. There may also be people appearing out of nowhere to either help or distort your positivity. Visualising will help you create and manage the atmosphere you need to succeed.

Let me tell you a story of mine. I was simply walking down the aisle one day looking for a book to read and got stuck at one section. The shopping aisles were not so wide, and I had a trolley I was pushing along with me. I was so passionate about finding a particular book that I was looking for and had all that pumped up feeling as I thought I had seen that book in this particular store once. While looking for that book, in this aisle, there was this lady who was just standing there without acknowledging that I was there wanting to pass through. She looked by the side of her eyes that I wanted to pass through, but first did not acknowledge at all even though knowing my presence. And when I said excuse me couple of times, she simply ignored me as if I was a big hassle coming her way. At that time I was minding my little two-year-old daughter, and minding a child of that age takes some effort, I am sure all with kids will agree. I just lost my cool, which I normally always maintain. I could not believe the fact that someone could behave in such a manner and I decided to squeeze through the aisle and did not say sorry when she turned around when my trolley bumped into her a bit. She surely had time to look at me then, but again even though I lost my cool while passing through I still smiled at her out of thought that; maybe she is having a real bad day and thanked her for giving me way to pass through.

She reacted with such a burnt red face that I can't even explain. The moment went by, but I just felt such a negative feel just by being around there at that point in time. The expressions on my face had changed. But I learned a lesson that day, to keep such people out of my way all together. If I can sense that feeling I just use an alternative, which helps me keep my calm, leaving me with better control over my senses. This control, after some time, also becomes one of those habits where you get use to staying calm. That way if you ever encounter a bad situation, your mind is not ready to get out of that peaceful state, it loves being in that comfort zone and helps you look at the situation in a different manner, just because you can't be bothered losing your peace of mind. Whereas, you may otherwise react to the situation differently and cause a scene to occur, leaving neither you nor the other person happy. I don't mean to say that do not stand up for yourself, but just imagine the angry moments you will avoid and the positive use you could have for that peace of mind, that energy.

So people are also a very important factor to include while directing the simulation of the future in your mind. The people you encounter along with the places you may end up going, or visiting, the effect those people and places, all may become a reason to mould the path for the future you want to live in.

The painting scenario is only a lightweight example just to help you in understanding how to simulate in your mind the future you may encounter. As there can be lots of possibilities as to where your life may reach in your FPS (Future Probability Sphere). The impact, which the decisions and actions have on the life that we live in the future is very much dependent on those decisions and actions you take at any given point in time. Which in turn are largely influenced by the beliefs, thoughts and feelings we have about the rest of the world around us. You need to make those decisions keeping in mind the effects it has on your own self and the people around you, and then the world, environment and Mother Nature and the whole Universe around you. Steve jobs of Apple use to say '**Make a Dent in the Universe**'. He surely knew how to do that with his decisions and actions, so can you.

If you have been trained in a general or a particular way since childhood, and you do not believe that that training is working the best to give you what you want in life, then it is time to change that. You must start to **Un-Learn and Re-Learn** what will work for you. Rearrange your memory and delete the old unproductive training you had. Eliminate the beliefs, which may be holding you back and fill up your mind with the resources and knowledge that you know will help you achieve your goals.

It's no different to what we talk about in the technology world that, you can't play state of the art graphics designed movies or games online, without a compatible hardware/software and the high speed Internet connection. If you just want a computer that types documents then it may be OK with a basic computer, if you want to play DVD's or CD's in it, you need to have CD/DVD drives, speakers added to them, and though long gone are the days of such basic computers. What I am trying to convey here is that a plumber cannot fix a tap with bare hands, or a bricklayer alone cannot build a house for someone, he will need architectures to design it to show what it looks like but not build it without them or without himself being qualified or trained, a 'geek' cannot build a state of the art computer with only basic hardware and software for computers. One needs to empower and up skill themselves to perform better tasks. So the right tools for the right trade makes a successful tradesmen and that is what we need to do in our lives. Recognise what you want to be, define your spot in our FPS, empower yourself with the training and knowledge that may be required to reach that goal. Trust your own self; believe in your own self and take that bulls eye shot! You'll never miss.

Believe Thy Self

To succeed in reaching any goal that you may wish to in your FPS; **believing in your very own self** is very important. And as we learn from mystics that God created man in his own image, the belief in the supreme creative power or God and his creation is also very important, belief in the laws that govern this universe is very important. God or that creative power is the reason for everything that exists; we can exercise the same abilities in us under his will and under his laws. It is equally important for our success that we also believe in those scientifically backed seven laws of the universe. Let's take a journey how different beliefs exist in science, in mystical world and practical world and try to build that trust and belief in our own self.

There is a great deal of in-depth links and connections between this mortal body of ours and the eternal world, the way it operates. God has done it all, created it all and science is exploring his creation and presenting it in the way we can trust what exists; then are **scientists** not **God's trust advocates**. The things we knew with science about the whole existence back in days have a lot been contradicted or redefined by science itself as we discover more about the universe, as we move ahead in time and technology. The planets and their moons once we believed to be in moving only in one direction; there are discoveries now that there are planets with their moons that actually do move in the opposite direction too. We are trained to believe what we see and mystics have seen what science is discovering. In biological world, our **body per square inch has thirty two million bacteria**

forming it. There are lots of species that we know once existed and there are some that we have seen in our lives but are listed as endangered species now by the relevant forest authorities in different parts of the world. The mechanism of life as per the mystics and what they tell us is still beyond the discoveries made by science on our planet till date.

We all have heard of the UFO's not many of us has seen them, but there is evidence provided that they exist. But the powerful vehicles and technology they seem to use appear to be far powerful than what we have here on our planet. In March 2013, US marines are told to have found an ancient plane referred to as Vimana in Afghanistan, hidden in a cave. The electromagnetic field around it is believed to be the reason it hasn't eroded but eloped the marines that were assigned the duty to get this machine out. Most allied partner countries including then US President Obama is said to have visited the location. I do not intend to say that we should or should not believe in UFO's; I will believe the day I see one. But at the same time, just think about the amount of time, space and discussions the topics on aliens occupies in the history of newspapers, the Internet, and the videos on the Internet. After all there might be some truth to certain extent. And at the same time, may be they exist not. I am happy to leave that believe as open ended, as I do tend to believe some evidences provided for their existence. And as I also believe in the astral plains, the spiritual truth about our existence, my trust on mystics about millions of universes; there must exist some sort of shape or form of life on those planets. So that is my personal belief to leave that as an open-minded discussion, until the day I may see them with my eyes. But what we must learn from possible Alien existence and their visits to us on earth is that such technology exists to travel and we as humans should believe and continue to persist and find the solutions for such generally promoted as impossible achievements for most.

Also relating to the Ghost stories that we may have heard or all those monsters that we try to scare our kids off with, if they don't listen to what we have to say, just imagine the impact of those feelings of scare that we create in their minds. Yet, we ourselves seem to be not scared of those so-called monsters. Why? Because a large amount of us believe that it's just created stories. There is a very small minority that would say, Yes – I have seen one, Oh Boy... Tell me the encounter story; I am always keen to hear those.

I personally believe that; if you believe in them, you will definitely see them. Same energies attract each other, and of-course the aliens are looking for friendly energy fields too. As I said, believing is seeing when mind and universe matters. If you do not believe in them, you will never see them. Again believing is seeing. However such stories mostly seem to be coming from or are being presented by the parts of the world where such beliefs are very common in people and they do encounter such stories. I actually heard some stories within my family from distant relatives who lived in some remote villages. As I was told, one cousin sister died after seeing some dead relatives while she was returning back home fetching milk one really early morning, still dark before any trace of sunshine. It was a common practice in those days that some farmers even ploughed their fields in the moonlights during summer. But was it a belief in scary thoughts she probably had or did the spirits truly showed up, I don't know.

My grandparents told me some stories all the time, which actually did relate to our long distant family too. And actually there is one that my uncle said he encountered too. First – there is this story of my uncle. There is this belief in Indian community that there are some souls or spirits of those who die of an untimely death that exists, their souls are left wondering around. There is this one kind, which always have a long white piece of cloth covering them all along. They only come out in the night. These particular spirits are known by a different name, rather than ghosts, but they do not mean real harm to you, it is believed that they come out just to have a bit of a fun out there or just to give you a bit of scare but they do not harm you in any way, only unless you are shocked to death by their presence near you.

My uncle told us a one off encounter when he was cycling his way back home late on a summer night. Every night, he passed by a cemetery on the way. One night, all of a sudden he felt that his cycle was heavy as if there had been a large amount of load put on the cycle in addition to his weight. He first thought the air may have been leaked out of the tyre and as a second thought even though he knew there was nothing on the bicycles back hanging there, he decided to look, and what he saw would have scared the hell out of those people who feel really scared of even thinking about such presences. My dad seemed to have the knowledge of such stories from his elderly on how to tackle such spirits.

He simply knew that all he had to do was just keep going without reacting and the spirit that was enjoying the lift on his bicycle sitting behind him will get off in some distance. So my uncle's knowledge of and belief in the problem and its solution paid off. Now, that to me was always a funny story instead of a scary one but it did keep us away from running out alone in the dark at nights when the streets are quiet and dark. For obvious reasons, parents do not like their kids going out in streets in the dark. For the teenager kids too, no matter how grown up they think they may be. Parents wouldn't like to have them out in the dark. One, because it's also a bit like you know, you are always a kid for your parents, no matter how old you may grow and two, because it's for their safety. But do parents for one reason or another falsely manifest the thoughts in their children's brain without the real need. And that now forms the belief system, which may trigger at some dark time and cause more harm than comfort of safety. Think about the beliefs and how they are born.

And then there was another story that my granddad told me about those 'ancient' days in India, when there were no bicycles then, you can probably imagine the times I am talking about. He was on his way to another village nearby. On the way there was a well of water (well is that deep dug holes into the earth to the water levels, generating the local water resource for the village) just outside a village on his way. When he arrived closer to the well, there appeared to be a number of people all of a sudden but he could not make up where they came from of course in the dark night, it seemed as if it was a groom side family of people bringing home the bride in a specially made cart carried on shoulders by people.

And all seemed fine up until they kept playing music and singing songs. He first asked one of them, where they were going and decided to join them as they were heading in the same direction as he was going too, just so he has company along the way rather than walking alone. After a while he realised that he passed the same well of water again. He used to go through that route a number of times so, he very well recognised the route, and was surprised that why would they have come back around again and how come he did not realise where he was going, and how come he had travelled backwards in his journey. He decided to ask one of them the question, and he just heard a scary voice telling him to keep quiet and keep walking, at that time he said it scared him to his bones.

I think in those days such stories would have been quiet common and people knew how to try some tricks to give them a chance of survival. This time he recognised this was not the breed of spirits that I have spoken about earlier, but these were the ones who can take control of you, and visit your body any time they like. Make you scare other people and do weird disastrous things. Scaring others does seem to be one of their favourite things. And he had learned that in such scenario one should walk with their lower body naked and the moment he did, he was lucky that he did. As at that moment they had all turned around to him for whatever they wanted to do with him. But this act of his worked and they all disappeared in anger, and now, you can imagine he walked like that through the night until next morning till the darkness started to fade away.

The third story is quiet a freaky one, it's a friend of mine who visited back home from Australia and learned that a cousin of his has been possessed by this not one soul but four of them, and he actually saw himself with his own eyes and could not believe what he saw. He saw four different faces coming out of his cousin's neck and making a scary conversation with this tantric (cult), who had done all the prayer and tantric arrangements to get this spirit out of his body.

Oh well, I do not want to make this book a ghost story telling book, but just to imply the fact that we have discussed earlier, life exists in all shapes and forms and souls and spirits. What we believe in does play a role in determining what we encounter in future. Those who passionately believe in spirits, they go looking for them too; they follow their passion. I have heard a lot of stories even in the developed part of the world; they've turned their amusing passion into potential living too by the methods of books and movies. There has been those TV shows as well, which take people into the haunted houses to see if any spirit really does exist in those places. It's all about what they do believe in.

Let's talk about a scientifically proven discovery that we can use to build our belief system stronger to achieve what we want in life. If we start thinking too much about one particular thing or task, it becomes the paramount of thoughts in our brain and we start to see related events, activities, happenings and things in material forms everywhere around us. It's the **Reticular Activating System (RAS)** of brain. What you want and what you start thinking towards, you start seeing more of it around you. This can also be related to the Law of Attraction, whether people believe in it or not, it works, just as I mentioned above, the RAS. I remember the day I had decided to buy this particular model of car. I started seeing more of them around me, not that they never existed before, but you just start to notice them more on the road. Similarly this applies to what we want to do in life. It starts to pick up and give your brain more relative data to analyse and design the solution of any given thought or task to your brain. Once we decide our mind on something, then the RAS process of the brain kicks in and we start moving towards that direction as discussed in earlier story of canvas drawing formula.

The RAS is this part of our brain which sort of eliminates the lookout for everything and focuses our attention on specific things that we tell it are important to us at any given time. We will start looking for things we do need to accomplish that goal. At the same time, you will notice more of the related options, even though you may have passed by them few times every day for years, but never noticed. So, in a way all you need in this world to be truthfully your inner self does exist; you just need to decide. Find your peace of mind that will help you see things clearly rather than being occupied with all the things that you do not need or want, but have to do or live with on daily bases. It's like one of those things like garden with lots of unwanted weeds you stop extracting. As someone said once -

'When you stop working towards what you want,

What you don't want automatically takes over you'

So you have to keep putting efforts in towards what you want, but first of all you need to be clear in your mind, you need to be clear in your heart, clear in your brain, and then apply it clearly in your daily life. That is when you will start living the life you want. I personally took a decision to do what I wanted to do. This is what I said to myself -

'I must at least give myself a fair go. If I were to work in daily routine jobs, I could do it any day in my life, whether today or next year or two years later. But If I want to do what I want to do, I must do it today. And that way even if I have not been successful in what I wanted to achieve, I will not tell myself for the rest of my life, 'I wish I did'.'

Eliminate the "I wish I did" from ever appearing in your life. I just cannot think about telling myself for the rest of the life, not any more that if I had tried what I wanted, may be it could have worked, and I would have been happier. Also I do tell myself that if I do everything I want to do, not half-heartedly, not 50%, not 100% but with 200% effort, then how can I go wrong? But one needs to be determined. If I were to live an average life as a computer techie, and just pay for the mortgage and car loans for a large amount of my life, then I can start to do it even a year or two later. But if I want to give myself a fair go, then now is the time to load up some smart and up-skilling programs to my brain. I decided on that destination point on my FPS. This is how I built trust in myself and believed in myself to do the hard work to smarten-up. **And I am glad I decided that when I did.** I am on the track for what I wanted to do.

When you look at things deeply, we are kind of always successful in what tasks we put ahead in front of our brain, whether it is daily or weekly, jobs and tasks etc. We are achieving in all those little tasks that we do every day. We plan for them, then execute with action and they are completed. We are successful in achieving something every day, then why not just switch the task, up the game and achieve that goal of dream life, the abundant life. We just need to shift the goal to the new goal, which we desire from the bottom of our heart. Something we would love to achieve and be happy with for the rest of our lives. Make a shift of the tasks to the tasks that would help you in achieving the goals you want in your life. Tasks that will build towards the way of life you want to live, and make all your dreams come true.

You just need to stop telling your mind whether that goal is too big for you to achieve. By saying this you have already lost your battle without even starting. Instead you should say to your brain that nothing is too big or too hard to achieve. Be bold and **listen to that inner voice** from your within, that's telling you that it will work if you did it like this. I did and I am living a lifestyle that gives me more freedom for what I want to do. I do have goals, and I am acting upon them to achieve them. I love the journey; the process and I will enjoy that for the rest of my life. I believed in my course of life I desired, I pursued and I succeeded. Though there were sacrifices made for good. As someone said –

> *"If You don't sacrifice for what you want, What you want will become the sacrifice."*

I believed in my natural abilities. I was a bright student in physics and mathematics in my school times, not that I made it as a scientist, but the decisions I took reacting to my family and life situations have actually got me to where I am today. And since I understood physics and mathematics as a natural ability of my mind, I always loved the fact the way it explained what happens, occurs and moves in this universe. It is so precise and in such a definite manner that the whole universe is moving and yet not colliding. The planets, their own moons and satellites move so perfectly, precisely without conflicting with each other's paths. I admire the perfect plan to provide everything that is required for life on planet earth. The days, the nights, the seasons, the harvests, the rain or whatever is required for the survival of life on planet earth. How can we not believe in that supreme power that created it all?

And for such reasons I have personally liked sophisticated things, the surroundings, things and even matters that exist around me that are a bit sophisticated in technology, and also people who act wonderfully with such personalities that doesn't really exist in a lot of people. Ever seen people who talk less, and behave in a mysterious manner yet holding a great amount of respect for others, and that actually also earns them the respect they give out as well.

It's all dependent on the way your brain works and thinks, how deeply and how precisely you think about things can make a lot of difference in how you would behave with everything else around you and how everything else behaves with you, whether it is people, the material existence, the environment or the energy particles in any shape and form. Physics also explains that everything in this universe is a form of energy and governed by the laws of the universe. The **plants grow** so huge just with water, **yet no soil is lost** which nurtures it and grows it to a sort of solid state. A child can never believe that a huge tree can be born out of a little seed until they see the seed sprouting and growing. The universe is so huge and yet harmonious and precise that we are not always capable to see its power but should believe in it and learn from those who have seen it. The science delivers digestible information. The mystics bring the deeper and obviously the mystical stuff. We should combine them both and believe in what they tell us we are capable of and only then we'll be able to experience the power within.

Choose your spot in your Future Probability Sphere and start taking action to travel towards that goal. Don't let the fear of failure overcome your wish to succeed because if Einstein stepped back then we wouldn't have had the light bulbs when we did or Steve Jobs, Bill Gates, Elon Musk, there is a huge list of big brands and names today who wouldn't be where they are today if they didn't overcome the fears and dared to take action by believing in themselves. Are you a Star Wars fan, then you should know George Lucas and his story of when nobody wanted to buy his Star Wars story and rejected saying no one wants science fiction. With a lot of trouble and under budget with a 300% pay cut, he finally released with a low morale marketing team and on 25th May, which he recon was considered as the worst time for a movie release. Once released it spread out well and now has done over 27 Billion in business. What do you think he would have achieved if gave in after first few rejections. This is what he has to say –

"Always remember, our focus determines your reality"

Focus will come when you believe in yourself, he did and achieved his vision, and so can you. **Believe Thy Self**. Here's a quick visualisation of your Future Probability Sphere, you can cut/copy them and pin somewhere to constantly remind you about your present position in your FPS. You can download them on the website www.AtamDhillon.com or www.TheKarmicRewind.com as well.

Future Probability Sphere – For Daily Visualisation

Decide on your Goal

All those little circles are your possibilities and probabilities around you to be recognised and prioritised. With clarity and full passion you must prioritise your one goal, which is indicated as the darker circle in the FPS.

Prepare to reach for your goal

Make every effort necessary to Learn or Unlearn, Skill up, and get ready to put all your mind, love and heart into it.

Transition through to your goal

While you put all your mind, love and heart into achieving your goal, be ready to face the challenges presented by the change. Keep at it with strong will, keep connecting with your inner self and that will help you stop not till the goal is reached.

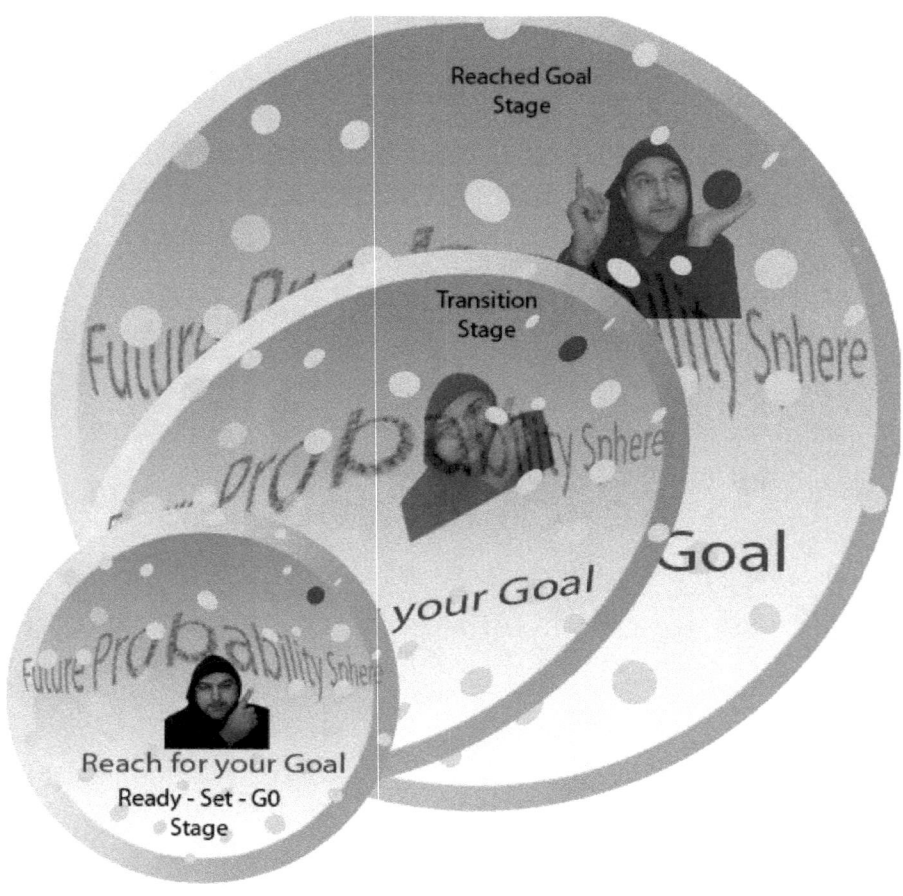

Achieve, Celebrate and prepare for next goal

Celebrate once your goal is accomplished and in your hands. Once at a new position in your journey of life FPS, everything around you would have changed, your approach to looking at life around you would have changed. That will bring you new aura of FPS around you, prepare to take the next challenge. There's always a lot more to live for in life.

It's Karma Time

Let's move forward to take the action now. As much as I believe in science, in humans being energy particles, being made of atoms and how they behave in this world based on frequencies we vibrate on, in the shapes and forms they exist in; I also believe that action needs to be taken to effect them to behave in a certain way. That law of action is the law of Cause and Effect, the law of karma, which I believe in very strongly and firmly; it does make even more logical sense with scientific evidence. In fact there is a very fine grey line to understand this well in detail. And not many people can understand and they start to get confused. I will try my best to explain the way I take it. This will really help you understand the relation between the sciences and mystical or religious beliefs. This theory of the Karmic Rewind will not only help you improve as a person, but also empower you as a person to achieve the goals in your life. Let's take a look at the Karmic Theory, and concept of Karmic Rewind. So you can Rewind, Revive and Re-live the life. Live life as you always wanted and the way it was always meant to be. It will help you invoke the powers within you like those of Brahma, the creator God as per Hindu mythology, but at a human level of course. So let's invoke the creator in you.

Part- III

The Karmic Rewind

REWIND – REVIVE - RELIVE

'If you've ever said in your life, Who has seen another or the next life; Then NOW is the time to say it again and make the most of your life, achieve the best you can in your life.'

The Karmic Theory

What is Karma, whether you believe in it, why should you believe in it?

There may be slightly different definitions among different groups worldwide, of what Karma is or what it may be. Karma is an ancient Indian word from Sanskrit language, the language of Hindu ancient history books that I also refer to as language of the Gods. To me –

"Karma is the mystic word for every action that takes place by a physically visible aura of the soul by any means, intentionally or un-intentionally in this world."

And as per mystics of India, we as human mortal beings are told to be composed of five elements combined. Those elements are – Ether (Space), Air, Fire, Water and Earth. We humans are also blessed to be able to use a very special ability- the *Sense of Discrimination* for the liberation of our soul. And we should make use of that power, the sense of discrimination in the best way possible to achieve one goal only in mind as per the mystics. That goal as per saints and mystics is - "The freedom from the cycle of birth and death and be one with God or merge back with the source and not worry about the agony and pain that one goes through in the world". We are also told that being Human is the highest form of all the physical forms a soul can get, out of 8.4 Million forms of life in this world. Being the most superior form of life, we are also told by mystics that the universal law of Karma is the prime instrument for soul to not being able to achieve salvation, karmic law affects us human beings the most. Why, because human life is the only life which is classified under Karma Yoni (form of life), which means we have the ability to commit or create karmas while bearing the fruits of the past. This also means that we are sowing for the future too. This is where all the action is whether creative or destructive; all other forms of life are classified under Bhog

Yoni, which means in all those other forms of life you only and only bare the fruit of your committed Karmas. This also means and is important to understand that in human form of life alone you actually have the **ability to create** that change through the medium of deliberate karma. A lot of people argue over freewill, here's what I say to that –

> *"If you say you are only bearing the fruit of your Karma, You actually mean you did commit or created some Karmas sometime somewhere somehow to be here now to reap the rewards of those actions, didn't you?"*

The very underlying cause of us all being where we are, becoming what and who we are is because of one and only reason of Karmas, the actions we either took in the past lives, or take in the present, or we've let things happen due to insignificant action on our behalf where destiny also had no set result for us to put us into. That part of life where destiny doesn't have to control us is where the freewill lies. I believe strongly in Karmas so I do respect the say of the destiny, which again is the result of our past actions anyway. Means we did have the ability to create Karma for that to result in a destiny, then why can we not do that again now with certain destiny in our mind, which we wish to reach in the future. All the other time that we have, when destiny decides to leave us alone is one sure opportunity where we have the freewill to effect change through our actions, our Karmas. Remember what we learned earlier about our fifth dimension. In our human bodies there exists a soul and the soul is bound to this world under unimaginable scrutiny and monitoring of Karmas that we commit from the very day the soul is moved into the universe from its actual supreme eternal source.

Have I surprised you yet by talking something that may sound out of this world? May be, maybe not, depending on the understanding you may already have about our eternal essence. Let me take you further into details and I will help you understand about the body that we live in as a soul. I will help you understand the influence of Karma that is conducted while living in this body, the deeds we commit and karmas that we accumulate. Whether those deeds, those actions those karmas are good or bad, whether they are committed knowingly or unknowingly, consciously or un-consciously, we are certain to be affected by those karmas, those actions.

Let's try and understand the Human body and its soul first a little more. In spiritual reality, we are all Souls in different bodies, and not just us human beings; every form of life we see on this planet or in this universe has a soul in it. There has been some scientific researches and advancement towards realizing the truth of the soul in a body. I was reading once about a Russian researcher; Dr. Korotkov, who has developed this specialized imaging system, called Electro Photonic Imaging EPI/GDV. These GDV cameras are being used as medical instruments as well for analysing the energy fields around the patients in hospitals. With these specialised cameras they have been able to very closely monitor and reveal a lot more about the emotional behaviours of even plants by studying their electro photonics.

In one of their experiments, they have been able to monitor that the energy field around a plant went down when destructive thoughts were developed around the plant and also increased whenever a happy person went close by or someone carrying water with them. As per the scientific belief, everything is just a form or particle of energy, there is no Inside or outside to anything, even human beings. Everything is some form of energy particles (atoms) that have come together to form the physical aura in some sort of shape and form. Research also conveyed that when they observe the play of light around either a human body, a drop of water or a crystal, scientists understand that everything in the world has interrelationship and any object - biological or inorganic - has its own inner energy. Understanding the fact that our life is not only material body and material existence but, first of all, it is energy, and therefore - Spirit, which makes us have new attitude towards our everyday reality.

As per Dr. Korotkov's research, it is possible to identify bio-electrographic correlates of Altered States of Consciousness (ASC). These are particular states, which a person enters during meditation, mental training, religious ecstasy, or when under the influence of drugs, psychedelics or anaesthesia. The research claims - "For many years we have been measuring Russian extrasensories, Candamblier priests in Brazil, participants of the Ayahuasca ceremony in Peru [Korotkov, 2002,

2003], Chinese Qi-gong masters, and healers in Germany, the USA, and Slovenia [Measuring Energy Fields, 2004]. And in almost all of these observations, we obtained signs and characteristic of ASC. Similar results, using the most diverse devices and methods, were obtained in the laboratories of different countries [Radin, 1997; Milton, 1996]. This shows that the processes of consciousness are apparent on the physiological processes measured."

The research does not intend to discuss the philosophical aspects of the process of researching consciousness. The experimental observations measure the influence of consciousness on physiological processes. In this regard they use a method called Electro Photonic Imaging the EPI method, which is very sensitive because it reacts to subtle changes in the working of the ANS (The **Autonomic Nervous System** is part of the nervous system that is a control system, functioning below the conscious level and controls visceral (instinctual or intuitive) functions. It affects heart rate, digestion, respiration rate, salivation, perspiration, diameter of the pupils, micturition (urination), and sexual arousal. Whereas most of its actions are involuntary, some, such as breathing work in tandem with our conscious mind). These sensitive measures make it possible to register subconscious and emotional processes. Another method is the registration of the influence of human consciousness on physical sensors. One of the most recent is water, or specially constructed systems. Many experiments have proved that such an approach is highly effective [Science of Whole Person Healing, 2004].

These scientists have also taken GDV photographs of a person as he was dying. It claims that in the photos, it could be seen that the area of the belly lost its life force (the purported soul) first, followed by the head. The heart and groin were the last to lose their life force, in that order. Scientists using the Gas-Discharged Visualisation (GDV) technique say that the aura of those who die unexpectedly or violently differs from those who experience a calm death. *The souls of the former remain in a state of confusion for several days and return frequently to their bodies, especially at night.* Korotkov ascribes that phenomenon to unused energy retained by the soul. He suggests that the GDV technique will also have applications for distinguishing genuine psychics from frauds. Source- Dr Korotkov's Research Website & Conscious Media Network Interview

As I believe and the fact, which should be commonly agreed upon is that the soul has no bigger or smaller size. It is all the same size regardless of the size of the bodies it may reside within. Lets start from ants, they keep moving, and they need some sort of food to survive on which they eat. So how do you think does the life mechanism works with them. If you think they are made of some sort of mechanical invention, then no, they do have a breeding process that keeps their numbers up and running all the time. The moment you step on them, their body mechanism is crushed to death, and after that death takes place, guess what is left behind, the very thing, that very physical form that was just moving around us a few seconds ago, and all of a sudden there is only one thing that went missing from that physical body, the life, that soul current.

The same applies to any creatures that we may believe are of higher strengths, the birds, the animals, the sea creatures, or whatever else, we all see that they are alive and when they are declared dead due to any reason whether accidental or natural or caused by human needs. The very same bodies are left behind and there is one thing that goes missing is the Life Current. And just if we think hard, what does this life current survives on! It is the breathing process. The body may still survive for few days, if it does not get the food or water but the moment one body is cut off from the free source available, the Oxygen, the body lives no more.

I often heard this holy song which we normally refer to as Bhajans from Sikh Religion of India; 'Hum Aadmi Haan ik Dami'. 'Hum' means 'us', 'Aadmi' means 'Human beings', 'Haan' means 'are', 'ik' means 'one', 'Dami' means 'Breather'. So as a whole what it suggests is that we as human beings are dependent on one breath. If we breathe we are alive, the moment we could not intake the air within our one feet vicinity, we are alive no more. How True, another reason we need to appreciate what we are provided by nature for free around us.

This current works very much the same way as the electric current in our real world. Do we see it? No, but what we do see are the effects of it, yet it very much exists. It is one of those things where we use electricity to cook a meal for a person using it in a particular controlled manner, and if not controlled properly, the same electric current can kill the person too. That electric current actually exists, yet we do not see it, we only see effects of it. Similar are the criteria happening in human or any other form of life on this planet by the means of soul current.

From the very day the soul has entered into this universe and resided in some sort of material body, from that day it has been reacting in this world, doing some sort of actions, and you can not escape doing some sort of action as that is what this planet earth is and was designed for. Even a thought that generates out of the memory bank in our mind is counted as an action, a karma with no consequences until materialised. If you study teachings of some mystics of the world and also those of the Hindu religion, you will learn some fascinating truths of Life in this Universe. Hinduism is the oldest religion on earth, a claim supported by science. Just search the Internet or libraries for the oldest religion on earth and you will have a lot of facts and figures from various articles and references published by some credible sources to help you learn more. Also if you dig deep in the history, Hinduism is the most peace loving, non-invading religion, a tribe of people who have never attempted to expand their horizons forcefully, whether the geographical wars or the wars for spreading their religion.

You can talk about any religion, the Hindu religion, Christianity, Muslim, Sikhism, Buddhism or Sufism; you won't have to go into much detail to understand that they all agree upon one reason about the beginning of the creation of this world, this universe. In Hinduism's ancient books, as well as Christ enforced the same as it is explained that – 'in the beginning there was Word, the Word was with God and the Word was God', and it still is. In Sikhism, it states the same and so does in Islam. Learn about Buddhism or other paths; they will all agree to the same.

A general human nutshell view is - we all entered the world as a soul and resided in some shape and form. When we entered the world, we started performing actions as we were supposed to. But there were different senses that were given to us as per the shape or form we were made to live in, along with the sense of discrimination and feel of power.

As per quotes in Bible - God made Man in his own image. It is in that context and with our ability of being able to commit karmas that we tend to believe in existence of our very own power when exercising everything else in the world, but not spiritual awakening. We completely ignore the fact, whether every action we are committing is in lines with the Laws of the Universe, the laws of Love, Peace and Harmony. More so often, it is not. We started committing certain actions that were against the laws of peace, love and harmony. That is where the sufferings began, when we started accumulating bad deeds, and such actions are what are called Bad Karma.

My view on Good and Bad Karmas being created is when some start to act under various influences of sensory passions such as lust, anger, greed, liking and pride, they create bad karma. They started using the power of action for their likings or benefits at the cost of causing pain to others. Those who act under the influence of peace, love and harmony, started to help those who were being affected by bad karma creators. So helping those in need, those in sorrow whether physically or emotionally is not just good Dharma (the call of duty) but also creates Good Karma.

Neutral Karmas are when you would simply take the life as it comes, take action as the life around you demands of you. It is the actual state of no leftover karma that can help reach the salvation of the soul. Though it is highly unlikely for a human being to achieve that without some spiritual guidance. At times, out of the human sense of feelings for other creatures around us, for instance; we may have seen someone in agony or need, we helped them by going out of our way. That has created the Good Karmas and on the other hand when our actions may have caused some grief to someone else for our own selfish purposes, or harmed someone whether physically or psychologically, we would have created bad karmas. We can practically never escape the play of karma but we do play this game of life and commit karmas. Sitting idle in meditative state may be the best for our soul's liberation but mindful practice is what we need to work on while committing those karmas so we may sort of plan for what we would reap into the future.

Now the way I understand the reason for our creation is that we were created to live in love, peace and harmony with whatever was manifested or created in physical form by God. He did this, as he may have wanted us to explore and appreciate what he had created. In other words he wanted us to explore and enjoy his creation; or should I say - **He's experiencing all probabilities and possibilities of his creation through us**. And if we go by the story of Adam and

Eve, the apple or the fruit from the forbidden tree of knowledge of good and evil, was not meant to be eaten. But, a Satan lured them into realising what they may gain and convinced to eat that fruit of apple that she was not supposed to. Some stories tell that she was told that once they have that fruit, they could become immortal like angels. Certain Religions and mystics call the planet earth as Mrityu Loka, which means the planet of Death and also a Planet of Karma. Adam and Eve thought they could disobey God's command and eat the apple to become immortal. From there on the story started far and beyond their imagination. They both were then descended to earth, to the garden of Eden but were promised the guardian angels to help them get back to their original homes, the heaven. Remember that the Satan is also a part of the creation. Perhaps God's way of seeing the negative end of his powers was Satan and positive end was the Angels or could they just be the names of the feelings invoked by negatives or positives within us.

So thus far by the research and studies that are available; all I can gather and as I mentioned it before too is that Hinduism is the oldest known religion on the planet. And below is the explanation that is derived from one of the Mystics of India, named, Saint Kabir. He is highly respected and referred to as a true saint and mystic of his time.

He was brought up by a Muslim weaver couple who taught him to be a weaver by profession. Kabir had a deep understanding of spirituality at young age. He lived his life somewhere near the town of Varanasi in India. He was very keen on progressing higher on the spiritual path. His desire did not bring him any fruit until one day, the day that was considered very auspicious for approaching a Guru for initiation. It is believed that to make any serious progress and achieve on the spiritual path; one must follow a spiritual Master, the Guru. It's not just a one-way street though, the Guru or Master must also accept the student for Initiation if the student is to progress in the spiritual journey.

The Guru, to whom Kabir followed and got initiated by, was Guru Ramananda, a Hindu. Kabir was a Muslim but wanted Initiation only by Ramananda. It was next to impossible for him to get initiation from a Hindu religious practitioner. During those days it was considered a crime if you went practicing a different religion. It is a common belief that you need to have a Guru, a perfect saint or master who can initiate you and give you further guidance on the spiritual journey. Without a Guru or Master, one can only go so far and even within the eternal world can be eluded by distractions to stop from progressing to higher and further spiritual regions. In a way true saints or Gurus are those guardian angels, the messengers of God as promised to Adam and Eve. But Kabir was so desperate to get initiated by a true saint, true Guru that he cared not for the religious barriers of the society. So, Kabir took recourse to a trick.

Ramananda daily went to the river Ganga for his early morning bath and prayers. Kabir was lying on the steps of the river Ganga in such a way that Ramananda stepped on him. He chanted the name of God realising that he had stepped on a human being. Kabir said that since he had heard the holy words from his mouth on that auspicious day, he was now Ramananda's disciple. Impressed with Kabir's intelligence, Ramananda took him as his disciple. Kabir also had shown very deep understanding of spirituality. However having a Muslim disciple caused annoyance in some of Ramananda's other disciples, who then stopped following him for that reason. His teachings were not to follow any idles, and to live an ideal life as to that of Impersonal Aspect of God. Kabir followed and progressed.

In his teachings in the book named Anurag Sagar, Kabir explained how and why the creation of us as human beings occurred. It explains how God created Kaal as one of his sixteen virtues, which we refer to as sixteen kalaas (virtues of God in a way) in Hindi or Punjabi. Then Kaal preyed to the lord for a large amount of years. Then he asked his permission to create a world of his own. Now Kaal will be able to create the accounts for actions of these souls in this world while in any form of existence of life. Based on their actions, intentions and wills and wishes as they go along enjoying life, he will keep them within his creation, the world as we see it.

Since the day the soul accompanied a physical form or body, it has been doing some actions, some good and some bad, which has been creating the Good and Bad karmas. The Karmas are committed and dealt by this body or any physical aura or physical contributor of the soul whether physically visible or not i.e. mind. Yet

Karmas are not related to the body, as it is just the medium and is mortal but they are related to the soul. The soul is accountable for those actions and must come back to bear the fruit for each and every Karma committed whether good or bad. You cannot offset one action against the other; so is the Law of Karma explains these mystics. Anything externally attached to the soul are the mediums for experiences that the soul has to go through. And all those mediums, various forms of life accompanying the soul exist for one reason alone, the Karma whether to create or to bear the fruit of past karmas. They are bound to accompany the soul; anything on this planet is mortal. Why, because when we die, we exist for no one and nothing exists for us, but the mortal bodies are run with soul current and what governs its journey in the world is the Karmas. All that's left behind is the legacy you create, so use your power of action to create a great one to lift the other fellow human beings. The Karmic account is what sticks with you and nothing else.

Knowing we have some spiritual component in us, I believe it will be a great help also to learn how our human body can be managed better with some spiritual awakening. This will be a great benefit if we consciously work on our actions, be more aware of Karmas we go about committing. We hear a fair amount of time about the statement, 'God created Human in his own image'. As per Hindu beliefs there are Seven Chakras of the body that are all said to be controlled by certain deities for the proper functioning. As per some mystics, there are a total of twelve Chakras as well and our creator, the Lord, The Eternal Source is sitting above all in the twelfth chakra. However this number may be due to them dividing the Crown Chakra into separate regions.

Let's learn a little about those Chakras. There is a vast amount of information available about this on the quickest reachable resource; Internet and I do recommend that you learn more if you wish to understand in deeper details. As in this book I will provide only some understanding to such concepts, so you understand the whole universal relation to us as human beings a little better. I am happy for any questions that you may post to me via my website www.thekarmicrewind.com or www.AtamDhillon.com.

Chakras of Human Body

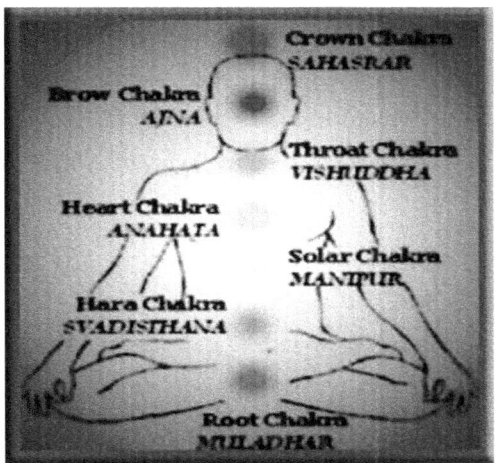

1. **Muladhar Chakra** - The first or lowest center is the Mul-Chakra, is presided over by Hindu Deity Ganesha, also known as root Chakra. This chakra is related to instincts, Security and survival, and also to basic human potential. This may be the reason why we have a famous saying of CYA (cover your a…) in the western world, just that this paragraph links that to the deeper meaning of why we say that.

2. **Svadisthana Chakra** - The second, the Indri Chakra, is governed by the god of creation, Brahma, the creator of the world. Also known as the Sacral Chakra, scientifically related to the sacrum and is related to the reproductive cycle by producing various sex hormones. It is linked to govern reproduction, creativity, enthusiasm and joy.

3. **Manipur Chakra**– also known as the third or Nabhi Chakra is controlled by God of Preserving, Vishnu, the one who nourishes or the sustainer. It's position is recognised as belly button area. Which clearly symbolises the stomach and its function of digestive system to the function of Vishnu. Scientifically linked to the organs responsible for the digestive system to convert Food or Matter into Energy for the well being and functioning of the body. Preserving what has been created.

4. **Anahata Chakra** - The fourth, which is also known as the Hriday or Heart Chakra, is ruled by Shiva, the Destroyer, the one that has the power to demolish what has been created whether bad or good. As being heart we all know it governs the blood circulation, and involves emotions of complex levels along with unconditional love. This Chakra is considered very important for realizing the clear light, the Devine light. Hence our hearts should be clean and free of any bad or negative.

5. **Vishuddha Chakra** - The fifth is the Kanth or Throat Chakra, presided over by the Goddess Shakti. Some also calls Shakti as Panchvaktra Shiva, God, the creator Shiva with five heads and four arms. In a physical aspect, Vishuddha chakra governs the communication, in emotional sense it governs independence, in mental sense it governs fluent thought, and spiritually, it governs a sense of security.

6. **Ajna Chakra** - The sixth Chakra, which is the highest stage ever reached by the yogis, is the 'Tisra Til' or the 'Third Eye', situated at the center behind our two eyes, and is referred to as the 'Seat of our Soul and mind', the 'Center of Consciousness' and the 'Thinking Center'. This is the center from where all our thoughts and energy go out. Science links it to Pineal gland. This is a Light sensitive gland, which produces the hormones to regulate sleep and awakening.

7. **Sahasrar Chakra** - The Crown is the Seventh and Top most Chakra, also known as Sahasrara and is generally represented by a Lotus flower referred to as bridal chamber in some scriptures. In Hinduism, this is where the Female energy from the Inner body rises and unites with the male energy, Shiva and a state of complete inner consciousness of being one with the God is felt. In scientific world its role as a place of pure consciousness is related with the role of the pituitary gland, which further connects to the central nervous system of our body and causes the actions, the Karma to take place.

Here we are on this mortal world or the planet we live on, within a mortal body. The planet where life exists and definitely has an end one day, we just don't know when. Time is the quickest one in dying sooner than anything else and at the largest scale than anything else. It is dying every tiniest fraction of a second, and if you take some scientific studies into account, our body itself is killing enormous amounts of tiny cells within our body, and that is also why we are eating all the time to make up for those loses in our body. Imagine how long your body will last or the energy within you if you do not supplement that loss in your body with something new. There's about two million red blood cells dying and regenerated every second. Just imagine and dig down deep into the reality of life and its existence.

It entirely depends on you that from which point of view you want to look at the world, as it exists. The bottom line is that the world we live in is mortal. Nothing materialistic exists with an infinite life, No, that just does not happen. And that is why it is so important for us human beings while living on this planet that we live it in the best way we can. Everything in this world is mortal, from tiny existence of certain bacteria to the plantation, birds, animals, ocean life and us humans. Anything and everything that exists as life in this world is mortal; it has a day and time when it will exist no more. The best-engineered machines even have a certain amount of life before they get scrapped, and there are other things, which may seem to have lost our interest in them, so we get rid of them. In other words, they are dead for us and more importantly; when we die, nothing exists for us.

Just imagine the life as a bubble made of soap water and air. It exists only while there is a perfect balance of surrounding atmospheric pressure and the thickness of layer formed as its body is keeping the air within the bubble. The moment that perfect balance breaks the bubble exists no more. Just imagine that everything materialistic around us has an average life. Take it as for the machinery that we buy, the furniture that we buy, and the wood used to build houses. The trees had to die first, the earth had to be dug in to first, for raw metals or other rare earth materials. But once we have had made full use of the things that were made from those materials, we will throw them away, so for us they exist no more. Also knowing us as human beings, our brain will very well get bored of those things and we will say we do not want it any more, it goes to the waste bins and crushed as rubbish. So what happened, those things all practically died for us.

There are other forms of life we know as living beings and creatures, we know they have life worth days, weeks, months years, and we hardly know many human beings who live past a hundred year mark. And some things may be made to last for average age of more than the human being but as we get bored, we will replace them, and eventually when we die, just imagine; we exist no more, the world exists no more for us as human beings. I hope that this does help you re-check your thoughts about living life. I hope you understand the reality of life and start Living life, Start living it the way it was meant to be. Create the world of Love, Peace and Harmony around you. Experience life deeply, as nature intended for it to be, don't live superficially as it seems to be becoming.

So, this somewhat explains the creation of human being along with the 8.4 Million forms of life, as explained by the mystics. A lot of us who may not be happy on this planet would be saying that what was the need for God to do that, why did he create this world. But, does it matter really? We are what we are and we are here to live a life. **What matters is how we recognise and understand the way life works.** That is why it's important to understand the Law of Karma and use it to move the life back to its very original purpose of enjoying the creation of God. Do your best and Leave the rest to God. At night, give it all to God and Go to Sleep with faith and trust in God, after all e's made sure that we wake up after we go to sleep completely unaware of the world around us. We can always only do our best. So do your best and let the life unfold but make sure you are doing your best.

What would we do if our kids (in a limited view, our creation) stayed under our guidance and loved us? We would always try our best to fulfil their wishes. We often will buy them something just because they have been Good, do we not! We may still exercise our control as to how much and what we buy them, but we do tend to reward them for their good work and love towards us. That is probably why (as per Saint Kabir) Kaal as a creation of God got rewarded with his wish of creating and managing the world under the Law of Karma. Kabir tells us that Kaal preyed to the supreme Lord for 64 Yugas (epoch or an era in a four age cycle). As I say, the logic flows throughout the universe; here it's the reward of love and devotion I am talking about.

We as souls are not any different from what God created in the very start. The first sixteen creations or identified virtues of his were in a way dimensions of his own and so are the souls. There is No such thing that was created from anywhere out side. And hence we are all part of that Supreme Being, that same eternal source. Souls were promised to kaal along with the grant of permission to create a world of his own. It is said that the materials that Kaal gathered were taken by force from another one of those sixteen creations of God called Kurma in Hinduism. And hence we are potentially part of God in the form of soul particle, living in a mortal body created by a mix of various virtues of god. So it is not separate and is connected energy particles as a whole one universe as is proven by quantum physics. We do not see that with our eyes, until we learn from and are spiritually awakened by the true masters.

One of the ways of looking at this creation may also be that God created the whole universe as he was feeling bored. And then, kaal (kaal interestingly enough also means Time in Hindi language) being one of his own creations; was granted a contract to build more variations of what God had created. Then Kaal created all different forms we see around us but he borrowed Life, which is soul particle, an extract of God himself to make things alive. Then finally, to see all that was created from all possible point of views, he created human with the best possibilities that he could in similarities with God, so God could see and feel all Kaal had created in all probable and possible ways.

That physically non-existing Mind of ours, is also said to be the agent of Kaal the creator within each body and hence the Mind's capabilities of Creating through the power of thoughts.

It is in that view we should look at ourselves. That is where the belief of us being part of God comes from. Hence with the abilities the soul current brings within us being the part of that supreme, supernatural power that creates all that exists. We should realise we have much more within us, much more than what we believe and know until we experience it.

If it was not for the saints and mystics, who always suggested that there is much more in the universe and if it was not for the human's sense of curiosity to discover more, there probably would have been no such ideas of exploring the astronomical world as we are currently. But think about it; did the telescopes fall from the sky for us to have a look at what's out there in the space? NO! Did the planes and rockets fell out of the sky for us to fly, NO. Did the boats, and ships that we travel in and around the world over oceans were born from the sea? No. It is the vision the human race had and started up with, which has lead us to creating what we have and what we can with our mind using the seed of thoughts and constant learning to apply improvements.

This is where you need to realise the potential of creating what we can, and we create what we start to think, imagine and start to see and then start to take action towards. Again, if someone said to you in the past centuries that we could fly in a box with wings and fans on it, what would you have thought or said. Yet there are evidences coming out that there has been civilisations who had built Vimanas, the ancient aeroplanes. So, We need to realise that potential, the power within and start imagining, then start believing, and then start taking action towards it. Once you take the action, things will happen, they are bound to happen as per the laws of Karma and the laws of action and reaction.

So getting back to the Logical flow of the universe. As per the Hindu religion beliefs, what was granted to Kaal as a reward for Love and devotion towards God, has actually been spread through the universe. The logic of love has been implemented from the very roots of where it all started. We do not need to look far. Just look around us, in our daily life, people around us, kids around us & us looking towards our parents in that, how they treat us and reward us when we live under their obedience and serve them with full love, care and obedience. They will do everything in their power to ensure the wellbeing of their child.

For such a child the parents do go out of their way to ensure their well-being. Now, this is the trend set at the very start of the world if we were to believe in the above-explained Philosophy of Kaal. And so far Hinduism does seem to be recognised as the oldest religion on the planet, as per what could be researched. So, *the trend set is that of the love and devotion.* The more you have and show the more you get and receive. And that brings the beliefs of Law of Attraction and the Law of Love into confidence. There on, the actions we take for and under that love, result in the Law of Karma playing its part. Which then follows on to cause the Re-

Incarnation, derived from the calculation, the results of Good and Bad Karmas accumulated on the judgement day after this mortal body diminishes to ashes.

The God, who created everything, has created everything based upon Love. We do have the common saying; Love is God, God is Love. The more you give the more you will receive. Out of Love rose the desire and Kaal is the controller of the Physical, Astral and Causal plains using Karma as the instrument of control. And it is under the influences of the senses we are equipped with that keep causing our eternal attention to remain outwards into the world.

Let's understand that there are nine apertures of the body to cause that. Two Eyes, that lets us see the world to attend to. Two for the ears to listen, so we can understand what is happening around us with the vibrations and frequency of sound waves or sound energy produced around us. Two for Nose giving us the ability to discriminate smells and lets us breathe.

And how smart is that, if you look from an IT system designer's point of view. One is the Mouth that was created. At the time of designing the nose, the air pipe was designed to give access to the mouth as well, or it could also be vice versa that, the air pipes were created for mouth but then God may have realised that we may not need to expose air directly through mouth all the time due to obvious risk of other creatures running into us all the time, He gave us Nose, a smaller access to breath with Hair filtering system. OK, I think that is enough of a system designers view.

The other two are the parts of body that runs the re-generative and clean up process of body to filter out the waste from what we take in as fuel for body. The food we eat is very systematically processed to ensure the required energy from it is extracted and then distributed properly to all parts of body. There has to be an engineer to design a system like that, and has to be a smart one. And if we can't see him, who else can we say it would be, other Than GOD.

We live because we all have that soul current within all of us. The moment that soul current is withdrawn, we exist no more. It may happen by accident, by sickness or by age naturally. It is bound to happen one day. That is how this body is designed. And if you think hard that who designed this body with marvellous capabilities, you have to give credit to some engineer, nothing constructive can evolve from nothing being done in a particular way except rot.

Scientific discoveries are great, but I do not think that they will ever be able to reach as far as the mystic world explains of the universe. And as per claims by the spiritual practitioners, there is a lot out there that may never be travelled by human being in the physical form, yet the ones who have meditated enough have reached those astral and causal regions with soul. A lot of Yogi's and Sadhu's of Hindu religion have explained of those astral and causal worlds. Jesus Christ's lost years are also discovered to have been spent learning from the saints and mystics of the Indian region. The Sikh Book of religion named – "Guru Granth Sahib Ji", also mentions that there are hundreds and thousands of such universes in existence.

Those who are non-believers in God, the supernatural power or energy could be more agreeable term. I would say that if you believe in science, then the supernatural power is the Energy that has created everything. Everything that exists around us is in the form of Energy as per science. Which also states that if we look under a relevant microscopic instrument, then we humans are also shown as just a form of energy as everything else.

The law of conservation of Energy is that Energy Can neither be Created nor Destroyed, but only transferred from one form to another.'

So, that should also add some support to the theory of Re-Incarnation, right. Or may be even start to get you thinking about yourself as a form of Energy. The soul current within us is causing the senses to stimulate in this body form. And when that is happening, there is a form of energy circle created around us as a result of those stimulations, and in this particular aspect of energy, the positive attracts positive and the negative attracts negative. Why, think of it in terms of like attracts like or similar attracts similar; do we not see that in everyday human life.

We know it and exercise it in our daily life. We know that people who are like us, we will associate more with them because they are like us. As human we tend to be attracted towards other human beings, if we see or notice something in common. We are okay with people who may have neutral personalities but we stay away from those who are completely opposite to what we are like. There is no secret to that, we know it, and we exercise it everyday in our life.

Now lets shift our point of view and talk from the view of a form of energy particle. That is what we are at a very microscopic level and that is also the medium we use to interact in this universe when you look at quantum levels. We all talk, but how does the other person hears us. It is that combined effort of energy that has produced certain amount of vibrations, which are called sound waves. These vibrations are then felt on the eardrums and interpreted to the brain, which again is a sequence of vibrations within our body at a deeper level. The brain is decoding those vibrations based on what has been fed into the brain's memory to help us understand intentions and then take action accordingly. This is just a simple example to help you understand why we are also a form of energy particles along with being human beings. A similar word or sentence has different vibrations based on what language you speak in and if you have not fed into your brain the vibrational frequencies used in a different language's sound. It will not be decoded by the brain and mean nothing except some words being heard. This again shows that our brain works based on what has been fed into it, similar to computers.

Getting back to attracting the same, as a particle of energy we are attracted towards the similar particles of energy. Similarly everything else that exists in the universe is actually a form of energy. The more negative you feel, the other particles of negative energy will love to be in your company, and similar applies to the Positive. The more positive feelings you have will help you attract similar energies closer to you, other positive energy particles will come to you as soon as they can or you'll reach them. Just imagine water, in a jug if you have half cold water and then add hot water to it slowly while trying not to disturb the cold water that is in the jug already. Now, you will notice that the cold water towards the bottom of jug will not mix unless you mix it well with a spoon. The hot water is lighter and cold water is heavier comparatively and particles with similar energies stick to each other. That is how we as energy particles also behave as well but we as humans have the ability to lift our energies up and create with the power of karma.

That is how the laws of universe work, that is how the law of attraction works. There is no concern of physical distance with the laws and powers of universe. I am sure you have heard of telepathy. Recently (July 2017) scientists in China have even successfully teleported from a location in Tibet to their satellite 300 miles in space. In teleportation, the complete properties of one particle are instantaneously transferred to another – in effect teleporting it to a distant location. Funny though, don't we humans take on properties of what surrounds us as people and their nature or habits. For us as humans, the closest like minded ones may reach to you quicker and could be a less hassle for the universe; but again, in the form of intense desire their is a force of Gravity around us all the time which will help the distant ones make their way a little quicker too. It all depends on the strength of vibrations that you are generating. Sakyong Mipham says there is a relationship between Karma and Gravity as explained *"Like gravity, karma is so basic we often don't even notice it"*. Sakyong Mipham Rinpoche serves as temporal and spiritual director of Shambhala, a global network of meditation centres.

It is not a wonder that a day starts bad mostly ends bad, or has a lot of negative happening more than positive if you have set up your mood to be bad. Such as starting up late to work in the morning will almost certainly bring to you the more consequences that will cause further delays with such mood. It may also surround you with people and circumstances that may not let you feel great for the day. You will be nagged even more at times, and even if you are not nagged, you will feel nagged because that is the mindset you are in. This is caused by the mode of energy you have started the day with. The negative feel you may have created around you will only help attract more negative, and just by changing few things in your surrounding environment, and most importantly your mindset, will help change all those things.

There is a great depth of impact in our reactions, which need to be understood - why we react in a particular manner and what could be causing those reactions. Let's try and understand. As one person looks at a glass as half empty, and the other one sees it as half full. The one, who sees the glass as half empty, will have different view of looking at things. Definitely lacks in higher level of positive attitude in the subconscious mind. It may even be that he is not really thirsty; as this will also play its part in the way that person would respond. On the other hand the one who sees the glass half full is definitely thinking positive and has a higher level of positive thinking in the subconscious mind. It may also be that such person may be feeling really thirsty and thinking about how to make the most of that half full glass of water. The difference between the thinking of the two may also be because of the attitude they have developed in life due to the circumstances they encountered. The first person may generally have lack of respect for what he has in life, whereas the second person does have respect. The energy field, which you create around you with such attitude, will influence the surroundings in conjunction with the laws of the universe and bring about circumstances accordingly.

    The attitude, with which you look at things around you, will determine and influence the next course of action you will take. And that action is going to derive some results. The one who is thinking negative is just going to think the bad results and so will he reap them. If one can change that energy field around them then that will instead help you make the situation better. Just imagine listening to that favourite music track to at-least change the emotions at that point in time. And you may be surprised by how much difference it can make to the rest of the day. Power of positive energy is much stronger than negative energy's power; **it's just that people put more belief behind negative than positive** and that needs to change. You tell someone something negative they'll immediately hold on to that as the truth and make that the truth. That is why it is important to watch your associations that are surrounding you.

    The world around us is full of energy particles and it behaves that way. It always did and always will. It's the experience we feel through the senses we have as humans that suffer. Because the bases of this supreme source of energy are love and harmony, it always will prevail and win. That is why we always see the movies or stories that show the good and the bad, but who wins at the end, the Good, the power of Love, the Positive Energy and as I said the logic of love flows throughout the universe.

    The more you concentrate on a particular thought; the mind with the laws of the universe begins to manifest what is required. The concentration is intense, so the intensity is high. The vibrations of you as an energy particle are very strong towards a particular form of existence, which you may be thinking about. So the rest of the energy particles around you will start making a way to accommodate the union of you and the other particle of energy you may want to have around you, which you will show a large amount of love and passion for. And for those things or events, which may need to come to existence for you, must exist in your thoughts first. Only then they can become reality. You must love what you want, and see it with clear vision.

Similar is advised in most spiritual practices. The more time you devote to meditation and fixing your behaviours in the manner as advised. The behaviours such as humble, loving, kind, helpful, living in harmony and noble respective practices will help you achieve a higher state of mind in spirituality sooner. You will never attain the higher state of mind if you do not practice the way you should in accordance with the laws of The Universe, Love, Peace and Harmony.

The only other way left otherwise would be the God himself holding you by hand and force you to do things properly by creating such circumstances, but believe me that may not be an easy ride to put up with. But that may only be necessary to eliminate the mighty evil, as has been scripted in Hinduism through incarnation of Lord Krishna in Mahabharata. We can imagine what we may need to face, to have the respect for others be born within us, if we do not have that already. We may not like the idea of our humiliation. But, how can we expect respect towards us if that is not what we give to others? So the more we pay respect, the more we show gratitude, only then we can expect that in return, not otherwise. *"What we sow, so shall we reap"* and *"What goes around comes around"* prevails in this world.

The same way as if your child was to return back home straight after school, but instead, they went elsewhere against the rules that were created for the house and the family, against your instructions or without your permission. What would you want to do? First you will be worried, and then you will go looking for your child. Then based on the reason, you may or may not be treating him or her with the special loving treatment, but instead a huge tell off, and probably imposing certain restrictions as punishment. However you are doing this out of care and love for your child.

Same applies with God's behaviour towards us as his children. Again as I said along the lines in Christianity: *"God created man in its own image"*. He may get us to go through a rough patch to realise him and stay close to him in the sense that we should be remembering him, living under his laws and be grateful all the time, respect him and his creation in every sense.

God – The Greatest Explorer

Let's just take a look at this reasoning of creation from yet another point of view. Let's just say that God is a mind of an explorer and wants to explore all the possibilities and probabilities of what he can create. Out of this curiosity, he created everything. One of his creations (which I also referred to as 'Kaal' earlier in this book.) loved him back and asked for God's permission to create and play the game of life becoming a creator himself and posing as the Supreme God to us humans. In this game Kaal wants to create lots of different creatures of all sorts of different shapes and size. Then, he wants to give those creatures ability to be able to enjoy this planet. The planet will play the role similar to the board of snakes and ladders game, which we played as kids. Now let's call Kaal the creation of God, 'Mr Manager' of our world in this story.

So Mr Manager started creating all these different kind of creatures. To give them life, so they can go around exploring this planet, he had to ask God for giving him a way to implement the life current. Life current of-course in this case has to come from God's own self. Mr Manager also told God that this way he can also explore what he created, with direct access through the soul current. He also said that, these souls would play by my rules in this creation to go through all the forms of life (as per mystics, there are 8.4 million in total). Mr. Manager will create the final form of life in resemblance to the God and that form of life will be their only chance to realise that they are part of God. It will be in this form of life that they can unite back with God. However, I shall still be able to keep them in the game, if they do not live by the rules that I create, the Law of Karma.

Those Rules will be based upon Love that you give us, Peace that we find being one with you, and Harmony that you have created among all you created.

With the law of Karma, I will ensure that they unite with you again the way you will give them to me, in pure form that you are. They shall remain in this game until they purify themselves from all karmas. Karmas, that they may have accumulated with their ability to commit actions while either abiding by or acting against the rules I create in this game. Those souls may wish to come back again in any other form of life if they want as I will give them re-birth as per their last wish in a given form of life. I will also keep them coming back for reaping the results of their Karmas. So, Mr Manager created us with soul current, which is part of God and God had created this Mr Manager, so eventually everything is created by God. Hence, what Kaal or Mr Manager came up with is also born with clues off God's mind, but controlled by this Mr. Manager posing as God. So, I also call God "The Greatest Explore of all that exists", the whole Universe.

Well not all of you may or have to agree on the way I look at this, but again, it is your life, you believe in what you find happiness in, if you do not believe in God. The science tells you that everything is a form of energy. Though science has made a lot of advancements, in fact huge leaps in the past decade: There are still many facts that science is struggling to find the answers for: things or behaviours such as consciousness, dreams, sure cures for diseases etc.

Science is a discovery and not the creation. It's about how things work the way they work not why they work that way. Scientists observe, learn, experiment and create knowledge to be understood on how things work. They cannot create what exists but tell us what exists and experiment on how it may have come into existence. So knowing that certain facts are still not explained by science may help a little more in believing that science does not have all the answers yet. Then why not incline the thinking towards existence of God. Even if it gives you an unseen shoulder to lean on and shed off dull and down to reduce the extent of pain by acceptance; it only helps you get by and get over some hard moments of life. But eventual truth is you exist, the universe exists and the phenomenon of creation exists; in terms of your goals, whatever belief you have, follow it with full heart, realise who you are and then commit related karmas accordingly. Realise the power and potential you have within.

This is where seeing your goals clearly will come into play. See your destination on your Future Probability Sphere clearly. That is when what science refers to as RAS – *Reticular Activation System* in your brain becomes active. Once you see your goals very clear and you want to achieve them; you will start to see and notice more circumstances relating to that. Just as we start noticing more of the cars or bikes of similar colour or brand that we may want to buy, when we decide to buy one of them by extracting our choice out from the all-else that exists. That is what we need to do with our goals in life as well and commit the Karma to achieve them.

The logic of love, the law of attraction flows throughout the universe. Once you have a strong desire and love towards something you want, how desperately you want it; will create the energy vibrations required as per the law of manifestation. Intensity of those vibrations will play part in how quickly you get it. You can relate this to any aspect of life, whether it's Work, Career, Business, Relationships, Love, Money, Health or Spirituality. For me it's the Spirituality that comes first, my goal is to make an effort for Nirvana.

To realise that purpose, whatever we sow, we must reap and try not to sow more if we can. This may practically be impossible to achieve for all of us. That is how this world was designed, to make it impossible to achieve that zero balance of our Karmic account with all the beauty created around us for us to enjoy and indulge in. Some mystics often refer to this world as a drama stage, where we all come and play part as assigned to the actors. In this case however, we get the roles as per our Karmas, our wishes and desires. The director of this drama stage, The Kaal as per Hindu beliefs is really enjoying the show very well, enjoying the world of illusion he has got us trapped into.

Only if Nirvana is your desire, there is only one way out to unite back with our supreme source and that is to have the guidance of someone as a true Guru in spirituality. They may take up the role as your karmic accounts manager in place of Kaal and help you write off the karmic debts with their guidance and by teaching meditation practices. If Moksha (Escape of soul into the Eternal Source) is one's goal, then you do need to find such a Guru. And for those who see other goals clearly, the **power of creation through Karma is within you**, the mind is the creator; just see the goals as clearly as possible, love them from the bottom of your heart and follow through with Karma, the action. For spiritual gains, one needs to meditate with as much concentration as possible. That can only come with love and devotion from your heart. That is why I also consider meditation as the technique to love God; the more you love him, the more you will be loved through this medium of love, through the Meditation. And that is why we hear, Love makes everything possible, and I wonder, if that is how people obtain all those mystical powers to perform those miracles. They express their full love and devotion towards God or Deity they admire. They then ask for what they want as a boon. What they prayed for is given to them as a result of their love and devotion.

There has always been Mystics, Saints and Darveshas at all times on this planet, in different times, in different countries, in all different religions. All of them spread the same message. The message was that of union with God with love, peace and harmony. Some of those mystics have been recognised as re-incarnations of the holy messengers from the past. And not only those, there has been a lot of cases studied around the world, which shed some light on re-incarnation. Let's learn a little about the studies on Re-incarnation as a concept along with findings of modern science. A lot of people dust off their hands on committing a good deed by short-sighted views of temporary gains when they are told to commit to a noble act so they can benefit from it in long run or the next life. Their argument is - "Who has seen another life". I completely agree to that and here's my challenge to you –

> *"If you've ever said in your life – who's seen another life, then now is the time to say it again and make the most of this life."*

Keeping this challenge in mind let's learn a bit about Re-Incarnation but know that who has seen another life; so we must focus on life we have on hands.

The Re-Incarnation

'As the moon dies and comes to life again, So we also, having to die, will rise again.'
San Juan Capistrano Indians

There are scientific back-ups to such claims of reincarnation and it is a true fact as per the Mystics as well as the other religious groups on planet earth.

There have been researches and studies done by various researchers, doctors and scientists in relation to re-incarnation. I came across the research by Dr. Ian Stevenson. I found below article on him on a website called near-death.com, which has been abstracted from various publications by Dr. Stevenson. He is recognised as the pioneer of Reincarnation research. I would strongly recommend reading more on him and his findings. Here's a little brief of his findings along with my explanation and understanding.

****

Dr. Ian Stevenson, the former head of the Department of Psychiatry at the University of Virginia, and now is Director of the Division of Perceptual Studies at the University of Virginia. He has devoted the last 40 years to the scientific documentation of past life memories of children from all over the world and has over 3000 cases in his files. Many people, including skeptics and scholars, agree that these cases offer the best evidence yet for reincarnation.

Dr. Stevenson's research into the possibility of reincarnation began in 1960 when he heard of a case in Sri Lanka where a child claimed to remember a past life. He thoroughly questioned the child and the child's parents, as well as the people whom the child claimed were his parents from his past life. This led to Dr. Stevenson's conviction that reincarnation was possibly a reality. The more cases he pursued, the greater became his drive to scientifically open up and conquer an unknown territory among the world's mysteries, which until now had been excluded from scientific observation. Nonetheless, he believed he could approach and possibly furnish proof of its reality with scientific means.

In 1960, Dr. Stevenson published two articles in the Journal of the American Society for Psychical Research about children who remembered past lives. In 1974, he published his book, Twenty Cases Suggestive of Reincarnation, and became well known wherever this book appeared by those people who already had a long-standing interest in this subject. They were pleased to finally be presented with such fundamental research into reincarnation from a scientific source. In 1997, Dr. Stevenson published his book called Reincarnation and Biology. In the first volume, he mainly describes birthmarks - those distinguishing marks on the skin, which the newborn baby brings into the world and cannot be explained by inheritance alone. In his second volume, Dr. Stevenson focuses mainly on deformities and other anomalies that children are born with and which cannot be traced back to inheritance, prenatal or perinatal (created during birth) occurrences. This monumental piece of work contains hundreds of pictures documenting the evidence.

During his original research into various cases involving children's memories of past lives, Dr. Stevenson did note with interest the fact that these children frequently bore lasting birthmarks, which supposedly related to their murder or the death they suffered in a previous life. Stevenson's research into birthmarks and congenital defects has such particular importance for the demonstration of reincarnation, since it furnishes objective and graphic proof of reincarnation, superior to the -often-fragmentary - memories and reports of the children and adults questioned, which even if verified afterwards cannot be assigned the same value in scientific terms.

In many cases presented by Dr. Stevenson there are also medical documents available as further proof, which are usually compiled after the death of the person. Dr. Stevenson adds that in the cases he researched and 'solved' in which birthmarks and deformities were present, he didn't suppose there was any other apposite explanation than that of reincarnation. Only 30% - 60% of these deformities can be put down to birth defects which related to genetic factors, virus infections or chemical causes (like those found in children damaged by the drug Thalidomide or alcohol). Apart from these demonstrable causes, the medical profession has no other explanation for the other 40% to 70% of cases than that of mere chance. Stevenson has now succeeded in giving us an explanation of why a person is born with these deformities and why they appear precisely in that part of their body and not in another.

Most of the cases where birthmarks and congenital deformities are present for which no medical explanations exist have one to five characteristics in common.

1. In the most unusual scenario, it is possible that someone who believed in reincarnation expressed a wish to be reborn to a couple or one partner of a couple. This is usually because they are convinced that they would be well cared for by those particular people. Such preliminary requests are often expressed by the Tlingit Indians of Alaska and by the Tibetans.

2. More frequent than this are the occurrences of prophetic dreams. Someone who has died appears to a pregnant or not as yet pregnant woman and tells her that he or she will be reborn to her. Sometimes relatives or friends have dreams like this and will then relate the dream to the mother to be. Dr. Stevenson found these prophetic dreams to be particularly prolific in Burma and among the Indians in Alaska.

3. In these cultures the body of a newborn child is checked for recognizable marks to establish whether the deceased person they had once known has been reborn to them. This searching for marks of identification is very common among cultures that believe in reincarnation, and especially among the Tlingit Indians and the Igbos of Nigeria. Various tribes of West Africa make marks on the body of the recently deceased in order to be able to identify the person when he or she is reborn.

4. The most frequently occurring event or common denominator relating to rebirth is probably that of a child remembering a past life. Children usually begin to talk about their memories between the ages of two and four. Such infantile memories gradually dwindle when the child is between four and seven years old. There are of course always some exceptions, such as a child continuing to remember its previous life but not speaking about it for various reasons.

Most of the children talk about their previous identity with great intensity and feeling. Often they cannot decide for themselves which world is real and which one is not. They often experience a kind of double existence where at times one life is more prominent, and at times the other life takes over. This is why they usually speak of their past life in the present tense saying things like, 'I have a husband and two children who live in Jaipur.' Almost all of them are able to tell us about the events leading up to their death.

Such children tend to consider their previous parents to be their real parents rather than their present ones, and usually express a wish to return to them. When the previous family has been found and details about the person in that past life have come to light, then the origin of the fifth common denominator – the conspicuous or unusual behaviour of the child - is becoming obvious.

5. For instance, if the child is born in India to a very low-class family and was a member of a higher caste in its previous life, it may feel uncomfortable in its new family. The child may ask to be served or waited on hand and foot and may refuse to wear cheap clothes. Stevenson gives us several examples of these unusual behaviour patterns.

In 35% of cases he investigated, children who died an unnatural death developed phobias. For example, if they had drowned in a past life then they frequently developed a phobia about going out of their depth in water. If they had been shot, they were often afraid of guns and sometimes of loud bangs in general. If they died in a road accident they would sometimes develop a phobia of traveling in cars, buses or lorries. Another frequently observed unusual form of behaviour, which Dr. Stevenson called Philias, concerns children who express the wish to eat different kinds of food or to wear clothes that were different from those of their culture. If a child had developed an alcohol, tobacco or drug addiction as an adult in a previous incarnation he may express a need for these substances and develop cravings at an early age.

Many of these children with past-life memories show abilities or talents that they had in their previous lives. Often children who were members of the opposite sex in their previous life show difficulty in adjusting to the new sex. These problems relating to the 'sex change' can lead to homosexuality later on in their lives. Former girls who were reborn as boys may wish to dress as girls or prefer to play with girls rather than boys.

Until now all these human oddities have been a mystery to conventional psychiatrists - after all, the parents could not be blamed for their children's behaviour in these cases. At long last research into reincarnation is shedding some light on the subject.

****

That is an amazing study and findings by Dr. Stevenson. This has caused me to think about whether my Daughter is my grandmother's soul. She was really close to me and had passed away after I had moved to Australia. My mother and I could not attend her funeral as my mum was also visiting me in Australia at the time of her death. My Grandmother was told to be concerned about me being the first member in the whole family living overseas. That also makes me think if she was still thinking about me at the time of her passing away. Some comments by my daughter and a dream conveyed to me by my mum about my grandmother, just before my daughter was born, has got me thinking deeper.

The comments by my daughter at least on two occasions, after having her bath were that she also use to give bath to my wife as well as me when we were small. You may be wondering that, one of us would be ok but how come both of us. But it is possible as when we were little, both of our families use to live close by in same area and were very close to each other. The world is a small place statement can be applied to the Universe as well at times when you believe in these theories with some back up from modern science.

So, since we are living on this planet of Life and Death, Soul's Karmic accounts are given the review after the death of a body. Based on the wishes and desires and the Karmas committed, the soul will be reborn into a body and a place, best suited according to its Karmic account and wishes it had desired for, while living in the last body. This also tells us that God does listen to us and does what he finds fit to keep the world running. To us it all remains mystery unseen.

"Thy kingdom come, Thy will be done in earth, as it is in heaven." ---Bible (Matthew 6:10)

Karmic Balance Sheet

We go through one form of life and arrive at our judgment day. It is that day when our Karmic accounts are looked at and the Karmic balance sheet is settled. Based on that Karmic account, we may have to come back into this world, to reap the fruit of the Karmas we did in the past. That is when we have to go through a rough ride in life, if we did accumulate bad karmas more than good. And if we did more good karmas we will still comeback to reap the fruit of Good Karmas, hence that may give us a pre-destined luxurious life.

Enjoying a good life as a result of Good karmas in past life may sound really nice. But the problem becomes that when we are physically given a new body to go through our past karmas. We are given a memory wash out. And because of that, we do not see the reason why we may be encountering the circumstances that we do. And yet, with the ability to commit and create new deeds, actions or Karmas, we carry on in our present life. We know what can happen once we have all the luxury at our hand. We can indulge into activities that we should not or are not supposed to, in accordance with the laws of universe, the law of love, peace and harmony. And hence just imagine going through a lifetime again while the Karmic balance sheet may slide into the negative.

One will only attain Nirvana, with a lot of meditation and a Zero Balance of Karma's, by taking the life as it comes & live in harmony without hurting someone physically and psychologically. Only then, that zero balance of Karmas may be achieved. This is a seriously tough task for us human beings. We have to have a good relationship with God's authorized Karmic account manager. That manager is a true spiritual guru or a master.

One of the ways to accumulate less karma is following a vegetarian diet. In reality Vegetarianism is not promoted by any religion but only promoted by those groups who teach about higher states of mind, meditation and the escape of the soul from the worldly loop of birth and death to become one with the God. Living vegetarian not only has its advantages in spiritual success but in general living as well. The higher the form of life one kills for its survival such as any kind of meat, the higher will be the debt of Karmas one obtains. The lower the form of life one kills for its survival such as fruits and vegetation, the lower the karmic crime in other words, and so will be the punishment in terms of repaying those karmas. The Vegan diet is becoming increasingly popular too these days with medical evidences proving it to be much healthier for our bodies.

An interesting saying in India is - 'Jaisa ann vaisa mann', which means that 'like food like mind' or 'as is the food, so is the mind', the kind of food you eat has direct effects on your human nature and behaviours. I was so surprised once by the comments of this guy, whom I never expected to favour vegetarianism. Once we were visiting a friend's garage for some car repairs in a western Sydney suburb. We ordered vegetarian pizzas for lunch as per the diet we followed. There was this Samoan islander guy who was trimming trees around the block. It was a quiet and hot afternoon so we invited him for a cold drink and some pizza too. Knowing that islanders love meat, I lightly mentioned before offering that we had only vegetarian pizzas. I was surprised when he told me that he was following a vegetarian diet too.

He continued by telling his story that how he use to eat a lot of meat and drink alcohol every day in large amounts. He was fighting at home every day, beating his kids and wife. **Someone at church suggested to him to follow a vegetarian diet** for a while. Since he started that, he felt much calmer in his behaviours. He became less aggressive and calmer. His family tells him that they love him the way he is now and are not scared of him as in the past. He loved living more peaceful life too. I am not convincing anyone to become vegetarian but just advising some of the proven and practically experienced facts of vegetarian life that may help someone somehow. This is definitely a way to create less karma and will be easier to achieve salvation.

As we see in real life banking systems, some bad debts are written off. There are also some cases where the bank managers may use their power to write off some bad debts. The similar may be attained in spiritual life. And those managers are the Spiritual Guru's. They are the one with the power of helping you in writing that karmic debt off. You just need to find a true perfect master, a true perfect saint. For some it may even become the case as per Bible says – *'When the Shepherd comes and blows the whistle, the sheep will come running'*. You may not even need to go looking for him and you may just come across one of those holy souls and the inner you will know it is time to follow him.

You just need to find that inner peace which only exists within. That can be attained with pure practice of Love, Peace and Harmony. Once that happens you will start to feel happier and more content. You will see life in a completely different manner. And once you are living a content life, you may not be bothered about much material gains. The results of meditation will enable you to concentrate better and see things clearly as to what you want out of life. You will identify the deeper meaning and purpose of your life after you have attained that inner peace. It will bring you the desired results in any other field and aspect of life. As long as your intentions are clear and pure, your love towards the goal is in line with spreading love, peace and harmony. As we also know that with more power comes more responsibility. You must also be ready to bare that as well as be able to give more. As one receives more, they should only help more under the guidance of the Supreme Lord, God or good purpose.

Destiny with Karma & Mighty Nature

For those who believe in Destiny and may be thinking where does destiny stand in all this theory? I do believe in Destiny too, but in the context of Karma - **Destiny** is something that is a result of your past karmas, the only exception may be the First Ever birth, but how do we know if it is our first life or whether the first wasn't as some other form of life. We can't justify believing in destiny without believing in karma and reincarnation. Destiny becomes a must as a result of your past karmas. However at the same time, your mindset and the ability of creating new karma can heavily affect the actual impact of destiny.

If the destiny has a good fortune or good incidents for you in your life, the experience of the journey of life will be a pleasure while you arrive at such a point. If the destiny has something that will land you in some troubled waters in life, then by concentrating on positive, at-least you gave your best to create a positive or tried best to minimise the impact of undesired. *Keeping positive mindset works as an anaesthetic during a surgery. You may have the surgery planned by Destiny but pain is numbed down by the use of anaesthetic.* Keeping positive mindset and working towards a positive outcome will make the journey much more of a pleasure and it will either help you accept the pre-destined destiny or you'll create one. The journey of life would be with your full and sincere efforts, at-least you know you did the best you could. Any outcome, if not to your heart's content, will be overcome by the good feels of positive aura you created with your positive efforts.

The fact is that, survival of everything on this planet (if you think deeper) is very much dependent on the existence of universe around us. The mechanism it has and the accuracy it runs with is just a marvellous peace of work, beautiful engineering and art. The sun helps the Life on planet, eliminate the sun and we know Life as we know it, will exist no more. Eliminate the water, and that again will cause the same consequences. Eliminate earth or the fertility factor of the soil, and we know what we will eat. Eliminate the air factor and oxygen, which is the most important ingredient of air for our survival, as we breathe for our life, **the smartest creature** on earth along with a lot of others **will not be able to survive**.

Nature still has its governing forces that will ensure that nature will keep on recreating on this planet, as it should be as per nature. It's us, who may not survive, if those free supplies that we take for granted and have stopped caring about, cease to care about us one day. We don't have to agree with the concept of global warming, but we should have a natural instinct for **looking after what looks after us**, in this case the Mother Nature as we call it. It should be a general courtesy of care. We care for our clothes that we wear, the food that we eat, the cars we drive, but fail to do so for the very core that has provided all that we needed to even create these everyday living items that we use. We know that a lot of those items we use are a result of what exists already in the form of raw materials such as metals, coals, trees, plants such as cotton used for clothing. I just do not understand that, how we humans can fool ourselves in thinking that we can keep enjoying these developed products and not care about the very reason for production of all the raw materials, not care about the planet which provides all that for our existence.

We all exist in the universe as interdependent entities, or interdependent particles of energy. Hopefully we all know how we measure up in size compare to the size of the universe. We live on earth, which is 12,742 Kilometers in diameter. Earth as a tiny planet is running on its path in peace and harmony with all others in the universe. One of the largest find in our Milky Way Galaxy alone is called the star VY Canis Maloris, which has a diameter of about 2,800 Million Kilometeres, yet it is only a tiny small dot among several billion stars forming the galaxy. To compare we can fit Trillions of earths to that size. Are you Still feeling Big? Theory of relativity at play isn't it. There are also about billions of galaxies in the whole universe. We just need to **stop living superficially** and start thinking at a much higher level. Raise our consciousness to see and feel what exists around us, to realise what we are to the existence around us.

I personally from a human level of observation would think of earth as a balanced ball that is revolving in a certain way and still well balanced at the core. And compare to the size of the planet, we are very easily held to the surface of it just as tiny particles with the force of gravity. And we as humans for our own personal gains have modified this ball, the planet to a very large extent. We have created reserves and large water dams and boast to have altered the natural flow of rivers that are supposed to serve the purpose of maintaining the balance. We have started mining at the largest scales, digging millions of tons from one end to another. We think it's still not enough and we are now talking about mining from the Moon or even other asteroids floating close by. We are conducting nuclear bomb experiments deep down in earth, causing it to shake as hard as we can. Yet the cosmos keep adding to its weight; scientists add that earth collects about 40 Million Tonnes per year. They also add the Earth is losing 50,000 tonnes of mass every single year, even though an extra 40,000 tonnes of space dust converge onto the Earth's gravity, it's still losing weight.

I would consider this a logical common-sense that, if a well-balanced ball is shaken, damaged or imbalanced from somewhere, it is going to have effects on its natural path, eventually affecting all the atmosphere around it which is affected by its motion. Hence we encounter natural disasters on earth, which I believe are not so much natural but also caused by our tempering. We humans keep ignoring the care we need to give to our planet, which has given us everything we need for our care. I have set up a page on Facebook named – **Planet Sake**, and only if we started commenting about a single thing we did in care of our planet, imagine the impact it may have on all who may see those posts. We can spread and nurture something good at least.

Let the nature flow the way it wants to be, does that mean I back up plans to go back to the way life was centuries ago. Well we may not like the way things were centuries ago but why wait until nature puts us into such place again. One may argue that Humans would have developed technology to live in space by then. But think about majority of the human race. How many will make it in those spaceships. I bet that number won't even be one per cent. I recommend watching the movie 2012 if you have not, that will give you the idea of what a race to survive is. So, a common man is being fooled by those money and power hungry breed of people in the name of technological advancement. The advancement which boasts about conquering the extremes of space, but how is a common man benefitting from this. The environmental disasters caused in the name of technology advancements are harmful to most of the human race. I am **against the extreme use of technology not the balanced** use. We all need to start bringing that change in our life to maintain the planet for what it is naturally. Earth is showing signs of disasters time and time again with unpredictable behaviours in different regions and parts of the planet. We just need to start caring more, start appreciating more and stop from wasting more of what we have. We are meant to live life on this planet as humans not as Technomans as I stated earlier in the book.

We do not care much about planet earth but we do expect the nature to show no adverse effects to cause us any sort of grief. Despite the fact it provided us with all we need to survive for free. With our power, we have commercialised it and damaged it on the way very badly. We have seen consequences of it as well and yet we refuse to care for it in the manner we should. I am not a Global Warming research scientist, but I know something that is common sense, if someone is caring for you, you should also care for them. It applies in every sense possible, in human race itself, and towards the nature. All forms of life's existence must be taken care of in the same way as the nature had intended, the way the universe intended and provided for. Nature intended for all to live life, enjoy its span on earth and die as what we call as natural death.

Time and Technological Balance

One fact about us existing in this world is the time factor. No matter what stories we have heard about time travellers, we as per the scientific advancement to date cannot travel through and in time, backwards or forwards. Recently its been proven to be mathematically possible but not physically. Other than arguments of travel in space with speed of time being different in space than on earth, only mystical ways so far claim to be able to achieve that through meditation techniques. Now just imagine us moving in our physical form along the Time axis of our existence, we cannot go back in time at all. Just imagine yourself with closed eyes. Imagine your physical form traveling on the axis of time with the three dimensional shape that we exist in. The movement of time is just occurring every moment as it passes by. The fact is that in reality, one can not go back and see themselves in the same place, the same time in exactly the same way as they were even just a billionth of a second ago. *There is no rewind button for real life, only for the memories.* Just imagine how our TV screens work, flickering of light at an amazingly high speed.

In the same way we can only imagine what and where we would be in the time that we would encounter, time that we may see in future. Yet we do not know what else may be occurring that could quite easily influence our circumstances and throw us way out of our imagination, way out of what we thought about where we would be at a certain time in the future. Just imagine the scenarios for people in an earth quake hit zone. There would have been many who went out with certain thing to be done in their mind, but a lot of them did not end up being where they thought they would be.

We must move ahead with best in mind while making the most of our current, our present existence. If there is nothing else that the destiny or universe has in plan for us at a particular point on the Timeline axis of our physical form, then our actions will be manifesting the required for our desired future. So future is what remains unseen until it becomes our present. So let's live in the present, and let's make a better present that we will see as our past in the future. It's the karma, the action you decide to commit now, which will determine the results to be seen in the present moments we will live in the future.

"Plan well for the moments in future that will become our pleasant present."

We must realise our natural self. Why not walk into the pleasant future with a walk in a beautiful park we all love, for one-hour everyday. It feels so wonderful to be connected with nature. For us humans to remain the natural beings we are, we need to keep the planet more as a Natural Habitat. The habitat that does exist as external factor, yet it is the core factor in existence of us human beings in physical form. We need to maintain it more and in a much better way. It was made for our survival; we need to make sure it's not destroyed from its natural shape and form. We need to *ensure that we do not become gangrene to our own habitat*. All the development of the world is great, I greatly do support it but at the same time we cannot afford to forget what we are in reality. The stories of how the world may end, does not worry me at all, *what worries me is the human race going away from living as being human.*

One of the ways science has predicted that the world could end is termed as wishful self-destruction, which is a 'Robots Take-Over'. We will create robots that will take over the world. We may not see that sometime in near future but as per Hans Moravec, who is one of the founders of the robotic department at Mellon University, we may see that coming to very close by the year 2040. As per him, these smart machines will match not only human intelligence but human consciousness too. He sees a symbiotic relationship between humans and machines emerging into postbiologicals capable of extending own intellectual powers. We already know that Artificial Intelligence has been the buzz world in 2017. Facebook tried their experimentation but had to shut down as two machines developed their own language for communication. Whatever other reasons they may have but I do think if that happens among any community, everyone else would surely get suspicious.

The story of Robots, who may take over the world will only happen because of us becoming weaker human beings, we want robots to do everything we do. Are we the Inventors or we are growing into a lazy imbalanced breed. I believe majority of us human beings are also satisfying the curiosity of those so called intelligent but imbalanced or extremist scientist brains. I call them *Science Extremists*, as they are now experimenting with the territories of human form trying to modify our own self. Why? *Are we not happy with what we are?* It seems a little obvious by now. Especially, when we are all involved in one way or another for funding such researches. Just watch a movie from 2001 – 'A.I Artificial Intelligence', and it may help you understand a little more about why we should push for balanced use of technology. The story is about a highly advanced robot wanting to become real human.

If we can maintain our identity as human beings as that is what we were created as and that is what we are, and then innovate technology for certain help, we should be able to prolong human survival on earth. Innovate but only as far as we can benefit from it under our control is great. At the same time trying to develop super smart robots to an extent of them starting to function on their own can be dangerous. Especially when they will be equipped with inputs of best of knowledge of humans, takeover of our race is always going to be a possibility. Not all the human race will be smarter than those robots, we also feel pain but they won't and if they will be equipped with the tendency to think the way we humans do, we know there are destructive minds that will take over the poorer and the weak. That will happen because we have created that to happen by means of equipping robots with best information of all humans combined.

WHY did we create that? Because we started to get so lazy in our daily life that even for living and doing things that we should do as human beings, we created machines to do those tasks for us, or we did not work towards stopping hatred amongst different races but would send robots in wars instead to kill their human soldiers and save ours. It is ok until we are using the machines for farming, and excellent mechanical engineering machines in the factories, but not robots for doing everything what we humans should ourselves be doing. And we already know that our lives are so much taken over by the use of technology, that we hardly see anyone not on a smart phone or a laptop/tablet or on an I-pod or such high tech devices. Soon there's going to be smart glasses full of Augmented and Virtual reality features everywhere; have we started hating our real lives that bad?

Using all that was fine for the matter of convenience or work but that very thing has developed *anti-social habits in the name of social media.* You may not care who is sitting around you but you care to put a note on the face-book, that only a few of people who you probably never get to see in months may read it. Even that was OK if you did pay some attention to the ones that are close to you all the time. We are seeing a gradual loss of love and respect for own family members because as we have grown up into the modern society so much that, the society is all that we care for the most over the very own members of family, over those who are the very reason of us being on this planet, our parents. I see a desperate need to restore the balance in living life as humans, which we are and will remain.

It's good to celebrate Fathers day and Mothers day in a year, but did our parents only came to us to look after only on the day our Birthday fell? No. They coped us day and night sacrificing their own life to an extent yet when it comes to the payback time, we most likely are happy to move them into old age homes. We tend to do that to them in their old age, when they need similar care regardless of whether they are living and behaving the way we want them to or not. But imagine for a moment, did they do the same, and put us in a childcare 24/7 and came to see us only so often. Yet for that very reason, people would opt not to take care of their parents and are happy to send them into aged care homes. However we may go into legal battles over getting whatever they had left behind after they died, except if there was a debt. It may not exactly be relevant to people in some parts of the world and more in other parts of the world. But, this is one strong belief I live with -

> *'No matter what you do, in no way you can pay back what you owe to your parents, as they are the reason You ARE, Only if you think deeper.'*

That was a bit on reverse parenting but in this techno age that is what we are heading towards as our future. We only need to do a little research on how much of an Electro-Magnetism field is surrounding us with harmful radiations all the time, where there should have been just the pure natural air and breeze to nurture us in a healthy way. The pollution levels are all time high; there are different studies on how that affects our body's natural capacities. All those frequencies, radio signals, electromagnetic waves from power lines, radar systems, home wirings, mobile phone signal devices, transformers, substations etc. are instruments to cause all sorts of health problems such as brain tumours, cataracts, headaches, stress, heart problems nausea, fatigues or what not. There has been a large amount of studies on these beliefs, which in some cases has contradicted these findings and others have convinced that these are real threats. I would suggest reading some advice from EPA (Environmental Protection Agency), which has put together a very informative article and advice for avoidance. They have also classified Electro Magnetic Field frequencies, as a Class-B Carcinogen; hence it joins the ranks of formaldehyde, DDT, Dioxins etc. that are threats to human health.

From what I have also heard from some friendly talks with friends or their friends is that there are already some Oxygen Cafe's catering for fresh air substitute in some modern world cities. I do respect the noble Idea of providing something absolutely necessary in the world we are living in, or I should say that the polluted world we have created for us. But, what a joke we are making of ourselves, in the name of technology and progress, we are slowly heading into the polluted world, where we have come to a stage of commercialising the very free elements provided for us. We being the very cause of it, and just because we want to advance further and further in technology world and lose our humanity even in the physical existence let alone the morals most of the people are living with these days. On the way to modernisation, we have caused a risk for our own self.

We are influencing our development into a breed of Technomans and **going away from being Humans**. The worse is that we are doing it to ourselves, and not any UFO flown Aliens. We need to maintain a balance as human beings. At the moment we seem to be too inclined towards the Technologisation of everything on this planet. That is only turning us humans into Techno-breeds. And we will become that if that is what we all keep concentrating on. As that is the power we do have as human beings, **'Creating from our thoughts'**. Take a step back and think for a moment – Are all these tech companies **taking advantage of you not being happy**? Are they making you feel unhappy as a natural being so you must make use of the virtual or augmented reality apps so you feel artificially happy? Think about it, are we moving towards a state of mind continuously asking for this temporary short-term happiness and taking us away from the real world?

We have the power to be able to mould and create our future. But our nerves are not going to grow of steel in reality, even though medical science may have developed artificial biological limbs. We can replace some parts in our body with modern technology and such is where I love and support the research and technology. But, our body as a whole running bio-machine is and will always be made of the five core elements of Earth, Fire, Water, Air and Space. *Air*, is the prime spot holder for our living ability as it keeps our lungs functioning the way they should for the rest of the body to function. *Water* which is about 50-65 per cent of the body space in all forms of fluid and we know we cannot survive without water. *Earth* element indirectly means for solids that go into our body, the food, which is grown from the soil, we can not survive without this too. So, eat healthy to live healthy. The *Space or Ether* is the vacuum that is created within our body for what is filled by the rest; it is the most subtle of all. The *Fire* is the fifth and final element of nature in our body. Fire element creates the heat required for our body to sustain. We operate at 37 degrees as human form. It also creates Energy in our body; more we spend it the more we have it. Hardworking people always have more energy and strength than others.

If all is kept in balance, we will stay healthy. The logic flows in the universe too. *The **Balance** is the word here.* Hence we need to start looking at maintaining that balance on this planet, balance of living as human beings and yet enjoying the advancements of technology. We need to create that balance sooner than later. We should start with our own lives first and create abundance for living an abundant and well-balanced life, as we will play a vital role in the world we will leave behind for our future generations. We are simply mortal beings as humans, and everything in this world has a life span, it does not matter how long it may be and how it ends.

The universe may have its own plans to ensure we do not cause any hurdles in the way it runs. Us walking into space in our human skin and dying straightaway is the clear sign of telling us humans that those zones are not made for human. Trespassing is only going to result in penalties. We should limit the technology to fly planes around the planet but not into the deeper space. If we are meant to realise the space, mystics have always preached about achieving that by the medium of meditation. And when we travel in the form of that soul current, we can enjoy all that is there and not work against the rules of nature, as those mystics explain.

Humans: More than What We think We are

Esoteric and spiritual teachers have known for ages that our body is programmable by language, words and thoughts. This has now been scientifically proven and explained. The below study was published by various websites and such enthusiasts on the Internet as well. Below article was found on wakeup-world.com and I will add relevance to my message where required. The website provides that all information for this article is taken from the book "Vernetzte Intelligenz" von Grazyna Fosar und Franz Bludorf, ISBN 3930243237, summarised and commented by Baerbel. You can reach the authors at www.fosar-bludorf.com

****

THE HUMAN DNA IS A BIOLOGICAL INTERNET and superior in many aspects to the artificial one. Russian researchers directly or indirectly explained the phenomena such as clairvoyance, intuition, spontaneous and remote acts of healing, self healing, affirmation techniques, unusual light/auras around people (namely spiritual masters), mind's influence on weather patterns and a lot more. Also, there is an evidence for a whole new type of medicine in which DNA can be influenced and reprogrammed by words and frequencies WITHOUT cutting out and replacing single genes.

They suggest that only 10% of our DNA is being used for building proteins. It is this subset of DNA that is of interest to western researchers and is being examined and categorised. The other 90% are considered 'junk DNA'. The Russian researchers, however, convinced that nature was not dumb, joined linguists and geneticists in a venture to explore those 90% of 'junk DNA.' Their results, findings and conclusions are simply revolutionary. According to them, our DNA is not only responsible for the construction of our body but also serves as data storage and in communication. The Russian linguists found that the genetic code, especially in the apparently useless 90%, follows the same rules as all our human languages. To this end they compared the rules of syntax (the way in which words are put together to form phrases and sentences), semantics (the study of meaning in language forms) and the basic rules of grammar. They found that the alkalines of our DNA follow a regular grammar and do have set rules just like our languages. So human languages did not appear coincidentally but are a reflection of our inherent DNA.

The Russian biophysicist and molecular biologist Pjotr Garjajev and his colleagues also explored the vibrational behaviour of the DNA. Which suggested that 'Living chromosomes function just like solitonic/holographic computers using the endogenous DNA laser radiation.' This means that they managed for example to modulate certain frequency patterns onto a laser ray and with it influenced the DNA frequency and thus the genetic information itself. Since the basic structure of DNA-alkaline pairs and of language (as explained earlier) are of the same structure, no DNA decoding is necessary.

One can simply use words and sentences of the human language! This, too, was experimentally proven! Living DNA substance (in living tissue, not in vitro) will always react to language-modulated laser rays and even to radio waves, if the proper frequencies are being used.

This finally and scientifically explains why affirmations, autogenous training, hypnosis and the like can have such strong effects on humans and their bodies. It is entirely normal and natural for our DNA to react to language. While western researchers cut single genes from the DNA strands and insert them elsewhere, the Russians enthusiastically worked on devices that can influence the cellular metabolism through suitable modulated radio and light frequencies and thus repair genetic defects.

Garjajev's research group succeeded in proving that with this method chromosomes damaged by x-rays for example can be repaired. They even captured information patterns of a particular DNA and transmitted it onto another, thus reprogramming cells to another genome. So they successfully **transformed**, for example, **frog embryos to salamander embryos** simply by transmitting the DNA information patterns! This way the entire information was transmitted without any of the side effects or disharmonies encountered in cutting out and re-introducing single genes from the DNA. This represents an unbelievable, world-transforming revolution and sensation! All this by **simply applying vibration and language** instead of the archaic cutting-out procedure! This experiment points to the immense power of wave genetics, which obviously has a greater influence on the formation of organisms than the biochemical processes of alkaline sequences.

Esoteric and spiritual teachers have known this for ages that our body is programmable by language, words and thought. This mystic myth has now been scientifically proven and explained. Of course the frequency has to be correct. And this is why not everybody is equally successful or can do it with always the same strength. The individual person must work on the inner processes and maturity in order to establish a conscious communication with the DNA. The Russian researchers worked on a method that is not dependent on these factors but will ALWAYS work, provided one uses the correct frequency.

But the higher developed an individual's consciousness is, the less need is there for any type of device! One can achieve these results by oneself, and science will finally stop to laugh at such ideas and will confirm and explain the results. And it doesn't end there? The Russian scientists also found out that our DNA can cause disturbing patterns in the vacuum, thus producing magnetised wormholes! Wormholes are the microscopic equivalents of the so-called Einstein-Rosen bridges in the vicinity of black holes (left by burned-out stars). These are tunnel connections between entirely different areas in the universe through which information can be transmitted outside of space and time. The DNA attracts these bits of information and passes them on to our consciousness. This process of hyper communication is most effective in a state of relaxation. Stress, worries or a hyperactive intellect prevent successful hyper communication or the information will be totally distorted and useless.

In nature, hyper communication has been successfully applied for millions of years. The organised flow of **life in insect** states proves this dramatically. Modern man knows it only on a much more subtle level as **'intuition'**. But we, too, can regain full use of it. **An example from Nature**: When a queen ant is spatially separated from her colony, building still continues fervently and according to plan. If the queen is killed, however, all work in the colony stops. No ant knows what to do. Apparently the queen sends the 'building plans' also from far away via the group consciousness of her subjects. She can be as far away as she wants, as long as she is alive.

In humans hyper communication is most often encountered when one suddenly gains access to information that is outside one's knowledge base. Such hyper communication is then experienced as inspiration or intuition. The Italian composer Giuseppe Tartini for instance dreamt one night that a devil sat at his bedside playing the violin. The next morning Tartini was able to note down the piece exactly from memory, he called it the Devil's Trill Sonata.

For years, a 42-year old male nurse dreamt of a situation in which he was hooked up to a kind of knowledge CD-ROM. Verifiable knowledge from all imaginable fields was then transmitted to him that he was able to recall in the morning. To him it was such a flood of information that it seemed a whole encyclopaedia was transmitted at night. The majority of facts were outside his personal knowledge base and reached technical details about which he knew absolutely nothing.

When hyper communication occurs, one can observe in the DNA as well as in the human being a special phenomenon. The Russian scientists irradiated DNA samples with laser light. On the screen a typical wave pattern was formed. When they removed the DNA sample, the wave pattern did not disappear, it remained. Many controlled experiments showed that the pattern still came from the removed sample, whose energy field apparently remained by itself. This effect is now called *phantom DNA effect*. It is surmised that energy from outside of space and time still flows through the activated wormholes after the DNA was removed.

The side effects seen most often in hyper communication, also in human beings are inexplicable electromagnetic fields in the vicinity of the persons concerned. Electronic devices like CD players and the like can be irritated and cease to function for hours. When the electromagnetic field slowly dissipates, the devices function normally again. Many healers and psychics know this effect from their work. The better the atmosphere and the energy, the more frustrating it is that the recording device stops functioning and recording exactly at that moment. And repeated switching on and off after the session does not restore function yet, but next morning all is back to normal. Perhaps this is reassuring to read for many, as it has nothing to do with them being technically inept, it means they are good at hyper communication.

In their book 'Vernetzte Intelligenz' (Networked Intelligence), Grazyna Gosar and Franz Bludorf explain these connections precisely and clearly. The authors also quote sources presuming that in earlier times humanity had been, just like the animals, very strongly connected to the group consciousness and acted as a group. To develop and experience individuality we humans however had to forget hyper communication almost completely.

Now that we are fairly stable in our individual consciousness, we can create a new form of group consciousness, namely one, in which we attain access to all information via our DNA without being forced or remotely controlled about what to do with that information. We now know that just as on the Internet our DNA also can feed its proper data into the network can call up data from the network and can establish contact with other participants in the network. Remote healing, telepathy or 'remote sensing' about the state of relatives etc., can thus be explained.

Some animals know also from afar when their owners plan to return home. That can be freshly interpreted and explained via the concepts of group consciousness and hyper communication. Any collective consciousness cannot be sensibly used over any period of time without a distinctive individuality. Otherwise we would revert to a primitive herd instinct that is easily manipulated.

Hyper communication in the new millennium means something quite different: Researchers think that if humans with full individuality would regain group consciousness, they would have a god-like power to create, alter and shape things on Earth! AND humanity is collectively moving toward such a group consciousness of the new kind. Fifty percent of today's children will be problem children as soon as they go to school. The system lumps everyone together and demands adjustment. But the individuality of today's children is so strong, that they refuse this adjustment and giving up their idiosyncrasies in the most diverse ways.

At the same time more and more clairvoyant children are born. Something in those children is striving more and more towards the group consciousness of the new kind, and it will no longer be suppressed. As a rule, weather for example is rather difficult to be influenced by a single individual. But it may be influenced by a group consciousness (nothing new to some tribes doing it in their rain dances and Yagyas (grouped prayers) conducted by ancient Indian Rishi's). Weather is strongly influenced by Earth resonance frequencies, the so-called *Schumann frequencies*. But those same frequencies are also produced in our brains, and when many people synchronise their thinking or individuals (spiritual masters, for instance) focus their thoughts in a laser-like fashion, then it is scientifically speaking not at all surprising if they can thus influence weather.

Researchers in group consciousness have formulated the theory of Type I civilizations. A humanity that developed a group consciousness of the new kind would have neither environmental problems nor scarcity of energy. For if it were to use its mind power as a unified civilization, it would have control of the energies of its home planet as a natural consequence. And that includes all natural catastrophes!!! A theoretical Type II civilization would even be able to control all energies of their home galaxy. And as in ancient times in India, whenever there used to be draught in areas, people will organise a group prayer and perform rituals to make the deity of rain named Indra, happy to bring rain. For non-believers in Deities, scientists have also proven the energy field vibrations in this article. I would assume that you have now better understanding of the relation of the purpose of such religious group prayers for creating the energy fields required, as explained in this research.

To come back to the DNA: It apparently is also an organic superconductor that can work at normal body temperature. Artificial superconductors require extremely low temperatures of between 200 and 140°C to function. As recently learned, all superconductors are able to store light and thus information. This is a further explanation of how the DNA can store information. There is another phenomenon linked to DNA and wormholes. Normally, these super small wormholes are highly unstable and are maintained only for the tiniest fractions of a second. Under certain conditions stable wormholes can organise themselves, which then form distinctive vacuum domains in which for example gravity can transform into electricity.

Vacuum domains are self-radiant balls of ionised gas that contain considerable amounts of energy. There are regions in Russia where such radiant balls appear very often. Following the ensuing confusion the Russians started massive research programs leading finally to some of the discoveries mentioned above. Many people know vacuum domains as shiny balls in the sky. Now the Russians found in the regions, where vacuum domains appear often and sometimes fly as balls of light from the ground upwards into the sky, that these balls can be guided by thought. One has found out since that, vacuum domains emit waves of low frequency as they are also produced in our brains.

And because of this similarity of waves they are able to react to our thoughts. To run excitedly into one that is on ground level might not be such a great idea, because those balls of light can contain immense energies and are able to mutate our genes. They can, they don't necessarily have to, one has to say. For many spiritual teachers also produce such visible balls or columns of light in deep meditation or during energy work which trigger decidedly pleasant feelings and do not cause any harm. Apparently this is also dependent on some inner order and on the quality and provenance of the vacuum domain. There are some spiritual teachers (the young Englishman Ananda, for example) with whom nothing is seen at first, but when one tries to take a photograph while they sit and speak or meditate in hyper communication, one gets only a picture of a white cloud on a chair. In some Earth healing projects such light effects also appear on photographs. Simply put, these phenomena have to do with gravity and anti-gravity forces that are also exactly described in that book and with ever more stable wormholes and hyper communication and thus with energies from outside our time and space structure.

Earlier generations that got in contact with such hyper communication experiences and visible vacuum domains were convinced that an angel had appeared before them. And we cannot be too sure as to what forms of consciousness we can get access to when using hyper communication. Not having scientific proof for their actual existence (people having had such experiences do NOT all suffer from hallucinations) does not mean that there is no metaphysical background to it. We have simply made another giant step towards understanding our reality.

Official science also knows of gravity anomalies on Earth (that contribute to the formation of vacuum domains), but only of ones of below one percent. But recently gravity anomalies have been found of between three and four percent. One of these places is Rocca di Papa, south of Rome. Round objects of all kinds, from balls to full buses, roll uphill. But the stretch in Rocca di Papa is rather short, and defying logic sceptics still flee to the theory of optical illusion (which it cannot be due to several features of the location).

****

We are much more than we think we are than just a physical skin form. We are more than just the physical form that we believe ourselves to be. How about taking a little more time for understanding the Sixth Sense we often hear about. Read on and you will understand a bit more about higher level of existence of us as human being.

It has long been known that we all have the ability to sense things before they happen. Known as the sixth sense that we have. However a lot of us may not be aware of it and yet use what we call as our intuitions, our gut feeling may be. I was not exactly surprised to learn in a news article that when one of the biggest natural disaster occurred in the month of December 2004, when the biggest Tsunami had hit the shores, the birds and other animals had already started to move towards the higher areas before the tsunami struck to certain southern parts of India on the Islands of Andaman and Nicobar. I did know this sense as a myth though but this was when it got impressed in my brain as something significant. The humans at that time were not even aware what was coming their way.

It is suggested that the 'Sixth Sense' the ability to detect, in some subconscious way, Earth's magnetic field does exist in humans but we may or may not be aware of it. But the scientists have proven that humans really do have a sixth sense - that lets them detect the earth's magnetic fields around them. Though a work in progress, geophysicist Joe Kirschvink from the California Institute of Technology says he's identified it in humans. In an article published by Sciencealert in 2016 it seems the most promising experiment yet to prove we humans do possess the Sixth sense. Here is an excerpt from that article.

****

Joe Kirschvink believes in showing that magnetoreception is actually happening in humans in the first place. The problem with previous experiments is that they've failed to be replicated - thought to be the result of electromagnetic interference messing with results.

To eliminate that variable, Kirschvink has built what's known as a Faraday cage - a thin, aluminium box that can screen out electromagnetic background noise using wire coils - two floors underground at Caltech. Inside the cage, people sit in the pitch black, and are only exposed to a pure magnetic field with no interference, and no other stimulus.

Kirschvink hooks these participants up to EEG monitors to map their brain activity, and then applies a rotating magnetic field, similar in strength to Earth's, to see if the brain shows any indications of picking up any changes. He's been able to show that when the magnetic field is rotating counter clockwise, there's a drop in participants' alpha waves.

"The suppression of α waves, in the EEG world, is associated with brain processing: a set of neurons were firing in response to the magnetic field, the only changing variable," reports Hand for *Science* magazine.

But more than that, the neural response was actually delayed by a few hundred milliseconds, which Kirschvink says suggests an active brain response.

"A magnetic field can induce electric currents in the brain that could mimic an EEG signal - but they would show up immediately," explains Hand.

A similar response was also seen when the magnetic field twisted into the floor - but not when the magnetic field twists upwards or rotates clockwise, which could reflect the polarity of our internal magnetic compass, suggests Kirschvink.

There's a lot more work to be done - a team in Japan is now replicating the experiments, and a lab in New Zealand is beginning their own study following the same protocol. The results then need to be scrutinised by other researchers in the field and published in a peer review journal before we can get too excited.

We've got a long way to go, but it seems like we might be closer than ever before to showing that humans haven't totally lost touch with our sixth sense. And that's pretty exciting. "It's part of our evolutionary history," says Kirschvink. "Magnetoreception may be the primal sense."

****

So, this was our journey from the mystical beliefs and from the scientific community as well backing up the beliefs and concept of us being of much higher consciousness rather than just the 3D form of a human being. I hope that, now we have a much deeper understanding of our inner self, the soul and the energy. What we face in our life is the result of Karmas we commit, the actions we take based on all those thoughts, beliefs, instincts and intuitions.

Let's now understand what we are today, what karmas we conducted to be where we are today. Let's take a look at how we can learn from our own actions and behaviours in the past to make a better future. Let's use a tool to *Rewind, Revive and Move Forward to Re-Live*, not only with ease, but also with comfort and joy. So, let's take a rewind look at our Karmas that we have committed so far in our present life.

THE KARMIC REWIND

Now with better understanding of who we as human beings are, how we unknowingly carry the living of life activities based on our surrounding environment, the society, the beliefs and influences that mostly gets imposed upon us but are not always desired, that mostly comes not from within, not from our heart and soul but mind that builds a cage around itself with thoughts and limits our potentials. We now better understand the way the Karmic theory and the sophistically designed body works and how modern science also shed some light on how life works on this planet. No matter what your goals are, if you are committed, you are able to achieve them with the help of the process that I call - *"The Karmic Rewind"*.

Use this tool to **Rewind** through your stages of life to learn for improvement, give yourself some time and techniques to **Revive** and think deeper into the meaning of your life and then get fully equipped to take steps to move forward and **Re-Live** as your true higher self.

With the understanding of the Karmic theory, you know that you are where you are today, because of the past Karmas or actions you had committed; whether in the past of this life or previous life. Based on those karmas that we committed, we are surrounded with certain situations and atmosphere around us to make us go through results of those Karmas, which also somewhat places the destiny component in our life. **While we go through those karmic results in our present life, we still have the same tendency and capability of committing new Karmas. And this capability is which will do the trick to realise our goals.** Recognise this fact very clearly in your mind. Empower your brain with the knowledge of existence of this ability, this is the most important factor that will play a major role in seeing the change we want in life, the change you desire, and the life you desire.

> *'Knowledge, Wisdom, Intellect and skills, will all burry in the dust without the Karma committed for their purpose, for Your Life's purpose.'*

You will need to **promise yourself** to start sowing the seeds of related karmas, to see them flourish as the time passes by to reap the rewards and benefits that you want to reap. Once again, what you sow, so shall you reap? If you sow the seeds of sunflower that is what you will reap. So –

> *'Start thinking and start seeing clearly what you want to reap,*
> *so you may start sowing the right seeds.'*

It is that commitment of committing new karmas, in the direction of better life, which will bring you the karmic results in the way we want to see our life in the future. If we can learn from our own karmas, karmas that we have committed so far and then analyse them to help us commit better karmas in the future that we face every second of time as it passes by, what better way can there be than learning from our own way of committing karmas and modifying those ways to commit something better to bring about something better.

In Indian culture it is very commonly believed that if you see someone with a lot of wealth; the people will relate to the belief that the person must have committed very good Karmas in the past, or must have donated a lot to the needy people, even in past lives so he or she is reaping the rewards in their present life.

Why you committed the karmas that you have so far were largely because of the beliefs you were fed with, the kind of training you have had since you were a child, the circumstances you were brought up in, the sense of discrimination you developed based on those beliefs. These are all the factors that have caused you to take that certain action that has landed you where you are as of today. We will learn further about this mind of ours and shift the mindset to better tune in with what we want to achieve. You need to find and lock down your new landing destination and *define it clearly in your Future Probability Sphere*. And this tool *'The Karmic Rewind'* is going to help you assess and learn about your own self. Learn about the type of personality you are. Learn how you behave in certain circumstances and then step-by-step backward story of life situations, and what derived those situations in a reverse manner. So get ready to perform some **reverse engineering** on this biological gadget of yours "Your existence as human Being".

Realising Your Own Self

You will need the quietest moment possible in your life today or now or the moment you decide to sit down and work with this tool on your life. This is to learn about and knowing your enemies well so you can defeat them with ease. The enemies holding you back from your life and your happiness here are not just outside but also within. I need you to stand in front of the mirror and do not treat yourself as your own self that you see in the reflection. Keep looking in your eyes, as if you are looking in another person's eyes to search for the truth in what they are saying. It is vastly believed that *"The eyes never lie"*, some real experts or some thugs may disguise it, but when You are standing in front of that mirror, You know you can never lie to yourself. You may wish to run away from facing certain truth and if you do, then the results will also be as far away from what you want yourself to be. It is time to brave up and own up to who you presently are and whether that's in sync with who you truly are within your heart and soul. Whether who you are resonates with your future true self that you want to become.

If you want to achieve some results for yourself then You must be truthful to yourself as best as you know yourself. If you believe you may need someone's help after you have recognised the main composing factors of your existence as a whole, feel free to discuss with someone faithful and truthful. Feel free to send me an email if you would like. If you think you are not ready for it yet, as this may be because of some story that may be a bit bitter for you to realise about yourself, or some decisions that you may have taken which have turned out to be bitter and you do not want to think about it at all, then I recommend that you become courageous right away, give that fear up now or work with any other way that will help you find courage to face yourself, the reality of your own self, and how you would confidently be able to remove that fear out of yourself. We all have that one trustworthy soul around us, if it's not our mother.

Some people take certain outcomes in life as a failure. But, that is how one may look at them, if they do not want to succeed. Let me tell you one very important thing, *no unsuccessful attempt at any goal in life is a failure*, you will be surprised by the lessons you have learned from that previous attempt to make it further towards success the next time around, to keep having a better go at that goal and finally succeed. Imagine the feel of succeeding with your own hard work, and more attempts you may have to have will only make you the best teacher and a role model for others when you succeed. You are bound to succeed if you do not stop attempting.

If you would like to then go ahead and read part four (Time for Four Changes) of this book first. You will find the courage, motivation and ways to deal with and get rid of that fear to move ahead in life. Recognising them clearly is the first step though so **lets just do it**.

When you are ready, the next step is that of being prepared to take responsibility and hold yourself accountable for the life you have lived so far. Life could have been better, only if you had realised the true potential you have within. It moves forward with decisions we make every moment, every day while living.

'Life is a Decisions based Actualisation of time so make informed, well thought out decisions with awareness and actualise what you want your life to be.'

Hold Yourself Accountable

When you are looking at yourself in the mirror, look at yourself as a person whose behaviour has landed you where you are in life today. You may even print and hang a poster of yourself for that sake. **Become an interrogator** to that person, and ask questions aligned with the situation you are in today. Then align the answers to those questions, analyse how it affected you, why it occurred that way, and why that person in the mirror has acted in a particular manner during a particular situation.

There will be few different topics you will need to choose to interrogate your mirror image on. Questions like, where I am at today in different modes of life, such as personal, career, business, financial, physical or psychological health, spirituality, love or any other aspect of life that you can identify. Then take time to step by step analyse each and every question, situation, achievements, and unsuccessful attempts. Below are some examples to wake up your questioning skills. You may not always start with precise questions, but slowly you must come down to ask direct and specific, to the point questions to pin down the exact causes.

1. Who am I? Where Am I now, today in my life and in my Future Probability Sphere (FPS, part-2)? Am I Happy here or Is this where I really wanted to be?
2. How did I get here? What brought me to this situation? Would it have been any different to what it is today if I took a different approach? Would I have been better if I acted differently back then, at the initial stage of reaction to the cause that has caused me to be where I am today? Should I push for the next level?
3. What were the circumstances that caused me to take a certain decision at that time? Was it my Mind? Was it someone else who influenced me? Was it my own analysis through knowledge or lack of it that helped or caused me to make that decision?
4. What caused me to think in that manner to make that particular decision? Was it the beliefs in my mind? Was it my own assessment based on my beliefs? Was it the way my brain was trained ever since and formed certain

habits? Did my parents or someone else played the role in training my brain in this manner? Was it my friends at school who influenced my thinking in the manner I think? Or was it some other kind of social influence?

5. Was it a situation that I was stuck in, that has left an impression that I cannot think in such situations ever again? Or even was it that I saw someone resolving a situation in a beautiful manner often enough that has given me the ability to resolve any situation in my own life in the best manner possible?

There are a lot of factors, positives and negatives, it is kind of a complete psychological analysis of your own personality, your own behaviour, your habits, the way you act and react to situations, it's the whole lot of you as you are, as you exist in this universe. Once you know who you are, every little piece of information about you will help you control or manipulate your own behaviours in different situations. And since you will know how best you perform and in which manner under different situations, it might just be a slight change in your attitude about the way you would look at a situation. By just tweaking that attitude a little, you may very well be able to get a much different outcome to the same situation or a problem. But you know you can never get a different result with same old approach for the given situation.

Persistence is the only action to be repeated with improvements until success is achieved. The new altered outcome obviously should be a better outcome for you as you have tweaked and fine-tuned your actions for the better performance by your own brain, your own mind, and your own behaviour.

'You are the owner of your strengths and weaknesses. You have the ability to better nurture your weaknesses to strengths.'

The weaknesses that you will identify are the ones you want to get rid of ASAP. You need to nurture those weaknesses to strengths or give them up to make more space, to have less burden caused by non-supportive elements, beliefs or habits on your brain so it can learn and develop new strengths while enhancing your existing strengths. To be able to do this, all you need to start doing is to believe in yourself and concentrate more on the Positives and Strengths that you have.

You have been somehow using those weaknesses to define your future rather than using your strengths, which is one of the reasons one may not have been successful. Just **think about the importance or weight you give to a negative thought than to the ray of hope**. Everything you want to do and wanting to go for has been postponed or eliminated due to existence of even just a slight fear of not succeeding. You simply need to realise more of your positive strengths and completely stop walking into the vicinity of negativities. As said earlier, even if it takes getting away from those negative people, friends, friends of friends, environments then '**Nike it**', I mean to say is that '**JUST DO IT**'. You will do a lot of good to yourself and others reliant on you.

You will need to pick up your pace before you can pull others along. And you can only do that when you can get away from and break free from the strings that are holding you back. Someone may always feel left behind but if they are not resonating with you, you can always come back and pick them up rather than killing your dreams with them; but to do that, you must build yourself up first. You need to hook yourself to the strings that will pull you up, the family and friends who can help you and support you to rise and shine. You may need to look for mentors to help you raise your game, but before all that you must believe in yourself, have faith and the rest will happen through Karma.

Faiths, Beliefs, Friends and Self Realisation

The friends, people and family or even relatives who we associate with frequently do have the effect on us in one way or another. One very important factor to ensure is that the people you accompany are the ones who believe in you, are in line with the way you want to live your life, the goals you want to achieve in life. Ogyen Trinley Dorje, who is also known as Living Buddha as per Central

People's Government in Tibet, has the following advice on the friends and people we accompany.

Friends – Although each of us has our own personality, our circle of friends can influence and change us. So, it is important to rely on friends who have intelligence and integrity.

Good Company – Are your friends taking you in the right direction, Think about it. Judge for yourself if their advice is helpful right now, or if it will lead you to something better in the long run. Friends have brought ruin to many – don't trust them blindly. Discrimination is the key. This doesn't mean you should totally disregard their advice. All advice has to be scrutinised. If the outcome is harmful, so what if it was given with good intentions. Sometimes our enemies can give the best advice. If it's helpful, take it.

What ever we may be and where ever we may be in our life, on this planet, in our careers or relationships. Learn to be more than what you think you are, act to be more and you will become more. Always believe in yourself and the inner source of our existence. We need to develop our own personality stronger but also wisely.

'Do not let that Inner You, die of the beliefs of others.'

This is so interesting that we always live our life according to the beliefs and faiths we have and the values we have in our mind, why because that is what we were fed on and we accepted to operate our life upon them. Yet, we fail our own beliefs at times based on a comment someone else may have made according to their beliefs. If one has ever faced that, what a bizarre situation we have developed our life into. How can someone else's beliefs and in physicality, just the words out of someone's mouth shatter your entire confidence to achieve something you like and you believe you are good at doing. If we were to analyse this from the scientific point of view, which suggests we are also a form of energy particles, then it simply suggests that the strength of vibrations of those negative words was stronger than the strength you held in your own beliefs.

First we may have very well been deceived by our own beliefs. Beliefs that are effected by what our parents fed into our brains and also the people, surroundings and situations around us, which may or may not have been suitable to nourish the best of our natural talent and abilities. There on we simply got comfortable in that mind-frame. Then one day again, when we may have realised our potential again and wanted to change those beliefs for a better outcome in our life, someone else may have simply come around again and daunted our confidence with certain unsupportive words. We may have let that happen to us. Nothing in the world can be worse than this for a person, that when they want to rise, they have let others affect their true self again and fallen backwards to let their dreams die.

This is what I tell everyone who talks to me about someone else who came along and said something to them that has made them upset for the rest of the day or week or month. What I tell them is that you need to strengthen up your core self. How fragile can you let your personality be if you really want to grow stronger? **Be flexible for accepting wisdom but fragile - not at all**. You need to believe in you, you need to believe in your strengths. And once you concentrate on these two hard enough, you will have overcome your weaknesses. Your life would by then be automatically designed in a way that those weaknesses will become negligible, in fact transform into strengths or disappear altogether from your life.

An important motive of this book is also to help **self-realisation**. The self-realisation is the most important part that will affect at large how our future will be designed and constructed. **It is about exercising the Brain, the mighty Mind that we are going to turn into our Friend, the best friend and then unleash its power to the full in the direction we want to head in**. The first aspect should be to realise who we are as a person. What personality we have and what has influenced our mind, our brain in becoming what we are today as a person, are we comfortable and happy with that.

Before you can analyse any other aspect around you, you need to assess the **core of the cause** that is going to take a decision, and that is **you** as a person yourself. So let's get started. And please be sure to write it all down. Do not miss any thing that comes to mind. And if there is something that seems negative and you don't want to remember it again. Be brave and you will be surprised how soon you can get over those feelings. That is where we go wrong a lot of the time when we tend to not face up to things and run away to ignore them instead. I would rather have you write them in the list of negative aspects to be eliminated and ensure they are not used ever again in the reviews you will conduct of your karmas by eliminating them from your life, and your personality.

I always believed that *ignorance* of such kind is not the way of living and a real *bad tool* for designing your life. I always tried my best to face up to any hurdles whether mental or physical. And I always urged my close by friends and family to do so too. And Now, I Encourage You to do the same. Be brave and stand up to all that has happened in the past. And if there is something that is positive, Brag on it within if you like as this is going to raise the **positive energy of confidence** within you. And that is what we need to ride upon from this point onwards. **Writing and seeing clearly** is important and you see and realise **your goals** more clearly if you do write them. There has been a study that showed that university students who actually wrote their goals down had achieved more of the goals than the ones who did not. So I strongly encourage you to start getting into the habit of writing, as *you will be putting your thoughts into physical existence straight away* in written form and repeat and review them to bring better results.

Out of the whole wide world, the **most important existence** right now is **You** as a person. So, you need to realise that; where do you see yourself today as a person? Lets take the core of you, the core of your existence, your own personality, your behaviour, your ethics and assess your own self, assess the aura of the person you see as you. Whether you believe that you are a Nice, Average, Humble, Emotional, Grumpy, Dumb, Talented or Angry kind of person or whether you have positive or negative Attitude, you are Greedy, if you are a Motivator or anything else that you see within yourself. Just start to think about yourself and then ask questions; 'why am I like that?' Start writing the reasons whether good or bad (tool – page 226). Sometimes you will find influences from people in life, and you will fall into asking 'Why the person who affected my personality in a particular manner did those things?' If those were great things, then you know the answer to that why straight away, because he or she wanted you to be something good that you are now. But if that had bad effects on you, then please let me suggest that, you need to restrain yourself from concentrating more on why they did that and try to **practice forgiveness**. Just make a note of the reason, which affected you in that way and *lesson should be learned for selective isolation* of such people. That note will be something in the list of removal items from your mind and will help you create and expand the positive aura of your personality, which we need to move ahead on the positive road.

Learning about your own behaviour is important so that we may also be able to exploit our own self for our behaviours to achieve better results. Now when something occurred or happened, how did you react to that situation, write that down and then do a detailed analysis of your behaviour. Write down the reason for why you reacted in that manner. What were the **beliefs** in your mind? What were the **thoughts** in your mind? Did that thought help, did that belief **caused you to react** in a way that should have given you the positive outcome that you wanted or desired? If not, place it in the list of assessing the beliefs if you are not able to delete it from your memory straight away. Then you can go back and reassess that belief and find a **positive replacement** for it.

What were the **thoughts** in your mind at that time, what were you thinking when you behaved or reacted in a particular manner that made you the way you are today. You were obviously thinking in a particular manner, right? Obviously either you were or you were not aware of the results, which that action provoked by that thought would bring about in your personality or life. If you were thinking about and have become what you are today, then I would say that you were aware and knowingly acted upon or with that thought in mind. **Congratulate yourself** for a very important skill you possess – *Thought implementation with awareness*. Keep spreading your charm this way, you achieved what you could foresee as a result of your **thoughtful actions**. This means you already have certain level of skill and mindset that is needed to achieve further goals in life.

But, if you are not happy with what and who you are today, and you did not know that your thoughts and beliefs will make you what you are today, then you must **increase your thinking ability**. Make use of the walk your thoughts technique as mentioned earlier in the book (In FPS). The thoughts and beliefs that caused you to act in a particular manner or if they caused you to not even think about what you would become, how that action may mould your personality, at that moment of decision, then those beliefs and thoughts need to be erased off the memory straight away. You need to be more aware and more mindful of your actions in this Karmic world.

For me **Personal Life and Relationships** are aligned somewhat closely. You may take your Personal Life as a separate assessment to Personal Relationships, which is what they are, closely related separate aspects of life. I present myself as an open book to people, who I am related to and associate with not professionally. They very much are part of my life, only exception being my relationship with my wife; which of-course is even personal.

When you think about **Personal Life**, You must dig deep into your heart and soul, what gives your heart the feeling of never ending happiness, what gives your soul that divine ocean of love and contentment to swim in for the rest of your life in this avatar of human life. That is what needs to merge with your physical aura. You may also think about the kind of personality you are and have developed. Look at the factors that contributed and how to re-build your personality suit or dress to wear for the way you want to live, and the way you want people in personal life to see you. The way those people close to your heart see you should reflect your true inner self, full of love and care. And that true personality can only be great, if you feel that from within and create your personal life and atmosphere around you and in your house with that love and harmony. You will also think about the style, the fashion in which you do certain things and live your life.

When you start to think about **Relationships**, there can be many classifications but primarily you need to think about *personal and professional* relationships. For the most content outcomes, you would want your relationships **based on honesty** the most but also depends on how much love you pour out from your heart. You may think about the bases of those relationships and how strong they are? How much would you go out of way to do things for people involved, and what others do for you? Look for opportunities to appreciate and give back to those who Love you and care for you. There is a lot that is done for caring for each other that gets un-noticed all the time, especially within family members. We take it for granted, and only realise it when we stop receiving those caring and loving moments. If we receive more, then we should give more. And if we do give more, then if anything, we will only receive more. Letting go of such behaviour is not really spreading the message of love and harmony in our relationships and also the universe. Honesty, Love and Care are equally important in professional life.

When thinking about **business or career**, think about the profession you are in, the business you are in, whether it is something you love to do, assess your financial health all together. Whether the income is enough or not? What you really want to achieve? How can you create it and create more? What have you been doing that did not work, and what should you do or change to make things work? That may mean changing the profession all together or just making some changes in the approach you have towards the business and its marketing strategy may be. Even if that means looking into the option of retraining yourself for changing the career to the path of your choice, the path that you would love to follow for the rest of your life. Most people under estimate the power of investing in your own self; you must continuously **invest in you** to equip yourself with more tools of knowledge, skills and power through the forever changing times.

Also you can apply this separately to the **Financial Health**. Just take note of the account balance and assets to work out the possessions you have and hold. Work out what to keep or what to let go or re-invest in a better way, weigh them against what you would like to achieve. Most importantly, work out the reasons, why you want to achieve that. The stronger the reason, more you will be keen to achieve that goal. Create an action plan to achieve what you desire. This is closely associated with your business and career in most scenarios but at times you may see hitting the lottery numbers. For most of us, hitting the right area of business and career for wealth is no less than hitting the lotto numbers.

For some people **Physical Health** is a huge issue. So do assess that well before it becomes an issue for you. *'Healthy Body Healthy Mind'* statement, does also apply vice versa. Assess your Physical health; whether it is weight loss or weight gain, running more kilometres, those Karate skills for self-defence, cycling for longer or doing Yoga, every thing is possible. You just need to believe in yourself and develop that Can Do attitude. People have cured themselves of chronic diseases; I have talked me into loosing weight from hundred plus kilos to 81kg in 7 weeks. Every day I did not feel like going and wanted to take a break but every day I told myself – "**Let's do it today and worry about rest tomorrow**". I cut down on all fizzy drinks and sweets and cut most food and only ate a little just before going to gym, to ensure I don't collapse down. Set yourself the goals even if you start with small. It's just a switch in the brain, if you turn it on; it's well and truly on. Write the goals and make them visual to your eyes as a reminder if you need to. Strengthen your mind to believe in what you want, your way of life and a healthy one. Do not forget '*Health is Wealth*'.

Spirituality is being in touch with your higher conscious, your soul and its source, it is the divine energy within you waiting to be nourished and prosper. This is also an aspect that can heal and fast wheel everything else related to life. When assessing Spirituality, if it is a new term for you, then you may need to think deeper about what spirituality means and its importance for you and how being spiritually inclined may help you. You may need to satisfy your intellect first and then find a spiritual teacher or true master for guidance on the path. Right guidance is absolutely necessary and important on the spiritual path. And yes, I agree that not all of them may be true saints or masters, so do your diligence but never indulge in unpleasant arguments. Your heart will tell you when it all feels right.

Now that you have warmed up your mind and brain to few aspects of life and know some questions you can ask yourself to start cleaning up to create your path, you must learn about keeping an eye on those milestones while you travel on that path of living the life of your dreams. You must set some goals and keep them in check within your Future Probability Sphere framework and achieve them with the help of The Karmic Rewind tool.

Art of Pursuing Your Goal

Goal Setting is very important part to achieve your dream milestones, to reach your aims set in your FPS. We may at times think that a certain goal is not achievable, but that is not the case at all. Where there is a will, there is a way but you must know what you want, what you are aiming for and it's positive or negatives or even neutral effects on your life. I classify goals to be positive, negative and neutral as well.

Positive Goals are those, which will take you towards higher standards of all aspects in your life. That may be your thoughts, wisdom, standard of living or being Happier in every sense. **Negative goals** on the other hand is primarily knowing your higher self, wanting it so badly and still not working towards that better aim in life. You are not intending to do any damage to yourself but you are still doing it unintentionally by not intentionally working towards your better self, your better life. Hence, you don't have to have a negative goal but not having a positive goal itself is a negative goal in that sense. **Neutral goals** are almost always there when you don't even know any better and whatever comes in the way, you'll go with that. Neutrality is the state of Nirvana should I call it.

In another way if we look at, we are quite successful in what goals we set to ourselves in our daily lives. The goals may be smaller at scale, but we do accomplish them. We have targets at work to meet. We have targets to meet relating to our family, we have responsibilities to meet towards our family, friends, society, and planet. There are some targets we are living up to and some we realise we need to do more about to accomplish them. It all comes down to how you prioritise and prepare for those goals or targets. You will achieve whatever target you put your heart and mind to and set as priority one.

When we are at schools, we have certain targets to meet, and that is what becomes our goal and we achieve them. The ones who concentrate with their full strengths, make use of guidance from experts and put their hearts and mind into it completely, they achieve the highest ranks, and the rest achieve the goal with certain lower marks, but they all achieved according to the goal they set for themselves, they achieved according to the amount of effort they had put in. So, end of the day if you look at your results in any aspect of life, you have actually achieved what goal you set for yourself based on the energies you put in to achieve.

Similar applies to if you go for any University qualifications or being an apprentice after school. If you choose the degree you are interested in, you will always put your effort to the scale of how much you like that stream of studies. An apprentice who chooses a particular trade is more likely to be the best at it if he or she chose the trade because they loved working in it, whereas others who do it for the sake of working, they may become good at it but will never be highly successful, as they will not have the drive within, the passion within that can drive them to be highly successful is missing.

"It is no point holding tight to a failure or an imperfect result for a goal; but it is important to fall in love and hold tight to the planning and execution of it to achieve the result. Results may not exactly be in your hand but the actions that bring about that result are."

That is why I have developed this attitude of doing the best as I can and then not worry about the results; yet keep persisting to achieve what I love. Here's a quick lesson from an ancient Hindu scripture, the holy book "Geeta". In "Geeta", Lord Krishna explained the similar to Arjun, one of the key role players in the historical war of Mahabharata. And the message clearly and simply was to *"Keep doing your Karma (actions or deeds), and do not raise expectations of the results"*. Anyone who may want to learn about the history is more than encouraged to do so. Mahatma Gandhi termed the holy book "Geeta" as The Gospel of Selfless Action. He also said –

'The object of the Gita appears to me to be that of showing the most excellent way to attain self-realisation' and this can be achieved by selfless action, 'By desireless action; by renouncing fruits of action; by dedicating all activities to God, i.e., by surrendering oneself to Him, the body and soul'. ---Mahatma Gandhi

That is why *I give my best in the present to create the present I will see in future, a better present.* Yet, not let my mind bother too much about the results so I can maintain peace of mind, which is much needed to progress ahead and further in spirituality. With that peace of mind, you get better control on your mind; you increase your mental strength so you can think well about the best possibilities for your future, yet not being attached with those lacking results. This in terms gives you the ability to perform your best, which otherwise may not be the case if you started to get worried about the results or even a possibility of getting over excited about the results. We have all heard of the words over-smart, the story of the rabbit and a tortoise is a best example to think. So the need is to hold your mind in the best possible state in the present, the present that we are living every moment as it passes by.

It is not an easy mindset to develop and again persistence with some wise thinking will help. After all, the worry and fear, both do not make things easier. They will only help you lose control. If you have fear or get worried, you will not be able to react normal as you otherwise would to a situation.

'It is the momentum you will set in every present moment you face, that will sail you through into the future. So your future will be presented as a result of the force, the energy received from the presented moments of the past.'

We all are very familiar with the term of 'Nerves are getting to him or her' or 'It's the pressure or stress of the situation', being used quite often to the sports people, when they are performing in a game, a match and specifically if it is of high importance to them. What do you think happened if they performed badly, which is unnatural and below even their own standards? Is it their game that has degraded all of a sudden? No, it's the thoughts of the importance of the game and what would happen if the result did not go in their favour, it's that worry, that fear. And the feelings of those end results have overpowered their concentration and hence it starts to affect their performance. We have often seen in those high profile matches that the one who holds on to those nerves, keeps control over nerves and fear is the one who often wins.

Just remind yourself of that very next moment when a tennis player hits the ball to win the final match point that he/she throws the racket away, falling down to the ground and lying there, thanking the one in the skies above, realising the moment, the feel that they have won it. Imagine that final score hit by the winning side in cricket on the last ball, or the wicket taken by the bowler to take that final wicket to have their team win the match in crucial moments. Imagine the expressions of feelings, the pressure going away and a large smile replacing that worried look on the face. Yet all they had to do was, to give their best performance. If they are doing that with best control over their mind, they will have that extra capability to think about what they may have learned about the opposition and implement the techniques to encounter them. That way the results are very much likely to be in their favour. But the most important bit here is to keep your concentration, hold your nerves together without letting the worries and fear enter the mind.

If you can control your nerves on any given situation, at least that gives you the ability to perform the best you actually can. You must not worry about the results but only giving your best to achieve what you desire. How would the result matter if you have and could only do your best? Yet if it is not in your favour and you love to achieve that win so much, you will only want to come back with better preparation the next time. However, sometimes you do undermine your own potential to perform, which you can overcome by setting yourself for higher goals when there is nothing at stake other than improving upon or beating your own past performance. I love this quote I heard by an Air Force Officer –

'The more You Sweat in Peace, the Less You Bleed in War.'

Even though this belief may be hit hard by the opposition in war time but the pilot has given himself the best chance to equip himself with all the necessary training and practice to fly the war birds in best manner possible, whether its a defensive or offensive situation. And that is all he can do. If you have trained well and practiced hard, there is a good chance you will win in the situation. Otherwise we often see teams, players, and people, giving up under pressure.

To most situations in my life, I simply respond with the best of my abilities by assessing the circumstances and surrounding conditions and then make a decision to follow it through. The result may or may not be always in favour, but if I have been able to maintain my calm, I have been able to get the positive results. If the result was not in favour, then I have never let that affect my mind and have accepted that as destiny due to my past Karmas. Then I move on ahead in life with better and more knowledge, better and more experience, which I can apply on my next or reviewed goal or task.

If we do not find an opportunity to accomplish a desired goal we must create one through our Karma. We may need to force ourselves if possible towards or into the circumstances that will automatically push us to achieve success towards those goals. Sometimes you must deliberately **shut some doors** to leave yourself with the option of no second choice but to **pursue the one and only towards success**. If we set ourselves a goal and cut out the distractions, then we start working towards that goal without deviation. We start taking action towards that goal, and hence one day we achieve that too.

I lived with a few mates in a house where we shared a 3-bedroom house among four of us. It was no real issue as one of them was a movie junkie and would quite happily watch movies all night and sleep on the couch always. But the real issue for me became was the issue of some friends who visited us with their girlfriend's. Not that I was against any such relationships of them, or I had any problems with those girls, but as per my beliefs I did not want to get involved in any such relationships. I just wanted to get married as a good family guy, but then living in such environment could easily have an effect on my strong willpower.

Often stories are heard of people with strong personalities with strong family ties but falling into extra marital affairs. We all know stories of the likes of World no. 1 Golfer, Tiger Woods and Bill Clinton and more. Even in Hindu scriptures there are stories of such a Rishi's or religious practitioners who had achieved a very high level of consciousness in the spiritual world, along with achievement of a large amount of mystical powers to perform magic and what not, they had even failed to resist themselves against the environment with an attractive female in a lonely place.

Then I was not to trust certain human instincts in me in that regard in my early twenties. And what I decided then was to create the bounds on me so I would never fall a prayer to any such circumstances ever. I did avoid any such encounters on purpose and parties as well where I knew what the rest of the group might get up to. But I often dropped friends at places and at times went back to drive them back home as being a good mate and probably the only non-drinking sober one out of the lot. But the most important thing I did was when my parents had this marriage proposal for me. I at first was not ready, but then I was always going to get married with one of the proposals my parents would bring. I was born and brought up in such environment and could never think of going against their will to hurt them, or even at the least, if the things don't work out as well as they are seen to be in the mother in law and daughter in law relationship, at least no one could blame me.

That was another factor I considered, but later I agreed to where my parents wanted, as we knew my wife's family from long time ago, and our parents were actually good friends for years. My wife and I were born in the same year and around the same time, so unsure if our parents within themselves decided right then regarding this marriage. They probably very well may have done so, as were the trends among good friends in those days.

Anyways, I agreed to the proposal and this was also a way of me placing those boundaries on me. As once you are engaged, no good friend will insist on you to have a girlfriend, and in any such situations girls will also run away the moment they see that ring on your finger, or when you mention you are engaged and will be married soon. So this is also another example to impose an environment on you to get yourself into certain situation to avoid something you do not want to bother you or even to force yourself to get into an environment to succeed. That way you can effectively carve out a situation to be beneficial to your goals in life and at times save you from getting hurt or stepping backwards.

With the learned techniques in mind, the art of pursuing your goals basically comes down to these four things at the core – **Weigh** your options, **Decide** on one, **Eliminate** the distractions, **Go for the Kill**.

After all if you are addressing any circumstances in life, there can only be so many options and who else could know what's best for you. If in doubt always discuss with either an expert or some loved one who is suitably trustworthy. Why I say 'suitably' is because you must seek advice from someone who has the required knowledge or experience. There is no point going to a loved one who is no better equipped than you unless you have no choice, but then you and your gut feeling is as good as theirs but feel free to get that comfort too if the need be.

But sooner the better; **do not procrastinate**. This deciding to pursue period is where people stay stuck for very long and keep wishing upon their dreams to come true. So eliminate all secondary options by deciding on that one and only option and then do what ever it takes to pursue that. Stop not till the goal is reached.

While weighing in your options, you may wish to apply a widely popular strategy known as **SMART**. Your goals should be SMART as they say but let me add some context as to what we want to achieve with this book.

<u>**S – Specific**</u>, Be specific, even precise about what the outcome must be.

<u>**M – Measurable**</u>, You should be able to see something tangible to measure the progress and also the outcome. Helps in making your efforts visible.

<u>**A – Attainable**</u>, this generally means you should have everything in your possession that is required to achieve this goal. But, remember very importantly that now in this book, it is about You developing into everything that you need to be and attain that dream goal of yours.

<u>**R – Relevant**</u>, The goal must be relevant to you, your heart and soul, your inner voice and most importantly relevant to Master Plan of Your Life. We will help you design one further in this book.

<u>**T – Timely**</u>, most people act when a time limit is imposed; are you like that too? Place a time factor, by when to achieve the goal. Keep it realistically unbreakable yet flexible enough not to shatter the dream goal itself. Persist for goals but do emphasise to realise the time factor. Kill the procrastination behaviour.

Just put yourself in a scenario where your only option is to act in that manner and you knew in your heart that you would feel better in that situation but you just could not collect enough courage within to be there. Sometimes you can put the art of elimination to some intelligent and productive use and all of a sudden you will have pushed yourself into the situation you actually like, and you will start enjoying it. Ever remember those situations at school, when someone is to get on to the stage but are not able to go there just out of that little fear of being on the stage and then someone who is a good friend of yours or a well-wisher has given you that little push from behind that not only gave you some encouragement but also forced you to move to be where you should be.

That is the push you need to use to be able to achieve what your desires really are. If you can't do it yourself, have a conversation with someone you know, who will be able to help you and support you in your decision-making. Sometimes they may come up with an idea that you could not even imagine, that may make your achievement much more easier. You just need to decide, decide with your heart and soul, empower your mind, drive with your brain and instincts, take calculated risks, and do something different otherwise the results you are getting right now, the job you are working in are your baselines anyways. You can always fall back on to where you are now, but believe me, you will not have that need as you will know the better you once you have realised what you love and taken a step towards achieving what you love.

That is the concept I used to make the most of my natural talent and passion. The base line as a fall-back support can be set to the current place in life, set to where we are in life now. With the experience and talent I had, I could always get a normal expenses paying job any day. But What I really wanted was to achieve my dreams, dreams that involved a lot of social benefit, touching and benefitting people's lives, a lot of ideas, creativity and I want to get that out to the world. The way I could do that was by creating them in the way I wanted them to be seen, and who else could be my best friend in doing so except computers technology, and they were the ones I always loved working with too. So I decided to become an IT developer to satisfy that need. For writing I joined local writers society to surround me with like-minded people to help nourish my skills.

So this is a crucial stage, the deciding stage. It's now or never. The moment you have made a decision for yourself, the consequences will start to follow. And, for a lot of us, they will be with us for the rest of our lives. Yet there is no stage early or late, it just depends on how much heart and effort you want to put into it. That is why, making a decision with your full heart and seeing the goals you want to achieve clearly is very important. Let's take a look at **The Karmic Rewind tool** now with all the knowledge and stimulated brain from all that you've read so far. Let's look at how to use this **Eleven-Step tool**.

I chose eleven numbers of items in the Karmic Rewind tool, as in our culture, when we give money as a gift, the numbers ending in (1) is always considered Good Luck. It will always be like 11 or 21 or 31 or 51 or 101, 251, 501 and when higher, it's always of 1100, 2100, 5100 sort. All these figures are in Indian currency by the way. And the money gift value at weddings sometimes can far exceed these figures. Anyways, So I decided to make it eleven, a gift value number of steps for this tool. I want almost all people to make that Karmic Change that is required to **Live the Life for What it was always meant to be, on this Planet.**

Overview of The Karmic Rewind Tool

At the top level, the plan overarching everything about your life is going to be called the **Master Action Plan (MAP)**, the MAP of your life. Once created, you can even call it your very own personal religious book or personal prophecy to follow throughout life. This MAP is going to be a combined portfolio of realisation of **your overall and complete existence** and identified **aspects of your life**. Each identified Aspect will have an **Aspect Story and an Aspect Action Plan (AAP)**. The goals will be identified under each AAP and will be referred to as **Aspect Goals**.

To accomplish those Aspect Goals you will be creating a **Comprehensive Action Plan (CAP)** with the help of **Rewind, Revive, Re-Live strategy** used in the detail workout under this Tool. The detail workout will provide you with **Revival Action Plans (RAPs)** to specifically tackle or revive from a core problem or to nurture the required skills and also confidence revival. In the case of a brand new goal that does not require you to rewind and revive, you will call them NAPs in place for RAPs. **NAP** is your **Newborn Action Plan**. These RAPs or NAPs will feed into your Comprehensive Action Plan.

Your brain by now should have warmed up to what you should be doing and why you should be doing certain things. With all the wisdom and that thought in your mind let's go ahead, **design Your Life's MAP** to manifest your vision. You are about to **Unfold the Genius within** and **create The Book of Your Life**.

Here's how it will all fit together -

1. Master Action Plan (**MAP**) is the book of your life. It will pen down the core of you, your mind, create awareness, connect you within, with your heart and soul and your existence in this universe manifested through various **aspects of life**.

2. Then you will identify all the aspects of your life and create an **Aspect Story**. You will also create a **statement of happiness** to identify what will make you happy in that aspect of your life.

3. Then you will create an **Aspect Action Plan (AAP)**, which will consist of the identified **Aspect Name, Statement of Happiness** and all **Aspect Goals with Timeframes** to achieve happiness in that aspect.

4. Add a **heart score** to your Aspect Goals at a scale of 1 – 10 to have a feel of happiness once achieved. It may also help you with prioritisation.

5. To accomplish those Aspect Goals you will create, link and use the Comprehensive Action Plan **(CAP)** that gets created in step 10 of the tool.

6. The CAPs **incorporate Step 9 and any RAPs or NAPs** as per need from initial steps 5, 6, 7 and 8 of the tool where you would use the 'Rewind – Revive – ReLive' technique to craft the solution. You will then create **step-by-step, specific actions** to take to accomplish your desired goal.

The figure below shows the hierarchy of fitting it al together.

Figure 1 Tool Overview

Happiness Score on achievement - ♡♡♡♡♡♡♡♡♡

Note: Once you are working within an aspect AAP, the Immediate connecting boxes will always be your Goals in the aspect of life you are assessing. Your Goals will then be connected to your Comprehensive Action Plans (CAPs), which is made up of your steps to take along with Revival Action Plans (RAPs) or Newborn Action Plans (NAPs).

You will see an example and a guide Life MAP here. For creating Your Master Action Plan, use the copy at the end of this book or the separate 'Book of my Life'.

Book of Your Life - Your MAP

Step 1 – As a very first step you will **Identify the Existence of Your Core Self and Your Life**. Realising your self-existence must become your first priority to strengthen yourself from your core and connect within, feel your roots and learn to strengthen them so you can stand strong in life. You will also create your own unique **"I Am" statement** to connect within regularly, to read and impress upon your mind.

Step 2 – Once you've strengthened within, it will be time to move next to the life that exists around you. You will now **Identify and Plan for All Aspects of Your Life** and write an **Aspect Story** to connect with and assess it better. With that story in mind, you will create the **Aspect Action Plan (AAP)** by recognising the **Aspect Goals** to fulfil your desire of that aspect. The **AAPs** purpose is to provide an overview of your Aspect Goals and guide you to the respectively created **Comprehensive Action Plans (CAP)**. Sometimes you may choose to create Sub-Aspects (Explained further in examples). CAPs are crafted from RAPs or NAPs and Action Steps within the tool. Let's get going.

Here's an overarching view of your MAP of Your Life -

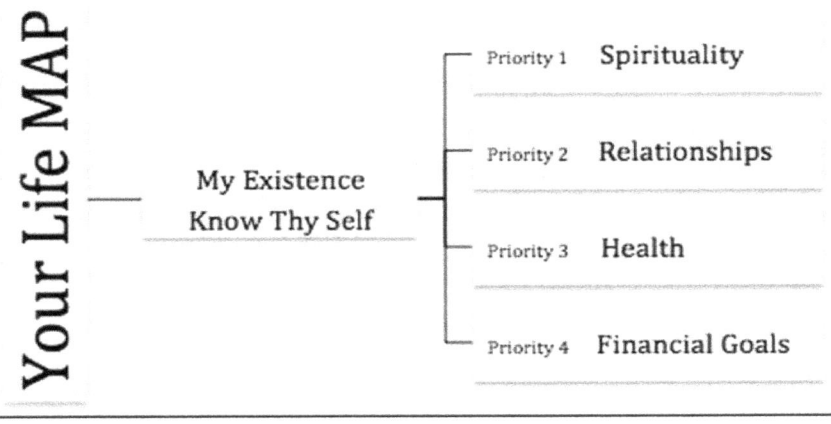

Figure 2 Map of Life

First identify and name the aspect you wish to work with; place it in bold writing when working in the tool or workbook. This will be the start of the section for that aspect.

ASPECT (Name)

Example below

ASPECT – MY RELATIONSHIPS

Next you must write your Aspect Story in the given section. This will help you connect better with life in current state and eventually design a perfect plan to live better in coming future, to Re-Live better.

ASPECT STORY

Example below

MY RELATIONSHIPS Story

(Add as many pages as you need but stick to the aspect only if you can. If you find **connections to other aspects**, make note and thoroughly think through and classify it under relevant aspect to address effectively.)

--   -----------
----------   ---

Once you are done with the Aspect Story, you should have **identified some goals** you want to achieve in this aspect of life to be happy and feel accomplished. It's time to **create the Aspect Action Plan** to make this aspect flourish with happiness. You will also be **prioritising the aspects** themselves **as well as Aspect Goals** within an aspect. Just remember that the priority is not necessarily the weight of importance as well. They are all important aspects of life but what you may trade for the other at times is where priorities will play their part.

ASPECT ACTION PLAN

1. **My Aspect** – (write the Name of aspect of life you choose to work on.)
2. **Aspect Priority Rank** (__)
3. **Happiness Statement** – (this helps you identify happiness within)
   My (aspect name, e.g. -Spiritual) **Happiness is in** _ _ _ _ _ _ _ _ _ _ _ _ _ _
   _
4. **Aspect Goals** (Add as many goals as needed for an aspect but list them all together only in this 'Goals' section for that aspect. Keep the related action plans for that goal in the following section identified and connected by the plan number and page number mentioned with the goal listed here in this section.)

It is now time to identify the goals that will help you achieve your happiness. Remember that initially you may not be very clear about the goal. You **must use The Karmic Rewind Tool** (in next section) now and establish all that is needed to be transferred here in the AAP section.

Goal – 1   **Priority** (____)

Specific Goal - _
_ _

Target Completion Timeframe –

    Achieve By Date - ___ / ___ / ___   By _ _ am/pm

    Note: _
_ _

Plan Number – Priority 1 Goal 1 | Created - ☐ Page No. ___

    Note: Mark your Plan number at the top of The Karmic Rewind Tool to keep proper references.

Happiness Score on achievement - ♡ ♡ ♡ ♡ ♡ ♡ ♡ ♡ ♡

THE KARMIC REWIND TOOL

REWIND | REVIVE | RELIVE

Plan Number – Aspect 1 Goal 1

Aspect of Life- _ _ _ _ _ _ _ _ _ _ _ _ _ _ _ **Goal Priority** (_)

I would love it if _
_ _

Note the aspect area of the goal you wish to work on. How do you rank it in priorities of your life in this aspect? What would be ideally the lovable situation of this aspect goal in your life? The goal will relate to one of many aspects of life such as Financial, Health, Spirituality, Relationships or any separately identifiable areas in your life. This may also be a subset of another major goal. Such broken down sub-goals if identified, will help you work on achieving a top-level goal in the hierarchy. In such case, maintain a clear and connected hierarchy through Priority ranking.

REWIND stage

1. Where Am I currently in this area of life or on the path to achieve this goal?

Here you will note down where you are at in this particular area of life at present. Be open, be clear and be precise. Write an essay if you like, on a separate paper and then pick primary points here.

Currently in this aspect of my life I am/have _ _ _ _ _ _ _ _ _ _ _ _ _ _ _ _
_ _
_ _

2. How did I reach here? What decisions played a role?

When, at what point in life did you make a decision that has landed you where you are today in this aspect of life. This will help in backtracking. And while tracking back, you may find some other potential incidents that you may need to apply the Rewind to Realise technique to, to dig deeper to learn about yourself while detailing the incidents. In that case just take another print out and start over to rewind that particular aspect. In this case you may end up creating a hierarchy of related aspects to achieve a desired outcome of the primary aspect that you identified. It may be as simple as I did this, this and this or even – this happened, then this happened and then this and I got here.

I got to this stage because I _____
_____
_____
_____
_____

3. Why I made the choice?

Note down the **Actual Compelling Reason** for every decision that you made causing you to be where you are. Note those here with clarity.

Decision	Reason
1.	
2.	

_____
_____

4. What caused me to think or convince into making that choice?

Whether it was due to the circumstances in life, or you identified a need or a must do situation or even out of leisure. It could be your assessment through knowledge or even lack of it. Was it the Beliefs you had embedded in your mind, or you were left with no other choice. Was it just a thought, what went through your heart and mind for that **Decisive Reasoning** to occur? Identify everything and note it down. _____

_____
_____
_____
_____
_____

REVIVE stage

5. Beliefs That Played a Part

These are somewhat the beliefs that you would have identified in column above. Think a bit more deeply to dig out any beliefs in your conscious or subconscious mind. By doing this you'll recognise and perform necessary changes to your **Belief System** and steer ahead with a completely refreshed mind that believes you will achieve here on.

1. _____
2. _____
3. _____
4. _____
5. _____

Revival Action Plan (RAP)

Old Beliefs that need to be killed

These are the beliefs that you identified that have not helped you in achieving what you want to achieve in life. You will erase them of your mind or alter them. List all such as – "I don't think I can/they will ....". Why is your mind saying No for others, do what you must and should and let others decide.

1. _____
2. _____
3. _____
4. _____
5. _____

New Beliefs to Accomplish Desired Goal

These are the beliefs that you will identify to help you in achieving what you want to achieve in life. A **Believe in Your Own Self** is First and is a Must. Start activities that will consolidate your self-belief. Give your mind what I call a **Cannottocando** lolly (can not to can do). Say "Yes" rather than "No", say to yourself "I Can" rather than "I Can't", "They will" rather than "They won't".

1. _____
2. _____
3. _____
4. _____
5. _____

6. People who Influenced Decision

A major factor a lot of the times is influence. Was it your parents, your friends or relatives, your school and teachers, a social or religious organisation or even if it was a philosophical influence. They all eventually have influenced you, your thoughts and beliefs that have directly or indirectly affected your life.

Revival Action Plan (RAP)

You need to identify all persons connected with this aspect goal of your life and then work on either *selective isolation* and/or start making *new connections* to support your goal. Note the names here along with what role they play in your life, your support system. Whether they are a positive push or a negative pull down. Use below template as help but don't forget to listen to your heart. Loved ones may not be on this list but increase your effort to get them on your side if they are not already. In that case it may become a sub-goal to achieve in backdrop. Do not loose focus on your actual goal though. On a sidenote, you may also want to filter out any places or locations that may be limiting your mindset and eventually your growth.

Association Assessment

Name - _ _ _ _ _ _ _ _ _ _ _ _ _   Supportive – Yes _ _ _ No _ _ _

Association context - _
_ _
_ _
_ _

Associate More: Yes/No   Note: _

Disassociate: Yes/No   Note: _

Selective Isolation: Yes/No Note: _

7. Identify Your Weaknesses

Weaknesses - Identify the weaknesses if you believe you have any that may have caused you to fall below the expectations that you may have from yourself or if your family members had from you. I know we, as human beings do not like to admit we have any weakness. And if you truly believe you are being honest, then it is great and I am really glad for you. E.g. – Procrastination, excessive smoking, drinking or TV etc., fear of failure, fear of society, fear of technology, standing up for yourself, learning, lack of knowledge or training or whatever else that's failed you or stopping you.

No matter how much courage it takes, do identify them and put it down on this paper and realise the **cause** that is **costing you your dreams**, holding you back from exercising your true potential.

1. _____
2. _____
3. _____
4. _____

Revival Action Plan (RAP) – Identify the ways that will help you to get rid of these if identified or turn them into your strengths instead. My advice – Just Nike it, I mean Just Do it, get over them and take whatever action it takes, get out there and get rid of it. Take that training to learn a new skill if needed, build your strength with knowledge and skills. Get busy with the new and old will be left behind unnoticed, try it.

1. _____
2. _____
3. _____
4. _____

8. Identify Your Strengths

Now you should also be able to realise what **your strengths** are within. The strengths that you have as a natural talent, or a potential that you believe to have within but hasn't let out because of lack of support and motivation. You can even identify your love for something in particular. Now is the time to recognise it and put it to work. Unleash the talented you, that artist, that writer, that engineer, that archer, the player or that talented professional within you. The inner urge is what will guide you to know your hidden talents, pen them down and bring them out.

1. _____
2. _____
3. _____
4. _____

Revival Action Plan (RAP) - Now think of how to use your identified natural talents and abilities to realise this dream. Undertake the training if the need be, as that interest has come out as your area of strength from your within. Find someone who has and uses similar interests; don't be afraid to ask. People with similar mindset are always happy to help. Note them down and work out on how to improve, enhance and apply these strengths to achieve this goal.

1. _____
2. _____
3. _____
4. _____

Behavioural Strengths – Behaviours are kind of your automatic actions based on what's going on in our mind. Think about the way you behave in the environment relating to this aspect or goal. It is critical to note down any behaviour that will help you progress or even hold you back. E.g. – I get angry, irritated or rude very quickly or vice-versa.

1. _____
2. _____
3. _____
4. _____
5. _____

Revival Action Plan (RAP) – Imagine how you should behave or react in the situation in order to achieve the success you want, the goal you want to accomplish; is there a mismatch with the current behaviour? If yes, then imagine how you should behave in the situation to lead you up to that goal. Get rid of un-helpful behaviour and develop ways to encourage supportive behaviours by strengthening control over your mind. Identify the ways to improve, plan for more practice and activities that will improve your control on your behaviour, skills and abilities. Identify **training needs** for Sports, Meditation, and Yoga to better utilise your energies than on wasteful behaviours.

1. _____
2. _____
3. _____
4. _____
5. _____

9. YOUR GOAL – with Clear vision

Set a Specific Goal - Now that you have identified where you are at in life and where you want to be. You have filtered out any such thoughts and beliefs that were holding you back; identified your strengths, new beliefs, people and associations for good. You know what you need to do to revive and rise to shine; It is time to set a clear, refreshed or even new goal for you in this aspect of life. See it clearly in your mind, walk your thoughts over it, visualise it and finalise it to mark it in your FPS.

Specific Goal - Be Specific _
_ _
_ _
_ _
_ _

Target Completion Timeframe - After you have set and written that new goal you want to achieve. Set a target completion or achieving date for it. When you set that date and time, think, plan and only give any **levy for Persistence and Not Procrastination**. Be flexible so you keep persisting but do not let this be another procrastination story. Set the target Completion Date as if you are asking someone else to complete a task and if you think you work better under pressure then apply some such constraint. But most important is to *DO IT*.

Achieve By Date - ___ / ___ / _____   By _ _ _ _ am/pm

Notes: _
_ _
_ _
_ _

RELIVE – stage

Let's gear up; it is time to work on the Karmic aspect, to take action towards **living the life for what it was meant to be for You**. All your RAPs in a particular assessment will be combined together to form your <u>Comprehensive Action Plan (CAP).</u> Here you will build the <u>Comprehensive Action Plan (CAP)</u> that will link back to your Aspect Goal for a given <u>Aspect Action Plan (AAP)</u> and form part of the <u>Master Action Plan</u> for your life, the **MAP** of your life. That's what we talked about previously; one wouldn't build almost anything without a plan, a blueprint, then you must also draw your MAP to build the life by following your Heart and Soul. All CAPs for different aspects of your life, when acted upon, will combine to make up the life you will plan with this tool. Let's do it.

All your noted points, the **gems to create magic in your life** from the above nine steps will now be combined together to create a Comprehensive Action Plan (CAP) for you, the CAP you will wear from now onwards in this game of life. This will serve as your daily **start of the day pill**. You must read through it everyday at least for No Less Than Five minutes as a daily guide to achieve your dream. You must do this to impress upon your mind, your brain and remind your heart during the moments of turbulence that this is who you are, this is the divine purpose of your life.

<u>Newborn Goals</u> – Unless a young student, I believe you will always have travelled so far in life that you will always be able to take a rewinded look at where you are in an aspect of life. But, there may be times you might wish to set up new goals on a road not travelled yet in Your life. In such scenario, take hint from RAPs, replace RAPs and create your NAPs, I'll call that a **Newborn Action Plan** in that case.

10. **Comprehensive Action Plan (CAP)-** (copy details from step 9 here)

   Specific Goal - _____
   _____
   _____
   _____

   Happiness Score on achievement - ♡♡♡♡♡♡♡♡♡

   Target Completion Timeframe –

   Achieve By Date - ___ / ___ / _____   By _ _ _ _ am/pm

   Notes: _____

Revival Action Plans (RAP) or New Action Plans (NAPs) to be aware of –

RAP/NAP – Beliefs (Impress Positive and New Beliefs in Mind)

   1. (copy details from step 5 here)_ _ _ _ _ _ _ _ _ _ _ _ _ _ _ _ _ _
   2. _____
   3. _____
   4. _____
   5. _____

RAP/NAP – People and Social Associations (Keep or Avoid)

1. (copy details from step 6 here) _
2. _
3. _
4. _
5. _

RAP/NAP – Weaknesses (Remove or Convert to Strengths)

1. (copy details from step 7 here) _
2. _
3. _
4. _
5. _

RAP/NAP – Strengths and Behaviours (Build and Strengthen)

1. (copy details from step 8 here) _
2. _
3. _
4. _
5. _

STEPS TO SUCCESS – using Walk your Thoughts technique

Here you will create a step by step actions list to manifest and achieve your aspect goal. Apply your insights from the steps above and craft the strategy to accomplish your desired outcome. Be clear, specific and list every detail to get you there, to guide you step by step on the journey towards your goal. Call it your Action Steps or Steps To Success, but this really is your **Karma list** to manifest through Karma.

1. I will read this CAP for 5 minutes every day. _____
2. _____ ☐
3. _____ ☐
4. _____ ☐
5. _____ ☐
6. _____ ☐
7. _____ ☐
8. _____ ☐
9. _____ ☐
10. _____ ☐
11. _____ ☐

11. Sync with Master and Aspect Action Plan (MAP/AAP)-

Remember when it was time to set goals under Aspect Action Plan, we said we may not have clarity on the goal when we start and we jumped to the tool to get clarity and set a precise and clear goal. So now the last and final step of this process is to **transfer** this clarified **Goal, Target Completion Timeframe** and place it as a **Goal under step 4 'Aspect Goals' section** of the Aspect Action Plan of the identified Aspect of life we are working with.

Link this CAP using a **Plan Number** such as "Aspect 1 Goal 1". Whatever format you decide to use it should make sense to you and help you connect the Aspect Goals to its relevant Comprehensive Action Plan. **Mark** this Plan Number in the **heading area at the start of this tool** and also **under the Goal** (in Aspect Action Plan's 'Aspect Goals' section).

Give it a **Happiness Score** in Aspect Goals to help you assess how much it matters to you in comparison to another goal. This may help you prioritise your Aspect Goals.

<u>End of The Karmic Rewind Tool</u>

Now that you understand the nature of ingredients going into the recipe for your life, it **becomes much easier to understand and design the MAP of your life by taking the steps while wearing your CAP and doing the actual RAP**. Sounds like a bit of a rhythm going on here doesn't it? Let's create the music of our life with planned notes now. Using what we've learned so far, let me now take you through those steps of the tool using some examples from my own life. Let's create an example for Your Book of Life, Your MAP of Life.

Your Book of Life - Your MAP (with Examples)

Step 1 - Identify Existence of Your Self and Your Life

You must identify all integral aspects of your life. Many people break it down to some aspects that eventually are linked to four primary aspects. To me **we exist in two forms – Physical and Eternal.** I believe in what many saints and mystics teach about our existence – *'We are Spiritual beings going through Human Experiences'*. The happiness of both our existences can be achieved by addressing these four primary aspects - **Spirituality, Relationships, Health** and **Finances.** Every thing exists because You exist regardless of which form of existence you consider your Primary existence to be. So *Know Thy Self* first and then make the move to identify and work on other aspects of your life.

When you start on creating your MAP of life, in 'Your Life MAP' tag, you will write 'Your Name' Life MAP. Your **first Aspect** as an **Ultimate Priority** I want you to mark is for **Your Existence,** your inner self and then prioritise other aspects that you'll identify.

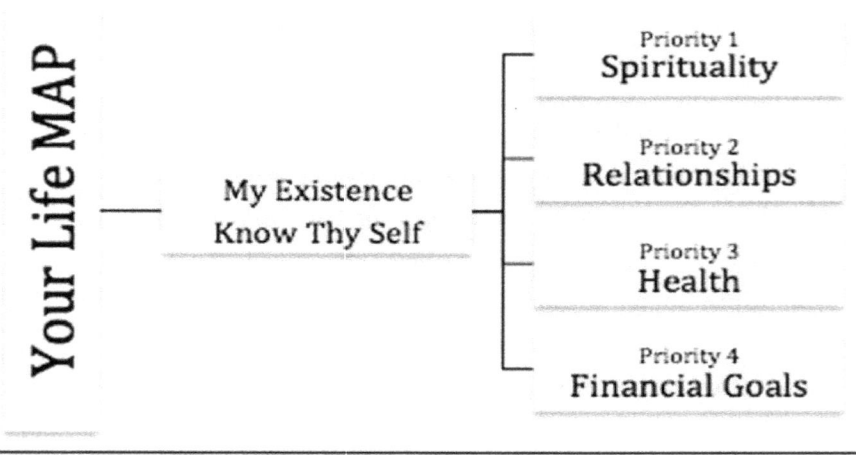

Figure 3 Master Action Plan (MAP)

Ultimate Priority Aspect– My Existence

Let's time travel, I know it's not physically possible yet but it is with imagination. So, let's imagine and travel back in time, set the day and time to the time and day you were born and ask this question; **Who am I**? Ultimate truth as per my belief is – *"We are Spiritual beings going through Human experience"*. Ask questions to know Your Soul, know Your Heart, and the reason that heart in your body started to beat for the first time. Know this body as an instrument to experience and enjoy life for what it was meant to be with virtues of Love, Peace and Harmony. Know what makes you happy within before linking your existence to the outside world in any manner. You can only help anything and anyone else only and only if you are standing strong on the very base of your existence, the bases of who you are at your core.

Past Karmas may be the reason where you are born and to whom you are born. Start from their and listen to your heart, think within for all the attributes you may feel belong to you, attributes you have as natural talents and instincts and then draw upon the question - Who am I? *Everyone is born a hero of their story of life on this planet*, discover your purpose from within and *write that heroic story with* a plan, the Master Action Plan, the MAP of your life.

Some people believe in astrologers, palm readers and tarot card readers to find their life events, purpose or some guidance. You may also, if your gut isn't helping yet. But remember they may only see the destined but not the destiny you can **create with the power of "Creation by Karma"**. Find a relevant coach, a suitable friend or your mother to guide you. Do what ever it takes but *you must "know thy self"*. Let's think back to when we were babies and afraid of nothing; **let's take those fearless, full of energy baby steps and grow** into who we are meant to be without worrying about who's watching if we fall or fail. Failure is told to be inevitable by all the highly successful people on this planet. So Learn and explore who you are, connect within. If you are going to fail, it's better to fail early and learn lessons early to move forward.

The final outcome of this realisation is to create an **"I am _" statement** full of attributes of who you are deep within. You must write one using the help of template provided further in this part and in the workbook. Here is a guide to fill into your MAP for 'Your Existence' part.

ASPECT – MY EXISTENCE

Priority - Ultimate

Now in this part, **"My Existence" is your aspect** and you will have to **create some goals** in order to learn about your existence **such as Learning about your birth.** To achieve that goal of learning about self, you will create an AAP and a CAP. For the CAP, you may have some RAPs using The Karmic Rewind Tool or you may create some NLPs. Getting the hang of acronyms yet (if not, check page 195)?

Aspect Story - MY EXISTENCE

I was born on xx June 19xx at xx:00 am, a summer day in India. I was born in a Sikh family in Chandigarh, the capital city of the state of Punjab. I was born at home with the help of a midwife and not at a hospital. My Father was a good looking and a hardworking man married to my mother who came from the Mukerian village of Punjab. They got married on 28th November 19xx. They told me it was pleasant morning that day with lots of birds chirping at the time. I think they had also mentioned the flute being played in the street by someone passing by. She also mentioned a dream she had as a spiritual message few days before my birth.

I had an elder sister when I was born and later learned that another eldest sister we had had died short after she was born. We did get another younger brother about three years after my birth.

There is a lot more I should learn about that time. I must speak to my parents more about those times and about the day and circumstances when I was born. I have never spent enough alone time to think even deeply about these things and to connect within, with my heart and soul. I must plan to know more of me. I must develop well and nurture well the relationship of **my physical being with my spiritual being**.

Note: I won't write my autobiography here but hope this gives you enough hint to get started. Go on and write as much as you can about you but stick to your birth and your heart and soul only, try to not dig too much into other aspects for the purpose of this exercise. Let's get to the Aspect Action Plan (AAP).

My Existence

(Overview map)

In the figure below are the hints and list of some questions to get you thinking right into the depths of your being here, being human.

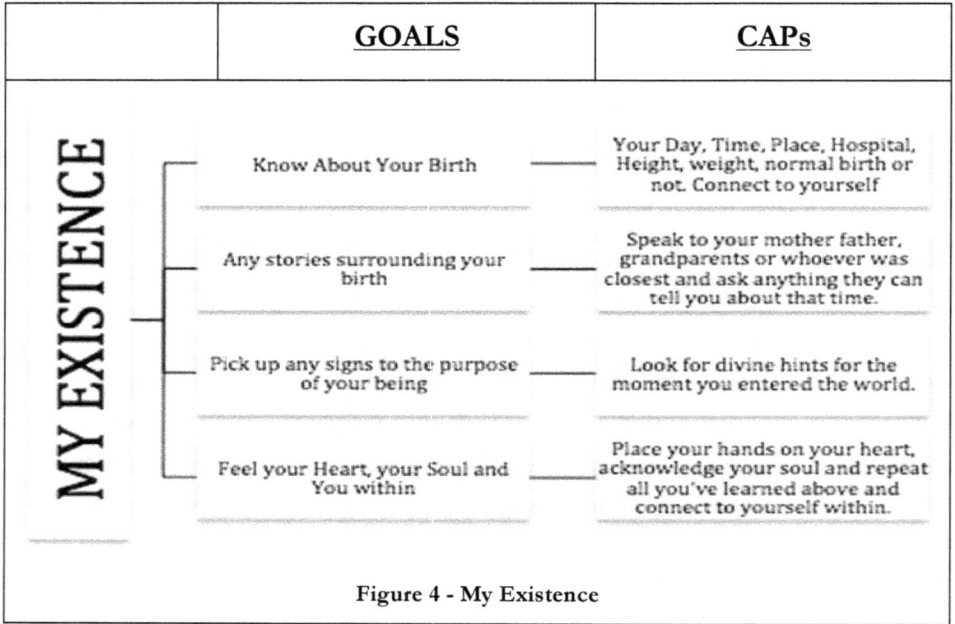

Figure 4 - My Existence

Note: Once you are working within an aspect or sub-aspect AAP, the Immediate connecting boxes will always be your Goals in the aspect of life you are assessing. Your Goals will then be connected to your Comprehensive Action Plans (CAPs), which is made up of your steps to take along with Revival Action Plans (RAPs) or Newborn Action Plans (NAPs).

ASPECT ACTION PLAN

1. **My Aspect** – My Existence
2. **Aspect Priority Rank -** (Ultimate)
3. **Happiness Statement** – My Happiness is in having well connected with my heart and soul. I must know my metal, my purpose in life and build a strong core to be me.
4. **Goals** (Add as many goals as needed for an aspect but list them all together only in this 'Goals' section for that aspect. Keep the related action plans for that goal in the following section identified and connected by the plan number and page number mentioned with the goal listed here in this section.)

It is now time to identify the goals that will help you achieve your happiness. Remember that initially you may not be very clear about the goal. You **must use The Karmic Rewind Tool** (in next section) now and establish all that is needed to be transferred here in the AAP section.

Goal – 1   **Priority (1)**

Specific Goal - Learn about my birth to connect with my own self.

Target Completion Timeframe –

Achieve By Date - 21 /02 /2018   By _ _ am/pm

Notes: _

_ _

Plan Number – My Existence Goal 1 | Created - ☐   Page No. 218

Note: Mark your Plan number at the top of The Karmic Rewind Tool to keep proper references.

Happiness Score on achievement –

♡ ♡ ♡ ♡ ♡ ♡ ♡ ♡ ♡ ♡

Goal – 2   **Priority (2)**

Specific Goal – Learn about any stories or incidents surrounding my birth to connect with my own self. _ _ _ _ _ _ _ _ _ _ _ _ _ _ _ _ _

Target Completion Timeframe –

    Achieve By Date – 21 /02 /2018   By _ _ am/pm

    Notes: _
    _

Plan Number – My Existence Goal 2 | Created - ☐   Page No. <u>224</u>

    <small>**Note:** Mark your Plan number at the top of The Karmic Rewind Tool to keep proper references.</small>

Happiness Score on achievement –

           ♡ ♡ ♡ ♡ ♡ ♡ ♡ ♡ ♡ ♡

THE KARMIC REWIND TOOL

REWIND | REVIVE | RELIVE

Plan Number – My Existence Goal 1

Aspect of Life- My Existence   Goal Priority (1)

I would love it if I can learn about time and circumstances of my birth to connect deeper with my own self. _

REWIND stage

1. Where Am I currently in this area of life or on the path to achieve this goal?

Currently in this aspect of my life I am/have limited knowledge about me at the time of birth. I need more information from my parents. _ _ _ _ _ _ _ _

2. How did I reach here? What decisions played a role?

I never made a point to learn thoroughly about the very start of my life. _ _

3. Why I made the choice?

Just never thought deeply about my existence but we all should. _ _ _

Decision	Reason
1. Unknowingly living under influences.	That's what we all do, don't we.
2. Just go with the flow.	No one told me any better.

4. What caused me to think/convince into making that choice?

Unawareness and blindly influenced into not finding ourselves within. _ _

REVIVE stage

5. Beliefs That Played a Part

1. It's just life, live it as everybody else. No need to connect with self-being.

Revival or Newborn Action Plan (RAP/NAP) -

Old Beliefs that need to be killed

1. It's just life, live it as everybody else. No need to connect with self-being.

New Beliefs to Accomplish Desired Goal

1. I was fearless as a child; I must connect with my core.

2. Every person born has a special purpose in their life, I have too.

6. People who Influenced Decision

Society around me simply pushed me into a rat race, a comparison living always relating to others but not emphasise to realise who we are at our core within. About my birth, my parents may have decided it was time for another sibling for my sister or it could be the social pressures of must try for a Son.

Revival or Newborn Action Plan (RAP/NAP) -

Must spend more time with parents to learn more about myself as a newborn and the times around my birth.

Association Assessment – not applicable

7. Identify Your Weaknesses

Weaknesses -

1. I have lost touch with my inner being. _ _ _ _ _ _ _ _ _ _ _ _ _ _ _

2. I am too busy doing things for others and exhaust myself. _ _ _ _

Revival or Newborn Action Plan (RAP/NAP) –

1. I must face my reality of being and discover my purpose. _ _ _ _ _

2. I must commit time to act and connect within. _ _ _ _ _ _ _ _ _ _

8. Identify Your Strengths

1. I love quiet time. _

Revival or Newborn Action Plan (RAP/NAP) -

1. I must behave like a child while with my parents to get more stories out of their memories to get more clues of my natural being.

2. Use the quiet time to think deeper within. _ _ _ _ _ _ _ _ _ _ _ _ _ _

Behavioural Strengths –

1. I can act like a child. _

Revival or Newborn Action Plan (RAP/NAP) -

1. Behave a little childish on purpose to get some stories out of my parents.

2. _

9. YOUR GOAL – with Clear vision

Specific Goal - Learn about my birth to connect with my own self.

Target Completion Timeframe -

Achieve By Date - 21 /02 /2018   By _ _ _ _ am/pm

RELIVE – stage

Note: In such scenarios, take hint from RAPs, replace RAPs with your NAPs.

10. Comprehensive Action Plan (CAP)-

Specific Goal - Learn about my birth to connect with my own self.

Happiness Score on achievement - ♡ ♡ ♡ ♡ ♡ ♡ ♡ ♡ ♡

Target Completion Timeframe –

    Achieve By Date - 21 / 02 / 2018   By _ _ _ _ am/pm

    Notes: Do it as first task when you start creating your life MAP. _ _ _ _

Revival Action Plans (RAP) or New Action Plans (NLPs) to be aware of -

RAP/NAP – Beliefs (Impress Positive and New Beliefs in Mind)

1. I was fearless as a child; I must connect with my core.

2. Every person born has a special purpose in their life, I have too. _

3. _

RAP/NAP – People and Social Associations (Keep or Avoid)

1. Must spend more time with parents to learn more about myself as a newborn and the times around my birth. _ _ _ _ _ _ _ _ _ _ _ _ _ _

2. _

RAP/NAP – Weaknesses (Remove or Convert to Strengths)

1. I must face my reality of being and discover my purpose. _ _ _ _ _

2. I must commit time to act and connect within. _ _ _ _ _ _ _ _ _ _

3. _

RAP/NAP – Strengths and Behaviours (Build and Strengthen)

1. I must behave like a child while with my parents to get more stories out of their memories to get more clues of my natural being.

2. Use the quiet time to think deeper within.

STEPS TO SUCCESS – using Walk your Thoughts technique

1. I will read this CAP for 15 minutes every day until marked done. _ _
2. Contact my mother and father. _ _ _ _ _ _ _ _ _ _ _ _ _ _ _ _ _ _
3. Check my Birth Record book. _ _ _ _ _ _ _ _ _ _ _ _ _ _ _ _ _ _ _
4. Know my dimensions at birth. _ _ _ _ _ _ _ _ _ _ _ _ _ _ _ _ _ _ _
5. Read them everyday until feeling a strong connection within. _ _
6. Use Twenty minutes daily quiet time to think deeper within. _ _
7. _

11. Sync with Master and Aspect Action Plan (MAP/AAP)-

The last and final step of this process is to **transfer** this clarified **Goal**, **Target Completion Timeframe** and place it as a Goal under the Aspect Action Plan of the identified Aspect of life.

Link this CAP using a **Plan Number** - "My Existence Goal 1".

THE KARMIC REWIND TOOL
REWIND | REVIVE | RELIVE
Plan Number – My Existence Goal 2

Aspect of Life- My Existence	Goal Priority (2)

I would love it if I can learn about circumstances and happenings around my birth to learn more about myself. _ _ _ _ _ _ _ _ _ _ _ _ _ _

REWIND stage

1. Where Am I currently in this area of life or on the path to achieve this goal

    Currently in this aspect of my life I am/have limited knowledge about circumstances around my birth. I need more information from my parents.

2. How did I reach here? What decisions played a role?

    Never thought of their importance on initial influences on my life. _ _ _ _ _

3. Why I made the choice?

    It wasn't a conscious choice not to learn but no one taught it as a way to 'know thy self'.

Decision	Reason
1. Unknowingly living under influences.	That's what we all do, don't we.
2. Just go with the flow.	No one told me any better.

4. What caused me to think or convince into making that choice?

That's what we see around – a lot of preaching about being successful and winners, but not about defining one's own success through 'know thy self'.

REVIVE stage

5. Beliefs That Played a Part

1. Life is a race to win above others. _ _ _ _ _ _ _ _ _ _ _ _ _ _ _ _ _

Revival or Newborn Action Plan (RAP/NAP) -

Old Beliefs that need to be killed

1. Life is a race to win above others. _ _ _ _ _ _ _ _ _ _ _

New Beliefs to Accomplish Desired Goal

1. I was fearless as a child. _

2. Every person born has a unique and special purpose in their life, I have too.

3. I am grown up but its good to learn what I was like as a child. _ _ _

6. People who Influenced Decision

My parents and siblings played a large role in my development at the start of life. But that was also with a small texture of social rat race.

Revival or Newborn Action Plan (RAP/NAP) -

Must spend more time with parents to learn more about myself as a baby and the times and stories or happenings around my birth and growing up.

Association Assessment – not applicable

7. Identify Your Weaknesses

Weaknesses -

1. I have lost touch with my inner being and confidence. _ _ _ _ _ _ _ _

2. I am too busy doing things for others and exhaust myself. _ _ _ _ _ _

3. It doesn't matter what I was like as a child. _ _ _ _ _ _ _ _ _ _ _ _ _

Revival or Newborn Action Plan (RAP/NAP) –

1. I must face my reality of being and discover my purpose. _ _ _ _ _ _

2. I must commit time to act and connect within to build confidence. _ _ _ _

3. I am grown up but its good to learn what I was like as a child. _ _ _

8. Identify Your Strengths

1. I am a deep thinker. _

Revival or Newborn Action Plan (RAP/NAP) -

1. I must behave like a child while with my parents to get more stories out of their memories to get more clues of my natural being. _ _ _ _ _

2. Think deep into those stories to find meaning in my life. _ _ _ _ _ _ _ _

Behavioural Strengths –

1. I can act like a child. _

Revival or Newborn Action Plan (RAP/NAP) -

1. Behave a little childish on purpose to get some stories out of my parents.

2. _

9. YOUR GOAL – with Clear vision

Specific Goal - Learn about my birth to connect with my own self.

Target Completion Timeframe -

Achieve By Date - 21 /02 /2018   By _ _ _ _ am/pm

Notes: _

RELIVE – stage

<small>In this scenario, take hint from RAPs, replace RAPs with your NAPs.</small>

10. Comprehensive Action Plan (CAP)-

Specific Goal - Learn about my birth to connect with my own self.

Happiness Score on achievement - ♡ ♡ ♡ ♡ ♡ ♡ ♡ ♡ ♡

Target Completion Timeframe –

Achieve By Date - 21 / 02 / 2018   By _ _ _ _ am/pm

Notes: Do it as first task when you start creating your life MAP.

Revival Action Plans (RAP) or New Action Plans (NLPs) to be aware of -

RAP/NAP – Beliefs (Impress Positive and New Beliefs in Mind)

1. I was fearless as a child. _

2. Every person born has a unique and special purpose in their life, I have too.

3. I am grown up but its good to learn what I was like as a child. _ _ _

RAP/NAP – People and Social Associations (Keep or Avoid)

1. Must spend more time with parents to learn more about myself as a newborn and the times around my birth and growing up. _ _ _ _ _ _ _ _

2. Speak more with my sister about childhood. _ _ _ _ _ _ _ _ _ _ _ _

RAP/NAP – Weaknesses (Remove or Convert to Strengths)

1. I must face my reality of being and discover my purpose. _ _ _ _ _ _

2. I must commit time to act and connect within to build confidence. _

3. I am grown up but its good to learn what I was like as a child. _ _ _

RAP/NAP – Strengths and Behaviours (Build and Strengthen)

1. I must behave like a child while with my parents to get more stories out of their memories to get more clues of my natural being. _ _ _ _ _ _ _ _ _ _

2. I am grown up but its good to learn what I was like as a child. _ _ _ _

3. Think deep into those stories to find meaning in my life. _ _ _ _ _ _ _

STEPS TO SUCCESS – using Walk your Thoughts technique

1. Read this CAP everyday about 15 minutes. _ _ _ _ _ _ _ _ _ _ _ _ _ ☐
2. Ask parents and learn about life and circumstances in those days. _ _ ☐
3. Ask and learn about any special or non-ordinary happenings. _ _ _ _ ☐
4. Write them down and assess for picking my own natural attributes. _ ☐
5. Read them everyday until feeling a strong connection within. _ _ _ _ ☐
6. Learn about natural abilities and behaviours to know thy self. _ _ _ ☐
7. Think deeper into the happenings to find their meaning in my life. _ ☐

> ## 11. <u>Sync with Master and Aspect Action Plan (MAP/AAP)-</u>
>
> The last and final step of this process is to **transfer** this clarified **Goal, Target Completion Timeframe** and place it as a Goal under the Aspect Action Plan of the identified Aspect of life.
>
> **Link** this CAP using a **Plan Number** - "My Existence Goal 2".

You may decide to just Know Thy Self with one goal but the above two are examples for you to get the hang of the tool and start designing your MAP of life. Once you are done with knowing yourself within, you must now create an "**I Am _ _ _ _ _ _ _ _**" statement to read and connect within regularly. **You must see, visit and meet yourself everyday to build confidence and impress your true self upon your mind everyday.** After creating the "I Am ____" statement, we will look at other aspects of life that exist because you exist.

Your "**I Am _ _ _ _ _ _ _ _**" statement must comprise of below

1. **Your name** and feel free to add a tag line to your name if you wish to. Someone I heard liked to call himself as David Miller the Problem Killer, you can have something that touches your heart for who you are at the core of your heart or what you want to be.
2. **Affirm your believe in your Heart and Soul** to be your eternal guides.
3. **List your natural talents and skills,** they are your natural attributes you are born with. Bring them on top and remind yourself everyday what your strengths are.
4. **List your heartily desire for what you want to become** as a person in this world, in the world around you that gives you the satisfaction to fulfil what you have recognised as a purpose of your life.
5. **List clearly, the purpose you have recognised for your life.**
6. **Affirm Your belief, Commit to your purpose in Harmony with the Universe.**
7. **Commit to doing whatever it takes to achieve your purpose.**

****

"I Am" Statement

****

I am _

(name, you can add a tag line if you like i.e. David Miller the problem killer).

I believe in my heart and soul to be my eternal guides on this planet.

I am born with Natural Attributes & Skills of _ _ _ _ _ _ _ _ _ _ _ _ _ _
_ _
_ _
_ _

My Heart and Soul desire to _
_ _
_ **so I can fulfil the purpose of my life.**

The Purpose of my Life is to _
_ _
_ _
_ _

I believe in my purpose of life and will do everything it takes to fulfil that Purpose and spread Love, Peace and Harmony that Supreme God intended.

I will pursue and take every action to achieve my goals to achieve my purpose of life.

****

Once you have created the above statement, Sync it with Master Action Plan under Your Existence part. **This becomes your very first page as you open the MAP** of your life. You must read this as positive affirmation along with the ones given on the next page or of your choice.

Positive Affirmations – As we have learned with scientific evidences that such techniques do work. We can use positive affirmations to help bring our energy vibrations to the levels where it will not only impress the courage, and confidence upon our mind but also help us heal our body, help in attracting and manifesting what we may desire in our life.

Often sports people repeat the words such as 'I can Do it' to bring their concentration and energy together before having a go. We often see team members or leaders saying 'You Can Do it' or 'Come on guys we can Do this' in various environments. People have repeatedly used **affirmations to create confidence and achieve goals** in life. You can use these affirmations too, to build your inner strength, to find that inner peace within yourself and realise your eternal strength. Below are some affirmations to use while you read your "I am" statement.

The world and Internet is flooded out there with the amount of positive affirmations that you can use for various circumstances and aspects in life. I have provided some examples below with a point of view of getting started with positively creating the change in life. No matter how many affirmations you may find, but no one else can ever know what exact words will work for you. What I would advise you do is to **create a set of your own positive affirmations** that will work for you. By being in contact with your inner self, you by now know what words will help you lift up and above the muddy puddle. You should be able to take clues from your assessments with the 'The Karmic Rewind Tool' and design your own affirmations. If not, then definitely make use of the ones given below and any other you may find floating around you to fit your desired outcome. The ones below are purposefully put in that order.

Examples of Affirmations

For Acceptance to be able to move forward

1. <u>Acceptance:</u> I accept who I was born as.
2. <u>Acceptance:</u> I accept that we are influenced beings.
3. <u>Acceptance:</u> I accept that my true potential and abilities have been affected by these influences.
4. <u>Acceptance:</u> I accept what has happened in my past.

For Accepting the Change

5. <u>Change:</u> I am ready to accept the positive change in my life.
6. <u>Change:</u> I am ready to create the positive change in my life.
7. <u>Change:</u> I am accepting the positive change in my life.
8. <u>Change:</u> I am surrounded with positive influences in my life.
9. <u>Change:</u> I am taking action to create positive change in my life.

For knowing the spiritual self

10. <u>Spirituality:</u> I am part of the supreme source of life (God) who is the source of all abundance.

For being grateful for present to receive grateful future

11. <u>Gratitude:</u> I am Grateful for having the chance to be able to change my life for the way I want to live with Love, Peace & Harmony.
12. <u>Gratitude:</u> I am Grateful for my life and all that exists for its existence.

For Minding your Mind

13. <u>Mind:</u> I am in full control of my Mind and Thoughts.
14. <u>Mind:</u> I am channelising my energy towards positive goals.
15. <u>Mind:</u> My mind is filled with positively supporting thoughts and beliefs.

For Peaceful & Healthy Living

16. <u>Peace:</u> I have a very Peaceful and Loving Atmosphere at my home and wherever I go.
17. <u>Health:</u> I am surrounded by healthy atmosphere and have a healthy body and healthy mind.
18. <u>Health:</u> The nature is healing me physically and mentally.
19. <u>Health:</u> I am following healthy diet and exercise.

For Happier Relationships

20. <u>Relationships:</u> I am surrounded by Happy, Like Minded, Sincere, Faithful and Supportive People.
21. <u>Relationships:</u> My family is very supportive of my goals.
22. <u>Relationships:</u> All our family members love and support each other.

For attracting Abundance

23. <u>Abundance:</u> I am attracting everything I love, in my life.
24. <u>Abundance:</u> I am like a magnet and am pulling Happiness, Prosperity, Money and Abundance towards me.
25. <u>Abundance:</u> I am attracting everything I need to fulfil the purpose of my life.

Create Your Own Affirmations

Once you have created your set of affirmations, transfer them to your MAP along with Your 'I Am' Statement.

1. _____
2. _____
3. _____
4. _____
5. _____
6. _____
7. _____
8. _____
9. _____
10. _____
11. _____
12. _____
13. _____
14. _____
15. _____
16. _____
17. _____
18. _____
19. _____
20. _____

Step 2 – Identify and Plan for All Aspects of Your Life

Once you have well connected within with your core existence and rejuvenated strength in who you are at your core, it's time to tackle the world and life around you. Everyone will have their own aspect priorities and goals in life. Hopefully by now you have already started to think along realising and revising your priorities in life. I will exemplify in this section through my priorities as they are. We will use The Karmic Rewind Tool for each aspect and look at how to use this tool to filter out what we need to get rid of, consolidate, build upon what we have, and would help us reach, realise and enjoy that goal of life sooner.

It always helps to put your life story together relating to an aspect of life. I call this your **life's Aspect Story**. Nothing is to be ignored as minor issues or minor negligible details while writing the story. It will take you back to the past and help you dig deeper so you identify the deeper strengths as well as any weaknesses or malfunctions and enable yourself to perform the revival maintenance better. This is the way to thoroughly clean and rebuild the mindset, the thoughts, the beliefs, the habits, the talent and abilities so we can **rewind well to revive and relive well** with the power of Karma to live our life for what it was meant to be lived for.

At the top level remains the Master Action Plan, which is a combined portfolio of realisation of your existence and identified aspects of your life. Each identified Aspect will have an Aspect Story and an Aspect Action Plan (AAP). The goals will be identified under each AAP and will be referred to as Aspect Goals. But remember that to establish the Aspect Goals clearly, we need the attributes from CAP, which is created using RAPs or NAPs in the tool. So the detailed work here is done using the rewind, revive, relive steps of The Karmic Rewind Tool and then to be fed back to the AAP and MAP of your life.

Just know that the priority of an aspect is not necessarily the weight of importance as well. They are all important aspects of life but what you may trade for the other at times is where priorities will play their part. Let's put it all together so we can start to create better – better life, better environment, and better world. Let's create the better for not only us, for all those who are associated with us in any shape or form via whichever means. Let's get started.

ASPECT – MY SPIRITUAL LIFE

Priority – 1

Aspect Story - MY SPIRITUAL LIFE

I have always been in touch with spirituality since my childhood, and probably my birth but obviously our memory only goes as far and to rare occurrences only for those times of life. I find a very peaceful and content feeling with spirituality. All that we take in during the early years of our life does influence the whole life of ours. I believe that a child when born and till next few years is like a raw computer memory where you start feeding all the data into their brain, obviously ignoring the re-incarnation memories as is the case with most of us. They cannot speak to express them so all their concentration and attention is on taking in all that they see and hear, the behaviours and actions they see around them. That is where the influence begins and that is why I call us humans to be influenced beings. That is why it is very important what environment you create around your kids as this has a direct impact on them.

My parents told me that when we were little young they never called our elder sister by name, as it was not regarded being respectful to call people by names who were elder than you, specially people you know and are related to you. Though, it is ok to call by name to those who are younger than you, this is not a rule as such but is a practice for more noble behaviours in Indian culture. So they always called her by the linguistic name for elder sister that is 'Didi' (Didi – means elder Sister in Hindi), and since we were always used to her being called Didi, we just always called her Didi as well. Yet I know some other families where they did not take up such value in their behaviours and in those families it is quite common and normal to call elderly by their names as is in the western world.

What I mean to convey here is that our brain is affected and conditioned by the circumstances we are living in, and when you compare that to western culture, it is preferred that everybody is addressed by their names, and often the word Sir or Madam is used to show respect. Again there is no right and wrong ways about living life from such a point of view; it's all about what you feel happy with, while maintaining the respect for others around you.

And since my parents were that cautious of the environment they provided us with, I believe it also led them to ensure that a touch of spirituality was always included in our daily routines. I still remember that our daily routine (in late 1980s and early 90s) would always start with some spirituality related prayers being played on the stereo every day. My mother played a large and important part in this, as she not only did this every morning but also in the evenings. And every evening when we would come home from school, have our meals and some rest, she got us to have a quick wash of faces just to get us freshen up a little, and got us to repeat a particular part of the prayer, referred to as Five Podian from the Book of Sikh Religion called 'Sri Guru Granth Sahib Ji'. She was not really a staunch practitioner of Sikh religion, neither was my father who still does wear a turban. But they had discovered this path of humanity, the path of spirituality, the path of meditation that was neutral to all as human beings and no discrimination against any other religion. The stream of practices they followed was never termed as religion, but a way of life, using the teachings of saints and mystics from all over the world and all religions.

When I asked my mum one-day, that why she does all those prayers related to Sikh religion even though my mum and dad both had initiation from the spiritual master we were following? I was told that one reason is because this had formed the bases of her spiritual behaviour since she was a child, and YES I probably did look at her as if questioning her truth that as if she was really a child once (Mums can never be child to their children until they understand how the growth procedure works) and I laughed when my daughter once raised the same question, saying Dads can never be small kids, as we appear to be as all grown-ups to our kids, and this is how they see us since they were born.

So, when she said that they had this Sikh temple close by their home and they use to go to temple really early in the mornings. Waking up early is still considered a really good practice as early morning is the best time and a bit of a quiet time too for meditation and prayers to God; before the whole world wakes up and starts off all the noisy business. Since then, it had become a practice of her to do this as daily routine. Now that habit, till this day is embedded so strongly into her mind that if she doesn't do it, she feels that something very important of her life is missing. This gave her a very peaceful feeling inside always and she called this routine the food for her soul. Although a little differently, but so it became a habit for me too as I grew up. The drowning incident, being declared medically dead and reviving played a part too.

Again that proves a point how the conditioning of our mind works with the influences of our environment, and how they can take up the form of a lifetime routine, a permanent roll in our lives. And because I was and always have been living in such an environment every day including our Sunday spiritual gatherings at a huge hall with numerous people, I am also in a constant touch with the spiritual belief of truth of human life and beings. No matter what I do, I try my best to incorporate those practices into my daily life. It is with that community as well that I learned a lot about respecting everything we have in life. That is where I learned to participate in volunteer activities, which have a very deep meaning and role in moulding our lives. It gives us a sense of responsibility as a human being towards all other forms of life and human life itself on this planet. It teaches us some real great lessons of life. It helps us to realise that living for our own self is not the only purpose of life; it's about living together while helping each other.

When you look at a larger scale that is what the countries are doing too in their own identity and capacity. The set up of the Human Rights Commissions, the Red Cross society, the United Nations, along with a lot of other smaller and local organisations in all parts of the world are examples of a common respect for all. My uttermost respect goes to those organisations and people who are participating in those activities with their true hearts and marvellous efforts of volunteers. That is why I feel the responsibility to be able to do whatever I can in my capacity with the grace of the God to help those around me in any kind of support I can provide. That is one part of my natural behaviour, which I pray to lord every day to nourish.

Spirituality gives you the ultimate sense of belonging, sense of the cosmic wonders within and helps to realise the ultimate power of being human. For me the Spirituality is my prime concern. I try to do my best to abide by the promises I made towards my spiritual life and seek guidance and assistance from our teacher, our master on that path. This is what you have to realise, what is the higher most priority of your life and why it is so. Once you know the strongest Why, you will be able to figure out, how you got to that priority being the number one in your life. And since you have the kind of ingredients of the situation, You will very well know how to go about things in the future and which ingredient to avoid to get that disliked taste out of the recipe of your life. This is somewhat the aspect story; let's use the tool now.

This figure on next page is a hierarchical overview of how the Aspect Action Plans will look like. You will name the aspect of life first and write the statement that relates you to your happiness in this aspect. Then you will derive or create Goals that will help you achieve that happiness with the help of CAPs, which include RAPs or NAPs for that goal.

Spiritual Life (Overview map)

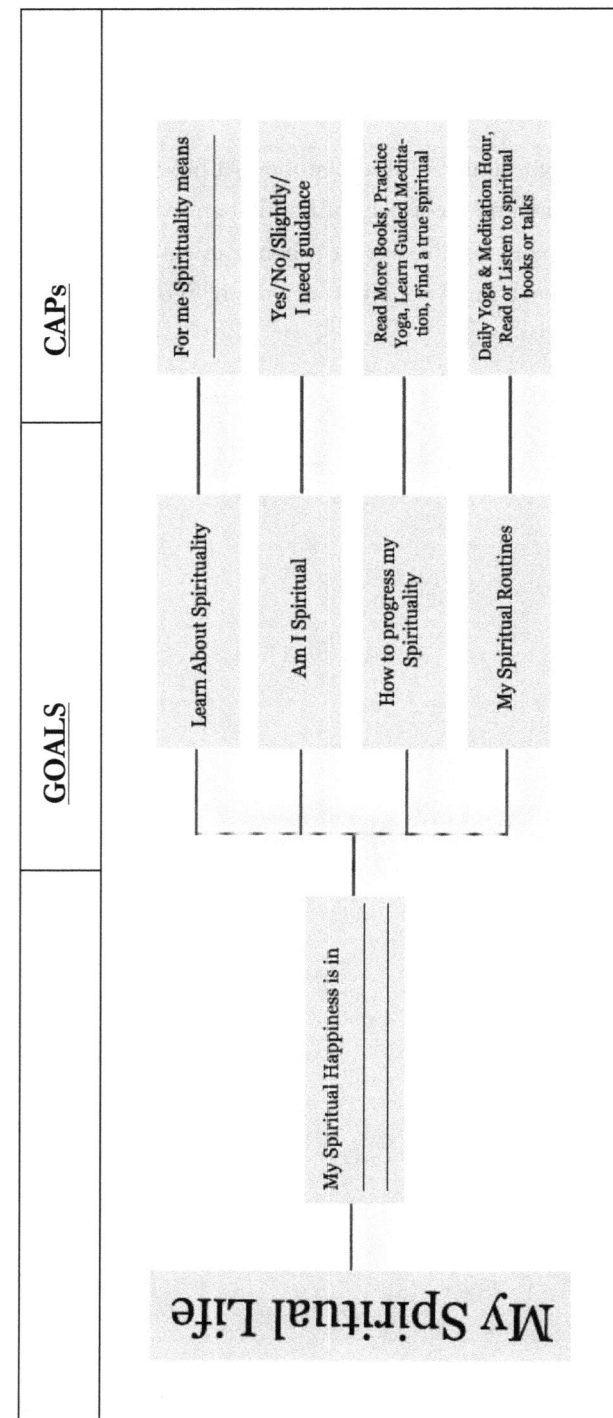

GOALS	CAPs
Learn About Spirituality	For me Spirituality means _____
Am I Spiritual	Yes/No/Slightly/ I need guidance
How to progress my Spirituality	Read More Books, Practice Yoga, Learn Guided Meditation, Find a true spiritual
My Spiritual Routines	Daily Yoga & Meditation Hour, Read or Listen to spiritual books or talks

My Spiritual Happiness is in _____

My Spiritual Life

Note: Once you are working within an aspect AAP, the Immediate connecting boxes will always be your Goals in the aspect of life you are assessing. Your Goals will then be connected to your Comprehensive Action Plans (CAPs), which is made up of your steps to take along with Revival Action Plans (RAPs) or Newborn Action Plans (NAPs).

ASPECT ACTION PLAN

1. **My Aspect** – Spiritual Life
2. **Aspect Priority Rank** – (1)
3. **Happiness Statement** –
   My Spiritual Happiness is in maintaining a calm and peaceful environment around me at all times to help replicate that within by meditating for a given time everyday.

---

4. **Goals** (Add as many as needed, be specific)
   It is now time to identify the goals that will help you achieve your happiness. Note that initially you may not be very clear about the goal. You **must now use The Karmic Rewind Tool** and establish all that is needed to be transferred here in the AAP.

Goal – 1   Priority (1)

Specific Goal - Meditate daily for two and a half hours minimum.

Target Completion Timeframe –

   Achieve By Date – 31 /12 /2018   By _ _ am/pm

   Notes: _

   _

Plan Number – Spiritual Life Goal 1 | Created - ☐   Page No. ____

Note: Mark your Plan number at the top of The Karmic Rewind Tool to keep proper references.

Happiness Score on achievement - ♡ ♡ ♡ ♡ ♡ ♡ ♡ ♡ ♡

THE KARMIC REWIND TOOL

REWIND | REVIVE | RELIVE

Plan Number – Spiritual Life Goal 1

Area of Priority- **SPIRITUAL LIFE** Goal Priority (**1**)

I would love it if – I can **Meditate daily for two and a half hours minimum.**

REWIND stage

1. Where Am I currently in this area of life or on the path to achieve this goal?

Currently in this aspect of my life I give my best to practice meditation everyday along with living by the principals I have been given to follow.

2. How did I reach here? What decisions played a role?

I initially followed the guidance from my family and then have taken Initiation from a spiritual master. I had developed the love and respect for the spiritual way of life, which I was always associated with and learned a lot from. I personally became very fond of this way of life that was all about learning and practicing something that is "Good for me and Good for all".

There were some basic requirements to get Initiation, which had me waiting till a certain age before I could get the Initiation to start my journey on the path of eternal realisation. As soon as I reached that age I wanted to get initiation. So, I did not waste any time to start on that path within from the moment I was considered eligible to start meditating with the special Mantras given by the spiritual Master.

3. Why I made the choice-

Decision	Reason
1. Listen to spiritual discourses or speeches to learn and practice meditation.	Because it gave me a spiritual feel, a level of peace and contentment within.
2. Participate into volunteer activities with the associated spiritual organisation.	It kept me away from over indulgence into this world that primarily is the cause of the process of re-birth. My goal is to achieve Nirvana, Moksha, the freedom of soul.

4. What Caused Me to think or be convinced into making those choices?

The pain and sufferings that are never ending in this world. Being rich and successful is not the real solution. If it was then why we see a lot of celebrities and successful people end up in trouble of one sort or the other. Inner Peace is the only solution and that can only be gained by getting in touch with your spiritual essence. I have been there done that. I came from an average earnings family, living in a small rented apartment style dwelling. Then my dad bought a small house with the money he could afford, about an 800 square feet property. He later sold it for me to be able to go overseas and study to be able to make a better future.

I have been able to buy them a nice property in a peak performing area, which has given them a billionaire status now locally. But realised that money was not the solution to inner peace and happiness, neither for them nor for me. If you bind your happiness with materialistic possessions only, then there is a good risk that you may never be satisfied; sky is the limit knowing the potential and abilities of human kind.

That may be OK if that is all you want, but for getting in touch with the spirituality, you will need to develop a mind-frame which lets you achieve those materialistic goals but yet not fully be attached to them at all. That is the secret which gives you inner peace, and that is when everything else is possible too, as also is the concept used in the movie series Kung-Fu Panda, for the Panda warrior to conquer the final fight.

REVIVE stage

5. Beliefs That Played a Part

God exists, Soul exists, Eternal world exists, and There is a higher source to life where one can achieve Peace Forever.

Revival or Newborn Action Plan (RAP/NAP) -

Old Beliefs that need to be killed

None, I feel peace and contentment with these beliefs and will keep practicing to reach higher states of mind.

New Beliefs to Accomplish New Goal

1. **I can** devote more time and concentration to advance in meditation and spiritual life.

6. People who Influenced Decision

People: Parents, fellow followers, Spiritual Teacher, friends

I always had a choice. They showed me the way but no one ever forced me for this. That is just not the way of practice for the organisation I became part of. It always welcomes anyone to satisfy their intellect before starting to believe in the path. I just always had this feeling of deep inner peace being on this path that I had decided at very early age to be on this path and follow to the best I can. The incident of me drowning gave me even more urge to practice more and more on this path of spirituality, the path of meditation. My inner feelings of peace and happiness being on the path had influenced my decision. All this started with what my parents had practiced. So, I am thankful to them for showing me this way of life.

Revival or Newborn Action Plan (RAP/NAP) -

You should make use of the association assessment template provided in the tool. For me All are helpful in achieving my Goal; only avoid in-sensible arguments but not sensible discussions. Accompany more people, who are spiritually sound, learn more from whoever has a say on spirituality. Knowledge can be gained from anyone regardless of their age, race, country, and language. There is always room for improvement and doing better. So associating with as many like-minded people will help in progress. I must spend more time in volunteer activities to have similar minded people and groups around me.

Association Assessment – Not Applicable

7. Identify Your Weaknesses

Weaknesses – Not devoting as much of time as I would love to for meditation being busy with family, kids and studying.

Revival or Newborn Action Plan (RAP/NAP) -

At-least spend 2.5 hours a day in meditation in any way possible. Find time in-between of doing anything else rather than chatting away time in time wasting activities.

8. Identify Your Strengths

My Strengths -

I do keep myself conscious of spiritual values at all times. This keeps my concentration in subconscious mind towards the meditation and makes it easier to withdraw mind when you sit in meditation.

Revival or Newborn Action Plan (RAP/NAP) -

Consistently remind myself to continue doing this in all decisions and actions I face in life.

Behavioural Strengths –

Patience and Love for spirituality

Revival or Newborn Action Plan (RAP/NAP) -

Find time in-between of doing meditation rather than chatting away time in time wasting activities. Find more quiet time.

9. YOUR GOAL – with Clear vision

Goal – Meditate Daily for 2.5 hrs. Minimum.

Target Completion Timeframe

Achieve By Date - 31 / 12 / 2018   By _ _ _ _ am/pm

Notes: Review every Sunday. _ _ _ _ _ _ _ _ _ _ _ _ _ _ _ _ _ _

RELIVE – stage

10. Comprehensive Action Plan (CAP)-

Goal – Meditate Daily for 2.5 hrs. minimum.

Target Completion Timeframe

Achieve By Date - 31 / 12 / 2018   By _ _ _ _ am/pm

Notes: Review every Sunday. _ _ _ _ _ _ _ _ _ _ _ _ _ _ _ _ _ _

Revival Action Plans (RAP) or New Action Plans (NLPs) to be aware of –

RAP/NAP – Beliefs (Impress Positive and New Beliefs in Mind)

1. **I can** devote more time and concentration to advance in meditation and spiritual life.

RAP/NAP – People and Social Associations (Keep or Avoid)

1. You should make use of the association assessment template provided in the tool.

2. I must spend more time in volunteer activities to have similar minded people and groups around me.

RAP/NAP – Weaknesses (Remove or Convert to Strengths)

1. At-least spend 2.5 hours a day in meditation in any way possible. Find time in-between of doing anything else rather than chatting away time in time wasting activities.

2. _

RAP/NAP – Strengths and Behaviours (Build and Strengthen)

1. Consistently remind myself to continue to be conscious of spiritual values at all times in all decisions and actions I face.

2. Find time in-between of doing anything else rather than chatting away time in time wasting activities.

3. Find more quiet time.

STEPS TO SUCCESS – using Walk your Thoughts technique

1. I will read this CAP for 5 minutes every day. _ _ _ _ _ _ _ _ _ _ _

2. Everyday remind myself to continue to be conscious of the spiritual values at all times in all decisions and actions I face. _ _ _ _ _ _ _ _ _ _ _ _ _ ☐

3. Have picture of spiritual guru to remind of staying connected with our spiritual self through his/her teachings. _ _ _ _ _ _ _ _ _ _ _ _ _ _ _ _ _ ☐

4. Find time in-between of doing anything else rather than chatting away time in time wasting activities. _ ☐

5. Sleep at 9pm. _ ☐

6. Set 4 am alarm to wake up and have quiet time for meditation. _ _ _ ☐

7. Increase 10 minutes weekly for meditation sitting time. _ _ _ _ _ _ _ _ ☐

8. Use time tracker or diary to keep note of time spent daily. _ _ _ _ _ ☐

9. Review daily-spent meditation time every Sunday. _ _ _ _ _ _ _ _ _ ☐

10. _ ☐

11. Sync with Master and Aspect Action Plan (MAP/AAP)-

The last and final step of this process is to transfer this Goal, Target Completion Timeframe and insert this CAP to the **AAP of your Spiritual life**. Place it as a Goal under the Spirituality Aspect of life.

Link this CAP using a **Plan Number** - "Spiritual Life Goal 1".

ASPECT – MY RELATIONSHIPS

Priority - 2

I am going to use relationships aspect as an example of how one primary aspect may be broken down into subcategories. You may have two or more subcategories such as personal, social and professional relationships and still work on them as major aspects of life. I will emphasise on also developing and nurturing a kind of **relationship you may not even have thought of**, and that is the relationship of **your physical being with your spiritual being**. Think about it and develop it well, nurture it well and the happiness will start to flow in all other relationships.

Whether you wish to work with subcategories of aspects or all identified aspects as primary aspects is entirely your choice. It's all about providing you with a framework to work within a flexible way as it suits you. It's your life and your priorities; you will give them required weight as per your choice while taking clues from examples here. As per the figure on the next page, you could work with this aspect in below manner.

1. Identify all types of relationships you may think of and create them as a sub-aspect under the primary aspect of My Relationships. For example Personal, Social and Professional relationships are all sub-aspects of the primary aspect My Relationships.

2. Now you will work with one sub-aspect and identify your relationship with all concerned persons relating to that aspect. For example when working on your personal relationships, you would identify your relationship with your mother or father or wife or children individually. With this identification, that particular relationship will either become your goal under personal relationships or become your sub-aspect to work on. How you categorise this part of hierarchy is completely your choice. So you will be working with a **goal "Improve my relationship with my father"** or a **sub-aspect of "My relationship with my Father"** and then set a goal you want to achieve in that relationship. Apply whatever works for you.

3. Once you have identified the goal or a sub-aspect, identify what will make you happy with that aspect. When you work with "Personal Relationships" or others as your sub-aspect, you will come up with a **happiness statement** for each one of those. You may also have each individual relationship identified as a **sub-aspect**, even for all identified people your relationship should improve with to be happy; write what will make you happy in that relationship and **set goals** in Aspect Action Plan. I am going to give an example using an overall perspective only so you can get the idea of the framework.

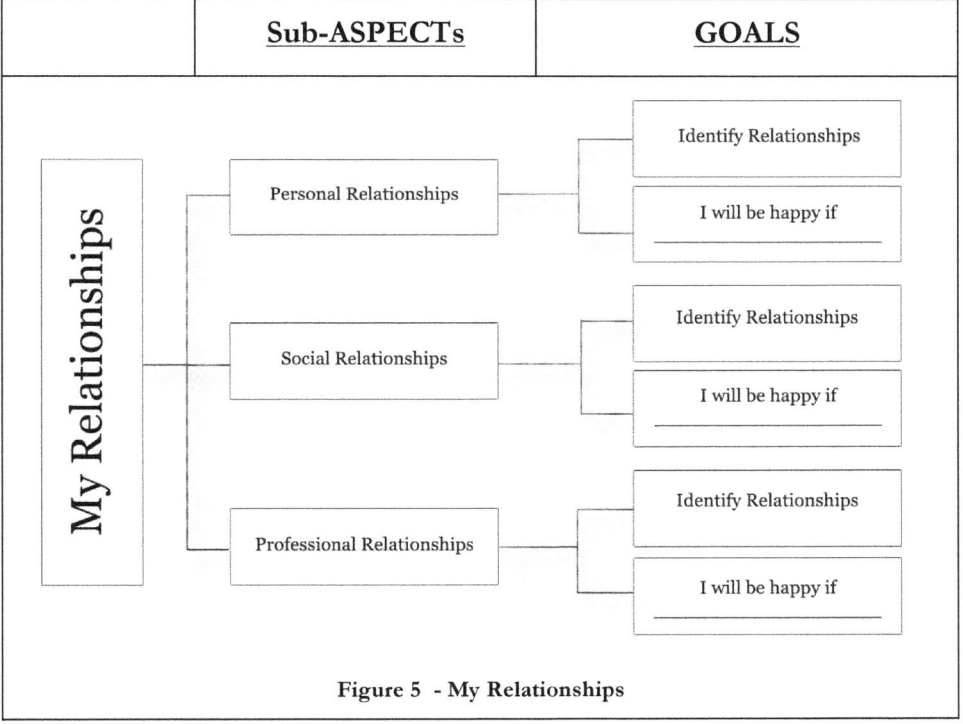

Figure 5 - My Relationships

Note: Once you are working within an aspect or Sub-Aspect AAP, the Immediate connecting boxes will always be your Goals in the aspect of life you are assessing. Your Goals will then be connected to your Comprehensive Action Plans (CAPs), which is made up of your steps to take along with Revival Action Plans (RAPs) or Newborn Action Plans (NAPs).

Aspect Story - My Personal Relationships

To me the personal life is very important factor in maintaining my First Priority. I am happily married with a loving and supportive wife and we have now two beautiful daughters. Our wedding was a family decision and we both agreed to get married as well. We both shared the similar spiritual beliefs so that would also be a great support for my first priority. Personal life plays a very important role in reaching the goals you want to achieve. Sometimes it also helps you in defining your goals for the love of your family members. As discussed all through this book, the environment you live in or create is very important to help you achieve your goals. My prime goal being the spirituality, it is very important for one to maintain the peace of mind all the time. Sometimes there could be very little things that can have a disturbing effect on your peace of mind, and that is what I do not want. And your personal life and relationships play a key role in living a peaceful and happy life.

And that is the reason why my personal life is so important to me to be able to create an environment that would help me make progress in my spiritual life. But, does everyone always get perfect circumstances though? Probably very few and others need to create it, once they have identified the need and have that will power. I tried my best to make sure everyone in family was covered for the basics in all senses and that should create the perfect platform for me to take next steps. I weathered few storms to ensure that. But it always came to them coming up with more demands thinking I had none of my own. After all that is how I had always treated them, putting their demands always before even my own needs.

I couldn't let that go on as I needed to revive myself to propel better the boat of life. Learned the lesson that they were not going to stop asking for more. Why should they, but the only issue was I was the primary provider. Doing what I was doing, I would have only burnt out myself with no one else looking to share the load but only becoming the load. Some didn't like it when I turned the emphasis back on me. I made sure that they had no problems meeting their needs but not demands while creating a platform for me to now take next steps to make bigger moves. I felt like a young horse who'll damage his feet because he started to run the race early and without even having the horseshoe on. I had to ensure to give myself a break, revive myself and equip myself with the required to carry on before I damage myself further.

Now after a few waves, things have calmed down a bit as they have started to understand and somewhat see the real picture behind my plans. I had to develop the habit of ignoring their reactions for some time as it only fed their desires and not mine. But this has successfully worked and I've realised a lot about me providing reliance for most of their needs rather than enabling them to cater for their own.

Now that I have brought back the calm again, I must give my best to what I attempt to do, and to be able to achieve that best performance; one needs to have much better control over mind and nerves. And if one has that supportive environment at home, the peace and support in your personal life from the closest people you care about and associate with, one will have all the courage to give their best shot at anything they do with love and passion.

ASPECT ACTION PLAN

1. My Aspect – Personal Relationships
2. Aspect Priority Rank – (2)
3. Happiness Statement –
   My personal relationships happiness is in ensuring everyone understands and work towards their purpose in life and are covered for all the basics and faces no harsh circumstances in life. _ _ _ _ _
   _
4. **Goals** (Add as many as needed, be specific)
   It is now time to identify the goals that will help you achieve your happiness. Note that initially you may not be very clear about the goal. You **must now use The Karmic Rewind Tool** and establish all that is needed to be transferred here in the AAP.

Goal – 1   **Priority (1)**

Specific Goal - Spend 2 hours daily with kids, parents and wife together.

Target Completion Timeframe –

    Achieve By Date - 31 /01 /2018   By _ _ am/pm

    Notes: Not Applicable, Review Monthly. _ _ _ _ _ _ _ _ _ _ _ _

Plan Number – Rel. Personal Goal 1 | Created - ☐ Page No. __

    Note: Mark your Plan number at the top of The Karmic Rewind Tool to keep proper references.

Happiness Score on achievement –

        ♡ ♡ ♡ ♡ ♡ ♡ ♡ ♡ ♡ ♡

THE KARMIC REWIND TOOL
REWIND | REVIVE | RELIVE
Plan Number – Rel. Personal Goal 1

Area of Priority- <u>Relationships (Personal)</u>   Goal Priority (<u>1</u>)

I would love it if – I can **spend more time with my whole family together.**

REWIND stage

1. Where Am I currently in this area of life or on the path to achieve this goal?

In my personal life. I am married, and we have two daughters. We are both high thinkers in life and at the same time deeply believe in spirituality and contentment. We try to do our best with goals in mind, yet not be attached with the outcomes. That is why we have maintained a very balanced approach to life in general, which is very important in creating and maintaining a peaceful and loving atmosphere at home. Things do get a bit whacky with little children at home and as parents grow older, but we manage with sincere discussions rather than heated arguments.

2. How did I reach here? What decisions played a role?

In my early twenties. I had realised the kind of life I wanted live, the kind of atmosphere I wanted to live in, which will help me on my spiritual path. It was obviously important to have a partner who shared similar idea about life.

It was when the first time we met with both sides of the family. We were given a chance to talk to each other and discuss anything if we wanted to. It was after that discussion that we found we shared common grounds of spirituality and ethics in life. We decided that we both were fine with this arranged marriage. We got married in very traditional way as an Indian wedding could be. Since then we had two daughters. Sometimes due to commitments, I don't get to spend much time with all family members together.

3. Why I made the choice-

It was a marriage arranged by our parents. Both sides of the family knew each other from the times when we were just born. Who knows if they had thought of it back then? But We only found out not so long ago before we got engaged. With family expansion comes more responsibility, which takes it's toll on time you have on hands to spend with your loved ones.

Decision	**Reason**
1. Thought about getting married.	Our parents had arranged this proposal.
2. Agreed to become life partners.	Everything that we both wanted as a partner in life, we believed we had found in each other. We discussed few things but nothing was an issue really. We both enjoy the same beliefs in spirituality and share same ideas on life.
3. Get busy with learning more and write a book	I had to push for the goals I wanted to achieve in life and that took family time away.

4. What Caused Me to think or be convinced into making those choices?

I had always seen arranged marriages being more successful and India I believe still has the lowest divorce rates. There was always more family support to resolve any issues if they ever arise. I also believed that both of us sharing similar beliefs would also help in maintaining the kind of atmosphere I wanted at home. With expansion in family comes more financial responsibility as well. I couldn't keep pushing myself onto the road I didn't want to travel. To change roads, I had to start making extra effort while still providing for everybody. That takes extra effort and time. Effort I loved but not the family time lost, but that was the sacrifice needed.

5. Beliefs That Played a Part

1. We need to maintain peace and harmony as much as possible to be in touch with our spiritual being.
2. Soul mates are decided to be together in heavens and do meet up on this planet.
3. I believe that in arrange marriages there is a more sense of responsibility towards the relationship than the Love-Marriages. That is also due to the family involvement in the decision.
4. There is a good chance that an arranged marriage can develop real love between the couple, but relationships based on Love and no marriage is fragile at any time. (I do not intend to say that Love marriages are not successful. I have seen a lot of successful examples in my close associations).
5. After marriage and kids the family expands, more time is needed to be spent on work to earn more to provide for everyone's needs.

Old Beliefs that need to be killed - None

Revival or Newborn Action Plan (RAP/NAP) -

New Beliefs to Accomplish New Goal

1. We can always work smarter and find time to spend with our family.
2. I can devote more time with my daughters in teaching them all I can, more importantly patience and guidance on spirituality. Her being in touch with these aspects will make impressions in her heart and mind, which will make her a better human being.

6. People who Influenced Decision

People: I guess it's the age and when your parents tell you that I think it's about time you get married. The culture we lived in, We cannot go to our parents and say, I think it's time I should get married. It's more like creating those conversations in a bit of a cheeky way before you could use that approach with your parents. And often parents are okay with that in this modern age. But in our case, it was our parents who talked to us about the proposals. I guess, the prime factor was parents, and then the mutual beliefs and views on life that we shared had influenced the decision.

It was also what I saw happening around me ever since I was a child, that one needs to work more hours and harder to feed the family. But you loose touch with your family when you don't see them and not connect well with them. That's when I had to seek knowledge about people who did everything with a lot of time on their hands. I had to look at the options of working smarter and not longer hours.

Revival or Newborn Action Plan (RAP/NAP) -

I must continue to pursue my purpose in life and goals to live life with balance. For that I must keep company of people who feed confidence and support to my purpose and balance in life.

(You may think of people who can help you resolve certain issues or think of people who should be avoided, who may not be helping you move towards happier relationship but keep adding bitterness.)

Association Assessment – Not Applicable

7. Identify Your Weaknesses

Weaknesses – I cannot stop thinking, researching and planning towards my goals. It's hard to get me off my computer when I am immersed in my work. Once I am on to it, I hate being disturbed but do put up with it using my patience stock. I need quiet and noise free environment to work in, which is a struggle when working from home. I do not enjoy loud behaviours all day along. Something I had to get use to since we have kids. Now we have our TV running for a lot more hours than Me and My wife both prefer to watch. I have developed more patience now.

Revival or Newborn Action Plan (RAP/NAP) -

1. Plan a set time to call it a day in the evening to spend time with family.
2. Get kids busy in activities other than TV when working and if possible.
3. Take regular breaks; listen to meditational or instrumental music with earphones hooked on to overrule the noises.

8. Identify Your Strengths

My Strengths -

Love, Care, Respect, Patience and co-operation.

Revival or Newborn Action Plan (RAP/NAP) -

Keep improving with time, experience and practice.

Behavioural Strengths –

I always behave in a calm manner regardless of the issue. It's only very rarely that I will get agitated but a smile will always do the trick. My patience bar is really high. I control my emotions very well.

Revival or Newborn Action Plan (RAP/NAP) -

Keep improving with time, experience and practice.

9. YOUR GOAL – with Clear vision

Goal – Spend 2 hours daily with kids, parents and wife together.

Target Completion Timeframe

Achieve By Date - 31 / 12 / 2018   By _ _ _ _ am/pm

Notes: Not applicable, Review Monthly.

RELIVE – stage

10. Comprehensive Action Plan (CAP)-

Goal – Spend 2 hours family time daily with kids, parents and wife together.

Target Completion Timeframe

    Achieve By Date - 31 / 12 / 2018   By _ _ _ _ am/pm

    Notes: Review every month end. _ _ _ _ _ _ _ _ _ _ _ _ _ _ _ _ _ _

Revival Action Plans (RAP) or New Action Plans (NLPs) to be aware of –

RAP/NAP – Beliefs (Impress Positive and New Beliefs in Mind)

1. We can always work smarter and find time to spend with our family.
2. Kids can learn more than we think.
3. _

RAP/NAP – People and Social Associations (Keep or Avoid)

1. When out of home, spend less time in unnecessary activities.
2. _

RAP/NAP – Weaknesses (Remove or Convert to Strengths)

1. Plan a set time to call it a day in the evening to spend time with family.
2. Get kids busy in other activities than television when possible.
3. Listen to my own meditational or instrumental music with earphones hooked on.

RAP/NAP – Strengths and Behaviours (Build and Strengthen)

1. Keep improving on Love, Care, Respect, Patience and co-operation with time.

STEPS TO SUCCESS – using Walk your Thoughts technique

1. I will read this CAP for 5 minutes every day. _ _ _ _ _ _ _ _ _ _ _ _
2. Set a definite finish time in the evening. _ _ _ _ _ _ _ _ _ _ _ _ _ _ ☐
3. Everyday remind myself to continue to be conscious of the spiritual values at all times in all family matters that I face. _ _ _ _ _ _ _ _ _ _ ☐
4. Have picture frames of our family in my office and home. _ _ _ _ _ _ ☐
5. Have more conversations with my wife/parents in-between breaks. _ ☐
6. Share more stories and experiences with family daily. _ _ _ _ _ _ _ _ ☐
7. Plan a holiday with all family members. _ _ _ _ _ _ _ _ _ _ _ _ _ _ ☐

11. Sync with Master and Aspect Action Plan (MAP/AAP)-

The last and final step of this process is to transfer this Goal, Target Completion Timeframe and insert this CAP to the **AAP of your Personal Relationships**. Place it as a Goal under the Personal Relationships Aspect of your life.

Link this CAP using a **Plan Number** - "Rel. Personal Goal 1".

ASPECT – MY HEALTH

Priority - 3

Aspect Story – My Health

I was generally an overall healthy guy. Always loved and wanted to be fit as I was a sports person from the school days. I started to play hockey for the school team from year 6 (year 1991) onwards. Captained and trained one of the Indian Hockey team captains Rajpal Singh as our junior in school team. Wanted to make it to a big stage somewhere but that didn't happen due to typical Indian parenting of pushing studies over sports.

Coming from sports background, my appetite was always big. When reached Australia in 1997, I weighed only about 65 kg at 18 years of age. Early days, it was hard to get use to the outside eating all the time but got use to it in some time. Finding purely vegetarian food was challenging in the start but slowly worked out the places and what to ask for. One Veggie burger at Hungry Jacks was never enough and it had to be more than one pizza to have my hunger satisfied. It didn't take me long to start piling up kilos and in about two years or so, I was touching over and above the 90 kg mark on the scales.

It was one of those days at my usual security patrol job, passing through the basement of a shopping plaza, I saw the weighing scale, checked my weight and it went over 101 kg. It was that day in year 2000 that I decided that something had to change. But soon I was to be struck by an accident that did my back and hurt my leg quite badly. I had to drag with that for a number of years and slowly started pulling myself back together. It wasn't until sometime in 2004 I think when I got myself back to walking a bit. Slowly I started to do jogging and there on built up some stamina while carefully watching the back, kept it intact.

I needed to badly loose weight to save my back as well. I went hard on restricting my diet. No more soft drinks, no more sweet stuff and completely avoiding stomach full of food. I only ate a little bit before going to the gym so I wouldn't faint. Every day I didn't feel like going and giving myself some rest but I pushed myself. I told myself in my head "buddy lets make it today and worry about the rest tomorrow" consistently every day, I pushed myself for seven weeks and there I was. Seven weeks later, fit with muscles popping out on biceps, chest back in its V shape, tummy tucked in. I never feel like wearing paint with shirt tucked in if my tummy is hanging out. I felt confident that day onwards when the scale showed 81 kg on it from over 95 kg about seven weeks ago.

I still remember one day this guy walked up to me and asked what I was working on that day. I didn't know really what to say because I was working as hell without a plan and on a bit of everything every day to get my fitness back. I was spending at least one hour and forty-five minutes plus the walk to and from the gym spending over two hours in total every day. Here's what I did every day for seven weeks of losing weight.

1. I walked to and from the gym a bit over 10 minutes one-way, so I would already be warmed up when I get there.
2. Spent about half an hour on cross-trainer machine to get simultaneous workout on my legs and arms plus shoulder/chest areas to shake off some fat.
3. Hit the weight machines to do three sets of fifteen to work on shoulders, chest, back, biceps, triceps and legs.
4. Slowly increasing the weight in first three weeks and a little faster in the next four weeks.
5. Then ten minutes light treadmill walk just before walking back home.
6. Add another ten or so minutes while walking back home pulling myself together in that tired body. This got easier after about second week.

All that hard work done in 2004, paid off for some time. Didn't quite join the gym but watched my diet and routine walks and jogging kept me fine for some time. It was a couple of years after I got married that the home-made rich food started to show up in the form of fat again. In year 2007, I got a big shock when a dream I wanted to achieve shattered in the hands of a medical condition.

I wanted to become an Air-Force pilot as plan A, this was in 2004 after I gained back my fitness. I was ready to start my life with a bang again. They didn't offer a position as a direct Pilot Officer but got two navy officers to spend almost two hours with me discussing options to join the navy as they could see a bright future for me in the navy. But I wanted to become a pilot, so refused the offer. Then a few years later after getting married, the dream again became alive and I thought about entering the commercial aviation industry as a commercial pilot. I was all set and booked for the training at Bankstown NSW training college, had resigned from my job at North Sydney, got my Trainee Pilot license from CASA (Civil Aviation Authority in Australia) and all set to go while still progressing paperwork on the medical sides.

It struck me when I read about being diabetic disqualifies you from getting the class one medical certificate required for commercial pilots. Both my parents were recently diagnosed with diabetes. I overheard a friend saying if both your parents are diabetic, there is an 80% chance of their child having the same. Panic struck, booked in to get it tested. Results showed me I was hanging on the borderline of 6.9. Once crossed 7.0, I will be officially diabetic. My heart started sinking for a bit. I took a decision to postpone the training for about three months and planned to control it and bring it fairly down and maintain it that point onwards. To my surprise, the dieting and walks did not do the required and ended up being declared diabetic instead. The reading showed up at 7.1. Discussed it with a dietician who recommended to give up on spending all that money on training and said - even if I maintained it well for few years, it will show up once I am flying more and exercising less. He said to imagine what it would be like loosing the license then. Having not the money to waste, I had to give up on that dream once again and work with plan B. Luckily on the career side, the day I decided that, I received a phone call from a Govt. agency which had kept me on their Merit list after I refused their initial offer to pursue my dream of becoming a pilot.

That double hit on my dream of becoming a pilot got me a bit and hurt me more because of my health issues which I never imagined I could have being the player and the fitness lover I was. Well, I still suffer from type-2 diabetes in 2018. I am still not a fit guy I would like myself to be and that is now my next challenge to take on. I am maintaining around 85 kg or so but not as fully fit while looking fairly healthy and a bit chubby. I so wish to get my toned and muscular body back to keep my fitness in check to last for long.

With that in mind, I'll do a quick example for you under My Health aspect. This again as relationships, can be broken into the sub-aspects of physical, mental, psychological and emotional health or others if you wish to and work with them as required.

My Health

(Overview map)

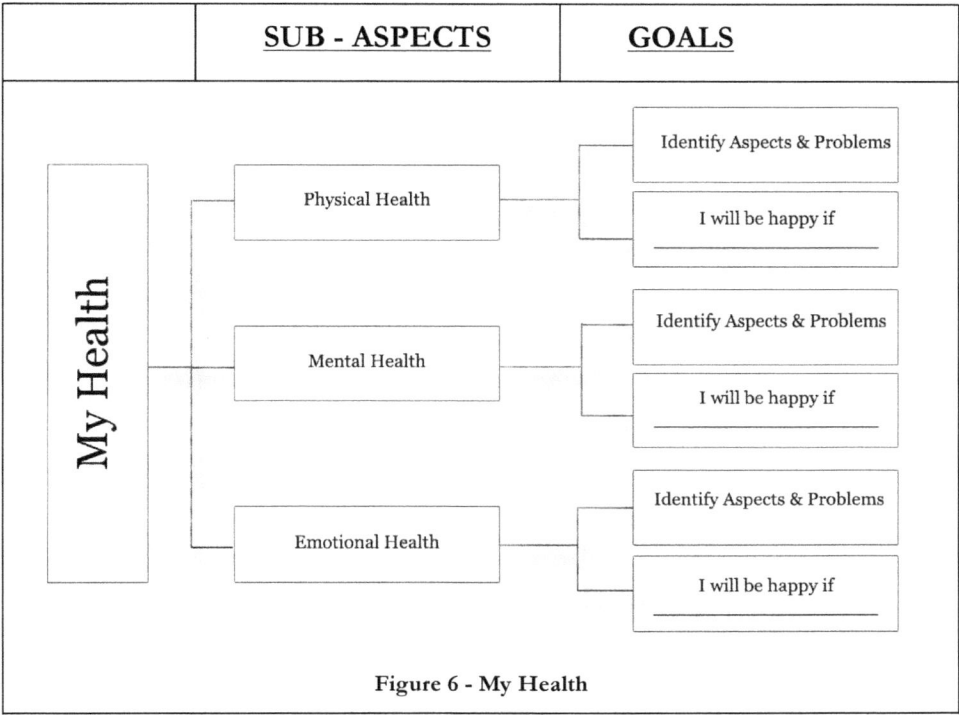

Figure 6 - My Health

Note: Once you are working within an aspect or sub-aspect AAP, the Immediate connecting boxes will always be your Goals in the aspect of life you are assessing. Your Goals will then be connected to your Comprehensive Action Plans (CAPs), which is made up of your steps to take along with Revival Action Plans (RAPs) or Newborn Action Plans (NAPs).

ASPECT ACTION PLAN

1. My Aspect – My Health (Physical)
2. Aspect Priority Rank – (3)
3. Happiness Statement –

    My physical health happiness is in being able to get my body back in shape, fit into my wedding time suits and develop stronger muscles and stamina to play sports with my kids, and live healthy for my lifetime. With a healthy body, a healthy mind always follows.

4. **Goals** (Add as many as needed, be specific)

    It is now time to identify the goals that will help you achieve your happiness. Note that initially you may not be very clear about the goal. You **must now use The Karmic Rewind Tool** and establish all that is needed to be transferred here in the AAP.

Goal - 1   **Priority (1)**

Specific Goal - Start Walking for 30 minutes Everyday.

Target Completion Timeframe –

    Achieve By Date - 31 /Dec /2018   By _ _ am/pm

    Notes: _

Plan Number – Physical Health Goal 1 | Created - ☐ Page No. ___

Note: Mark your Plan number at the top of The Karmic Rewind Tool to keep proper references.

Happiness Score on achievement -

♡ ♡ ♡ ♡ ♡ ♡ ♡ ♡ ♡ ♡

THE KARMIC REWIND TOOL

REWIND | REVIVE | RELIVE

Plan Number – Physical Health Goal 1

Area of Priority- Health (Physical)   **Goal Priority (1)**

I would love it if – I can **get started towards building a healthy routine.**

REWIND stage

1. Where Am I currently in this area of life or on the path to achieve this goal?

I am currently taking walks when I feel like at leisure and make no real point of going for a walk but find it easy to use an excuse not to. When I do walk, I am fit enough to put up with 8-10 km walks and some light exercises. I am always suffering from some sort of ache and do take medication instead of building a healthier routine and diet.

2. How did I reach here? What decisions played a role?

I am not sure because I always want to be healthy. It might be the stress of getting other things done first which pushes my healthy habits to a lower priority. Though I know if I am healthier, all else is easier to maintain.

3. Why I made the choice-

I don't think I am making the choices to be unhealthy but I am surely not making the choices that will keep me healthy. It is a case of - "When you don't work for what you want, what you don't want automatically takes over".

Decision	Reason
1. Not to go for walk daily.	It was too hot/cold outside. I needed some rest after an exhausting day on computer and building my social network profile up. I need to relax so rather take a tablet for diabetes and/or inflammation.
2. Not go for a walk today	I got to watch the game on television today. I can't miss this game.

4. What Caused Me to think or be convinced into making those choices?

I can always go for a walk when I am ready and have nothing else to do, though such time hasn't presented itself in years. I am at-least not as unfit as that big belly guy living next door yet.

5. Beliefs That Played a Part

1. I can always workout tomorrow and become healthier.
2. I can still do most of the stuff so I am not that bad as yet.

Old Beliefs that need to be killed –

1. I can always workout tomorrow and become healthier.
2. I can still do most of the stuff so I am not that bad as yet.

Revival or Newborn Action Plan (RAP/NAP) -

New Beliefs to Accomplish New Goal

1. I must go for a walk today and worry about rest tomorrow.
2. I must become fitter than just being able to manage to do things.

6. People who Influenced Decision

People: Myself based on other people I see that are in worse state than me. My wife and kids are always convincing me to go for a walk and do some exercise.

Revival or Newborn Action Plan (RAP/NAP) -

1. I must stop comparing with people in bad state of health.
2. I must bring my pride of fitness back as in school days.
3. I must find a fitness role model to help me visualise how I want to become in my physical health perspective.

Association Assessment – Associate with fitness conscious minds.

7. Identify Your Weaknesses

Weaknesses –

1. I always have something else more important and use it as an excuse to not go for walks or exercise.
2. I can't get my mind off work until I finish what I started.

Revival or Newborn Action Plan (RAP/NAP) -

1. Identify those tasks and manage them in timely manner ensuring they don't come in the way when it's time to go for walk.
2. If it can't be finished in half a day, it must be managed by ensuring time for healthy routines.

8. Identify Your Strengths

My Strengths -

Love for fitness and sports, ability to make it happen.

Revival or Newborn Action Plan (RAP/NAP) -

Get out there and get walking daily as a start.

Behavioural Strengths –

I love to be part of a team sport rather than solo running.

Revival or Newborn Action Plan (RAP/NAP) -

Find the nearest sports complex and become a member of a team sport of choice.

9. YOUR GOAL – with Clear vision

Goal – Start Walking for 30 minutes Everyday.

Target Completion Timeframe

Achieve By Date - 31 / 12 / 2018   By _ _ _ _ am/pm

Notes: Idea is to build a routine habit. Review monthly and add increments.

RELIVE – stage

10. Comprehensive Action Plan (CAP)-

Goal – Start Walking for 30 minutes Everyday.

Target Completion Timeframe

Achieve By Date - 31 / 03 / 2018   By _ _ _ _ am/pm

Notes: Idea is to build a routine habit. Review monthly and add increments.

Revival Action Plans (RAP) or Newborn Action Plans (NAPs) to be aware of –

RAP/NAP – Beliefs (Impress Positive and New Beliefs in Mind)

1. I must go for a walk today and worry about rest tomorrow.
2. I must become fitter than just being able to manage to do things.

RAP/NAP – People and Social Associations (Keep or Avoid)

1. I must bring my pride of fitness back as in school days.
2. I must find a fitness role model to help me visualise how I want to become in my physical health perspective.
3. I must associate with fitness conscious minds and look up to people with great fitness and health.

RAP/NAP – Weaknesses (Remove or Convert to Strengths)

1. Identify daily tasks and manage them in timely manner ensuring they don't come in the way when it's time to go for walk.
2. If work can't be finished in half a day, it must be time managed to ensure time for healthy routines.

RAP/NAP – Strengths and Behaviours (Build and Strengthen)

1. Get out there and get walking daily as a start.
2. Find the nearest sports complex and become a member of a team sport of choice.

STEPS TO SUCCESS – using Walk your Thoughts technique

1. I will read this CAP for 5 minutes every day. _ _ _ _ _ _ _ _ _ _ _ _
2. Find a role model or sports personality to look up to. _ _ _ _ _ _ ☐
3. Have a picture frame of the role/sport model in computer room. _ ☐
4. I will go for walk everyday in the evening at 6:30 pm. _ _ _ _ _ _ _ ☐
5. I will build this habit and slowly increase the timings. _ _ _ _ _ _ _ ☐
6. Find a sports complex with a gym near by. _ _ _ _ _ _ _ _ _ _ _ ☐
7. Join a sport of choice to help build more physical activity as well as network of people with fitness mindset. _ _ _ _ _ _ _ _ _ _ _ _ _ _ ☐
8. No matter what happens, continue to walk everyday. _ _ _ _ _ _ _ ☐

11. Sync with Master and Aspect Action Plan (MAP/AAP)-

The last and final step of this process is to transfer this Goal, Target Completion Timeframe and insert this CAP to the **AAP of your Physical Health**. Place it as a Goal under the Spirituality Aspect of life.

Link this CAP using a **Plan Number** - "Physical Health Goal 1".

ASPECT – MY FINANCES

Priority - 4

Aspect Story – My Finances

Career is number four in my priority list. It does not mean it is any less important. It is equally important yet lower in priority because I believe that once you have that divine inner peace through self-awareness, your existence in this world is healthy and your relationships are fully supporting your goals in life, then career achievement I believe is also not far from you. All three aspects ensure that you are working towards your dreams with all the necessary elements behind it to pursue for success. With these three priorities in check, I have the solid basic grounds needed to build that career I want to enjoy for the rest of my life. Writing and Web Development leading to online entrepreneurship are going to be the integral parts of my life, my love and my passion. However, it was not an easy ride to seeing those goals clearly and taking steps to realise them in life. One goal would be accomplished with the publishing of this book and the other I am well and truly on track to realise by the way of training and building more experience.

When I left India to go to Australia, I had not thought that things wouldn't be as easy as it looks when general public sees the NRIs (Non Resident Indians) coming back and have fun or when they see the foreigners and think life there is pretty cool and rich. The hard work behind the fun times that those people show off when they come back to visit India is completely hidden by those people as well as ignored by the locals. Back in July 1997, when I arrived in Australia, I went through a lot to get started on work life. While also managing the studies, I went job-hunting door to door at cafes, restaurants, car washes, and labour hiring agencies.

My very first job was a merchandise marketing getting reward only based on how much we sold. This was near railway station in North Parramatta, NSW. I still remember the first day, with my limited speaking ability and less known territory knowledge was quite an experience. I think I did that for about three days and left, declaring that merchandise marketing was not my cup of tea. I felt reward for my effort was completely dependent on other person's will and need without any basic reward for my time and effort. I kept looking for work and took up another completely commission based marketing campaign for a newly introduced telecommunications company AAPT. That sounded at-least better than carrying a bag full of merchandise and commissions were better. In fact the first two weeks were so good that I rejected a full time job offer at a factory only to regret after the third week in marketing went downhill and continued there onwards. This definitely made me quit marketing all up but did learn a lot of communication skills.

After that the next opportunity I got was at a property consultant's telemarketing company somewhere in North Sydney area. I think the name was 'Looker's & Associates'. That at-least paid a basic hourly rate and commissions on top for every lead provided. And fired after second week of not being able to generate enough leads, I got fired and surely I wasn't going to take up marketing any more ever in my life. I switched off my brain's marketing side of interests. I inclined more towards hourly rate jobs.

I remember once we even went to farms in Griffith NSW, looking for work and happened to get there at the slowest two weeks in the year when work could not be found. We made our way back to Sydney and applied for job at a subway. I got the job but resigned straight after first day's training, as I didn't want to handle meat in any shape and form based on my spiritual teachings I followed. I had done the same thing with my very first restaurant job at Hungry Jacks on Oxford Street, Sydney. Joined the job thinking I may request to be at the front counters only, but that wasn't going to happen so resigned straight after first three-hour induction training shift.

Somehow managed to get casual factory jobs here and there for a few months and then went for training as a security officer. Got lucky after a long while to get a casual call up with Chubb Security, which was contracted to patrol Sydney trains. Once I was running a little late and so that I don't miss my train, made a mistake of following the same path to get to the platform as the railway staff did from their car park. It involved crossing over a rail track that was very infrequent. But I wasn't railway staff so got fired for breaching the safety measures. It may be the demand for security personnel or I just got lucky again to secure another security job with another large company and worked at a prestigious retail store "David Jones" for a couple of years. Got an injury during some construction work happening on site and had to stay off work for quite a long time. This presented me with the opportunity to think better to retrain myself for better career and in something of my interest. I wanted to join defence forces as an Air Force pilot back in 2004 but I was offered almost any other starting position in Navy but not entry as an Air Force Pilot. They assured me they can see a very bright future for me but I only wanted Air Force Pilot position and nothing else.

I had gained good communication skills and computer skills so I started to apply for some call centre positions. I got lucky and got a job at a telecommunications company in their Technical Support team. We were technical support team titled as customer service so the company could make more money than us. It was ok for me to gain the experience but there on I switched the job for a better package. I always enjoyed technology and so working with it. I showed my skills enough to help me move into this new company's mobile technical specialist team. I loved that job, and I was successful in showing my talent and skills to achieve my goal of being able to work in the technical specialist team. At that point in time, that was my goal, and I wanted it so much that I put all my 200% effort into it and was able to achieve the goal I had set for myself.

Then I wanted to go for a higher position which will give me exposure to management roles, as I thought I was good at all the work in that department as in technical skills, but was I good at socializing with people? No. I was very friendly, and approachable and knowledgeable, but I was not very social outside the office. I never went out to work organised parties etc., simply because of the drinking, smoking environments, which I was never comfortable in. Smoking always caused me suffocation, and drinking was not in favour of my spiritual practices. I believed drinking alcohol was like wanting to travel through time without remembering it. I was probably influenced by the incident once on a wedding; I chatted away a good two hours on a useful topic with this friend, and next morning, he did not even remember we were awake that late let alone what was discussed. I also do agree what a lot of others said to me about attending social events organised by work – "a lot of useful outcomes can be achieved while being there and a glass of Non-Alcoholic drink would not hurt". Well, slowly I started to attend and learned to be a non-alcoholic socialiser.

These are some personal preference issues that people need to address if need be. But I am always happy to talk to someone for ages if it involved spirituality and sensible topics exchanging some wise ideas and advise. So, I had applied for a supervisor position and the job ended up with someone who was very good at socializing rather than his work (yes, he fell drunk in a gutter, ended up in hospital with a black eye). But after that set back, I figured out that I was forcing myself to make a career in the field I somehow liked but not loved, and I thought I needed much mature environment to work in compare to a telecommunication company's call centre technical support. So I decided to try a different job.

A job in one of the government departments where I thought I would be surrounded with a bit more mature minded people and possibly enjoy work and make progress fairly in a career that I thought I liked to be in, which was sitting at a desk in front of the computer and doing daily routine work. After a while you get so good at it that you start to get bored, even though Government departments offer much more variety in jobs that it sometimes is easy to make a switch between careers if you wanted to, but there was a creative instinct in me.

I always compared my way of working to some highly positioned people. From some I always learned more and there were a lot of others that I thought I could do their job better than them. And more or less I had this desire in my heart and mind to be able to do things differently, precisely and efficiently while adding creativity where ever I found room to fill that in. My fellow workers would tag me as a philosopher and a perfectionist at times. I always being shy in nature just passed a smile saying thanks. I always thought that there is much more purpose to my life and such suggestions and spiritual discussions I got involved in with colleagues and friends were mere a small amount of knowledge and experience that I shared with them.

I so wanted to break out of those boundaries of working in a set routine every day and being tired as anything. End of the day, I would never have enough time and money to be able to enjoy life the way I wanted to. In-between the urge to become a commercial pilot came along but wasn't successful due to medical issues. I ended up joining the government department in search of better and mature environment. The job was tax technical but not in IT but I took it to be able to join a government organisation just after finding out that I couldn't become a pilot. I needed to pay bills. After some time I was hit with back pain problem badly, took some time off work and joined back after more than three months. Being not exactly the job I wanted, I soon resigned and got back to cab driving for a while to earn the living and giving myself some freedom to think deeper about what I wanted to achieve.

Then I came around an opportunity that would give me same amount of income while working half the time that I was. I was looking for something different, but this would have meant that I would be working for myself, as I always wanted to and on a contract with one of the government departments. However knowing our nature as we always hesitate to take decisions for change, as most of us love procrastinating, I did the same. I kept on procrastinating for few months and one day I decided Why Not, it meant some investment but it was not my life savings to get qualified to do that work. It was also the habit of not letting go of my hard earned money for something I wasn't sure of in my heart.

I took this as an opportunity to dare myself and learn something different. One, I joined this MLM recommended by this lovely lady from Philippine getting into direct selling MLM company. This again being a marketing gig, I never pursued whole-heartedly. Two, I joined this training to become an assessor for the Department of Environment, Water and Heritage Australia (DEWHA as known in 2009-10). The training also made me more aware about how to help people improve their houses to make them more environment-friendly. Knowing the global warming issues that are being raised, I thought it would be a nice idea to get into that trade, where I will not only do some useful work but also add my share of caring for environment while still earning an income to pay for living. And what else could have given me the opportunity and the precious time that I needed on my hands so I could determine my direction in life, reassess and pave my path towards where I wanted to go, what I wanted to do and What I could enjoy doing for the rest of my life without thinking of the 9 to 5 Monday drags and Friday happy rides back home.

So, I joined that opportunity and when I started, I realised what an exciting opportunity I was about to miss and had wasted two months of it already if not more. Simply because of our procrastinating nature that we don't want to have yet we can't get rid off easily. And let me tell you one thing that I would have regretted if I had procrastinated any more. I would not have got that contract. I was lucky enough to receive the certificates I needed to get the contract just on a day before Christmas, and had I not posted them on that day as a lot of other people I know who waited till after x-mas, I would not have got that contract. I would have missed that huge opportunity which gave me the opportunity to change my life. I posted it on the last minutes of the post office closing before the Christmas break. From that point I thought there is no turning back now.

I enjoyed that job, it involved visiting peoples houses and advising them of how few minor things could be improved in their houses which will not only help them in living in a more comfortable house but also save them in cost of living. This way, they can have their contribution in looking after the planet by helping reduce their carbon footprint. It was an amazing experience. There were large amounts of different kind of people that I met during that job. This also helped me learn how different people have different ideas about the global warming and the carbon footprint reduction and the Carbon Tax, which was a huge issue of debate around 2009-10. Whether the global warming is a real issue or not? In general I am just a big believer in not wasting what we have. I take extreme care in doing so, why waste.

Even the time, why waste it in today's day and age, when we also hear that Time is Money. According to the spiritual practices we followed since our childhood, they have never taught us to waste anything and at least devote one tenth of every aspect of our life in the name of God or helping others. Hence I have also pledged that not just ten per-cent but also a lot more than 10% that I earn from this book will also go towards making the life better for a lot of others who are in need of financial help to progress in life. We were also taught that not only the money but also one tenth of the daily time which roughly sits around two and a half hours a day, should also be spent in meditation or such activities of showing your gratitude towards the Holy Spirit or the God. So, Life is not worth wasting, it's worth living and enjoying every moment of it.

Since I started this Job, I had the opportunity to get rid of all my loans that I had, a huge riddance of one major burden on mind. And no financial burdens always help your mind take a bit of a flight further. You just need to ensure that you are taking the right path forward. After making some sort of achievement, for some it could very easily become a destructive state. They start boasting about and indulge in certain activities that may lead them to a destructive path rather than path to success. So, at such stage I needed to decide and progress very carefully. But it was only few months after I started that work that the government announced some reduction to the amount of work we were doing; we were limited down to a minimal number of jobs we could do every week and this took a huge hit on the income we could earn. But for me that was still OK. Why? Because this will mean that I would still have some income to survive on and have a lot of time to work on getting things placed in right direction so I could pave my runway to the life, the life I was going to live for the rest of my life.

I started spending more time on the thinking process and started doing more investigations into things I enjoyed doing, which I would love to do. Even if I were to go and work for someone, which career path I should choose so that I am not dragging myself to work every Monday and the other days of the week, and just be happy on Friday because it's the last working day of the week. This only gives us two more days of enjoying the Not Working for someone else and not doing the work, which we do not always love to do. Yet, majority of us are doing it every week. And some of my juniors would hate me for those sarcastically teasing words every Friday; When they said; 'have a good weekend, so glad to be out of here', I always replied back with - 'don't worry dear, its only two days before you come back'. That is a feeling nobody likes and still we have been putting up with it for years and years and unhappily keep doing it for the rest of the life. And doing what? - Whinging about doing what we don't like.

I could bet you, if one of the non-ruling political parties took this as an agenda and offered everyone full assistance in finding work in the industry of their choice, or offer full support in training them in the field of their choice along with creating jobs in such sector. Imagine the number of issues it would resolve. The party will win (in my view most likely). And the productivity will increase and in-fact may even skyrocket, because a lot of the time it's the passion for something that drives people, and if you work in an industry that brings your passion out, you may also be *struggling again not to talk about work at home*. So it is very important that you choose the path to be what you would love to walk on for the rest of your life. When you walk with passion, you cover more distance with a pride ride. So why would you not want to make a decision that would lead you ahead rather than dragging yourself for the rest of your life.

I had made a decision that I was not going to let my life become a drag anymore. So, I kept on investigating, and investing more time in things I liked. One day another news followed from the department that the project we were working on would be discontinued in short time. That would not sound like a good news otherwise, but only because, I had decided to explore and taken steps to do what I wanted to do, I was not worried by that news as my debts were also paid off.

I explored few opportunities that would give me an opportunity to work for myself. I at one stage thought of starting Import-Export business from China or India. I even made a trip to Guangzhou in China and India together to explore the possibilities. I even registered a domain called "ChinImports", but I was exploring things on my own. I had a bit of a rough ride. I was lucky to have a friend who was in business and was regularly importing from China directly himself. He organised one of his Chinese partner's cousin to take me from place to place and help me explore as he could help me with translating English to local people and businesses. This was all a great help. But there were few problems I encountered during that trip. I am a strict vegetarian and was very hard for me to manage eating outside.

This was one thing that forced me to decide on not going to china myself, or at least not without my pre-packed food supplies to help me follow my Vegetarian diet principals. Second, not many people on street spoke English, but that may not have been a major issue, but when I brought some samples of goods from various wholesale suppliers, most of them did not work properly, and some were corrupted with virus. I loved technology always, and wanted to trade in technology gadgets as well. Moreover I enjoyed working with computers, as I always thought computers are more precisely controllable if you can give them right instructions or design them in the way you want them to behave. Anyways, for me, importing as a business initiative did not turn out to be a good start, and I gave that up. Maybe I needed more connections in China and with the community of importers in Australia.

I went back to India again to pursue my other plan that I had in my mind. I wanted to create and present things in my way to the online world. I loved the new buzz of Web World as the Internet technology advances. I wanted to start learning that so I enrolled at Canberra Institute of Technology. I started watching a lot of online tutorials, but in the mean while I thought I will also try the offshoring to India, which everyone is talking about for the technology work. I had a reference from couple of friends in India and a friend who runs a successful online business from Australia. He referenced me to this guy in India who had helped him in getting his website online. Not that I was impressed by the work he had done on that site, but He recommended him because of his after work support. OK, I thought I would meet up with him too.

I went there and had meetings with few web developers. I found this guy whose work looked fantastic and I was hundred per-cent sure he would be able to understand my ideas and the way I wanted things presented. I gave him the plans and what I was expecting, I had also given him a run down on the kind of ethics I was expecting from him in relation to communication and on time works or being informed on any delays if occurred. The guy was happy to work and agreed with me, conveying that they always followed such steps in all their work. But I only found out two weeks later that he was expecting me to call him every second or third day, so he didn't get stuck with other jobs they were doing and to ensure that my work was being attended to. Even though I had told him that, 'if you tell me one week for some work be done, I will not bother him for that week', as I respected his ethics as well. But that didn't turn out well in about three weeks time and I had to pull the job back from him.

There on I hunted the other reference I had for this developer that my friend in Australia had suggested. I got in touch with him. He did not seem like in touch with the modern design concepts but I was running out of time too. I wanted to work with someone I had met with. I decided to give him the project I wanted to start work on. It was for a community based website targeting worldwide audience. I thought I would make him understand what I actually wanted and it should all be OK. After all, a developer should be in touch with the latest technology and trends. It did not turn out to be a great experience either, and I had to send him repetitive instructions on the same thing. His English did not seem bad at all, yet he seemed to always do something different to what I was trying to convey to him.

At times he made me feel doubted for my own use of language, but I thought I could not make it any simpler than the way I was, to have any developer understand what I wanted. To him a uniform look of all pages on the website meant, leaving couple of pages with unworked backgrounds compare to how the rest of the pages were appearing on a website. How does that fit in the uniform and consistent look and feel of the website. When I asked; he said that was done deliberately for different experience on those pages! What the….?. Anyways, something that should have taken only about 5-8 weeks had now taken 9 months and site was still not ready. Yes we thought we would save some money by offshoring, but now you can see what we actually may have lost in that space of time. But is that a worry for me, Yes and No. Yes, because it has taken a lot more time than it should have, and by now we should have had a lot of audience on the site, and No, because that has triggered an opportunity for me to learn and become a web developer myself. And I know what I want to present to the world in my way and I will.

It was a great learning process and now, I have found my rhythm and got in touch with my essence, in terms of what I want to do and achieve in my life from my career's point of view. So the ideas of buying, selling importing have been shredded for now and concentration is full on, on web development in the IT services industry.

The most important change happened for me is that I have my mind made up on the change, the change I have already implemented in my life and am seeing different result and much more happiness in and around me. I am seeing my goals more clearly now and have implemented changes in and around me to give me more comforting and satisfactory environment. An environment that helps me maintain my peace of mind, an environment that helps me keep my focus on things which I want to do and goals that I want to achieve.

A minor but significant incident that added on to drive change in my life was, when I walked outside a bookshop one day. I was always keen on book reading, but wanted something that could help me learn more about life. I always read spiritual books and articles on Universe and Life relating issues. I was in this mode of life where I wanted to achieve some changes in life, changes for better and happier, abundant life. I knew I had what it takes, I could do it and I just needed some sincere help and a helping hand that could lead me through to the other side. It never happened till that day.

I had spent some money on all those, Internet and online gurus who could teach you anything in a matter of hours and also help you make money too. No, I don't want to place an unreliable tag on all of them, as some of them may be good and reliable as well. But I wasted some money on them and received no follow up help from them at all. All I wanted to do was to have a work life, which I can manage from home, giving me the time and freedom I wanted, to live my life and spend more time with my family and in spiritual development.

But What I did find that day on that bookshop's clearance desk was a book priced for just Two Dollars. I picked up this book; I was wondering about how they could sell a book like this so cheap. But I believe this probably was the only book they had left and put it on the clearance table. The books actual price was $26.99 and I paid only Two Dollars for it. I did not believe what I had found that day until I started reading the book. This was a book by John Assaraf. And when I read about the Law of attraction, I wondered why that book showed up in front of my eyes that day. Reading this book just gave me that little slight push that I needed to start acting towards the changes I needed to implement.

I so wanted to change things for the better, I so knew what I needed to change, but I just did not do it. Why, probably out of the fear of change, out of the fear of success or failure. The funniest part was I learnt what the fear of success could be. After all who should be afraid of success, no-one really; but I started to fear of the changes that may come along if I am successful in my implementations. And with that book it just gave me that extra bit of comfort to move forward.

Since then I read numerous articles on The Law of Attraction and the other laws of the universe. Then I started to align the logics with the spiritual, religious and mystical teachings that I had learned and seen around me in my life. That's when I figured out that all this is so logical. Aligning all those articles with my personal knowledge about spirituality and the practices we have been following for years do match up.

As I have mentioned earlier in this book about some religious scriptures, that there is an idea of becoming one with God. What could those practices possibly be? If you follow those practices, one is taught to practice prayers and meditation techniques to find the inner spiritual home, to find Nirvana, or Moksha (Mukti), all means the salvation of the soul, to become one with God. If you don't do those properly, you can't find that salvation and cannot avail the opportunity to be one with God, which is told to be only available in the human form of life. One must do prayers and meditation in a given way to realise the eternal truth. In simple terms everything and everywhere we look at such scriptures is asking to follow the same goal in different ways. The more you love God or Spirituality, the more you move towards finding it, feeling it and achieving it.

The same logic applies to whichever task you may set your target as. You may set the task of achieving success in any aspect of life. At the same time, if you set your energies and efforts too much towards negativity, that is what you start to see around you. Again, what you sow so shall you reap. If you implement negativity around you, you can only expect negativity to come on to fill the space around you. If you do on the other hand start to concentrate on positive things, that is what you can expect and that is what you will start to see.

But for all these to be implemented, you just need a deep sense of understanding and feeling for life and its purpose within you. As I previously mentioned with other examples in this book, the intensity of anything you do, intensity of feelings, intensity of energy you put in, intensity of love you show towards achieving something, all does matter and so does the opposite. So positive thinking and love towards your goal with full intensity is a must to pursue the actions that will take you towards realising them in physical form.

One will need to keep insisting, as it is not easy to get out of the mind-set that we have been in for years. And as that is what we have been taught from the start, from your homes to the school it may not be an easy task to conquer and kill the old beliefs. The only thing most people will tell their kids about schooling is to study hard otherwise no one will give you a job. No one says, study hard to learn well and to become what you want to and lead the world, but that is the only way you can succeed well, when you follow your passion and align it with your skills and love for it.

I did and I am glad that I did when I did. That has changed my life and now I am living happier. I have made my life to move on the track I would love to ride on for the rest of my life - Writing & Web Entrepreneurship. Writing was something I always loved since my childhood days, and web development is the way for me to put my ideas the way I would like them to be presented to the world, for creating a real social sense of responsibility towards humanity and the planet we live on.

I remember one day I came around this guy, I would have been only about 12-13 yrs. old then, and he knew I was a bit of bright student at school. He asked me if I could write an article to be published in a newspaper. I said OK I would. I remember sitting down through the night to write this article for him. I gave him the article next morning just before going to school. The guy said that it was very nicely written, then days went by but I did not see him again. Then I also got busy with my studies and thought maybe he was just encouraging me by telling me that it was a good article. Well one day I learned that he had moved to another city with his job and I never got in touch with him again. Mobile phones and even landline numbers during those days in India were not that popular among general public. So I could not try that, but that encouraged me more to learn writing skills.

One day after the home assessments program with the Department of Environment was scrapped, I came across that feeling again and decided to write the book about how I was able to turn my life around from living hard to finding happiness within by using certain techniques that may also help people to motivate, understand the deeper meaning of life, understand the logic of life in the universe, to find happiness and success in their lives. Success does mean different to everybody. I have implemented those techniques in my life and paved my way to happiness, satisfaction and contentment, which gives you that eternal peace of mind. The peace of mind which you need to Live a Happy Life, whether you choose to live with Richness of Money, Richness of Peace and Spirituality, or Richness of Love and Relationships. It's all about living happily, living an abundant life, living with peace and harmony to make one's own world a happy place and that is when you can help your loved ones too.

Now I have made a move to India, set up a nice home for family and a home office for myself. Not worried about basics of life and ready to make the next moves to the online entrepreneurial world. Do keep in touch and learn about the initiatives through my website – www.AtamDhillon.com.

My Finances (Overview map)

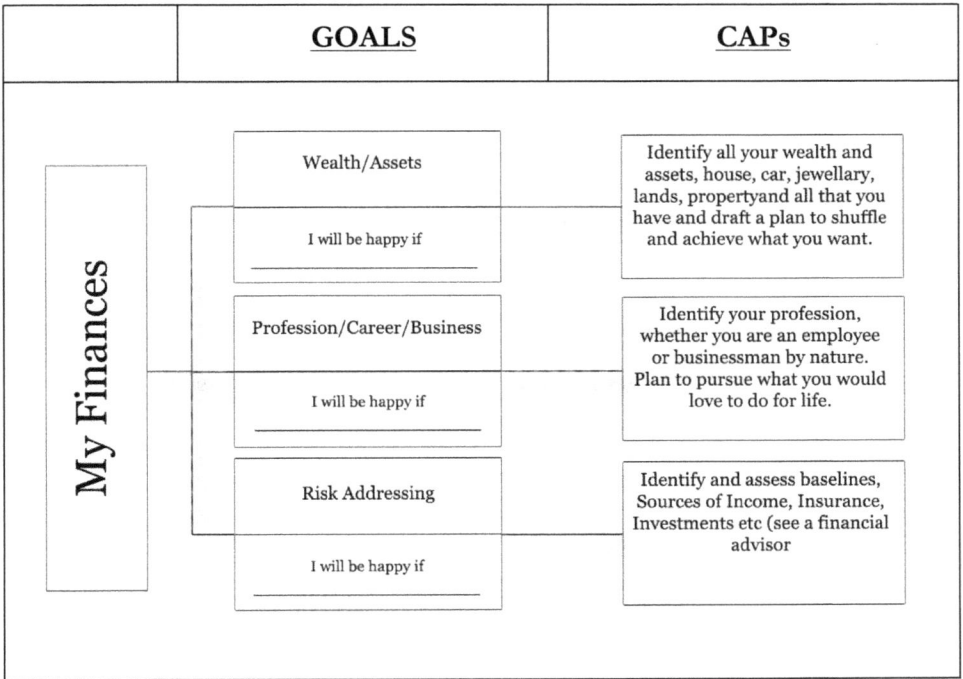

Note: Once you are working within an aspect or sub-aspect AAP, the Immediate connecting boxes will always be your Goals in the aspect of life you are assessing. Your Goals will then be connected to your Comprehensive Action Plans (CAPs), which is made up of your steps to take along with Revival Action Plans (RAPs) or Newborn Action Plans (NAPs).

ASPECT ACTION PLAN

1. **My Aspect** – My Finances
2. **Aspect Priority Rank** – (4)
3. **Happiness Statement** –
   My Financial happiness is in ensuring all the basics of life are provided for everyone in my family and a passive income stream is set up to cover for all running expenses, so I can implement next stage of success without any financial worries for basics of living. _ _ _ _ _ _ _ _ _ _ _ _
4. **Goals** (Add as many as needed, be specific)
   It is now time to identify the goals that will help you achieve your happiness. Note that initially you may not be very clear about the goal. You **must now use The Karmic Rewind Tool** and establish all that is needed to be transferred here in the AAP.

Goal - 1   **Priority (____)**

Specific Goal - Learn more about financial investment opportunities in Information Technology industry. _ _ _ _ _ _ _ _ _ _ _ _ _ _ _ _ _ _ _
_ _

Target Completion Timeframe –

    Achieve By Date - 31 /12 /2018   By _ _ am/pm

    Notes: _

Plan Number – Financial Goal 1 | Created - ☐ Page No. ____

<small>**Note:** Mark your Plan number at the top of The Karmic Rewind Tool to keep proper references.</small>

Happiness Score on achievement - ♡ ♡ ♡ ♡ ♡ ♡ ♡ ♡ ♡ ♡

THE KARMIC REWIND TOOL

REWIND | REVIVE | RELIVE

Plan Number – Financial Goal 1

Area of Priority- My Finances **Goal Priority (1)**

I would love it if – I can save more money and invest it to maximise the investment income on top of running regular home expenses and also provide for extra savings for investing in my own online projects. _ _ _ _ _ _ _ _ _ _ _ _

REWIND stage

1. Where Am I currently in this area of life or on the path to achieve this goal?

I have rejuvenated my career and I am glad I have done so. I am now enjoying writing and working on developing own project websites. I also refreshed and learned new skills and qualifications in IT to fulfil my dreams; the dream and vision that I have for developing and realising some entrepreneurial ideas. With a move to India, I currently have enough funds in bank to generate enough to cover my monthly expenses while I concentrate on writing and my online projects. Savings are not enough though to make some further and high-risk investments into new options like BitCoin, Etherium or other such digital currencies.

2. How did I reach here? What decisions played a role?

In October 2009, The opportunity came up with a government contract that helped me take a back seat and take a rewind look at the life I was living. That helped me recognise what I wanted out of my life. It helped me make a decision to make a career that I could work without getting tired for the rest of my life. I became desperate to do what I wanted to do in my life. A normal life routine was working well but not giving satisfaction to my heart and soul for what I believed my purpose was for life. I sold my house in Australia and built one in India to live mortgage free and have some savings to cover for living expenses to be able to concentrate on my goals with free mind.

3. Why I made the choice-

I had done about more than a year worth of research in finding what I would love to do for the rest of my life, which will also give me a better Work Life balance with more freedom. I had a passion and love for technology and a creative eye for doing things differently and in elegant way. I am also kind of a philosopher. So it made sense for me to start writing and start learning skills that will help me work in the stream I want to while giving me the freedom I wanted from the peaceful atmosphere of my home.

Decision	**Reason**
1. I Invested in myself to jump on to new opportunity.	I became desperate to do what I wanted to do in my life. I needed to dare myself to jump into change. I was holding back my savings rather than thinking they could bring more value by investing in my own self.
2. I moved to India.	I just wasn't getting time to spend on what I really wanted to achieve in life. I had to find balance in living life and having time to devote to my goals to feel satisfied with what I was doing in my life.

4. What Caused Me to think or be convinced into making those choices?

I got tired of living hectic life of working hard, giving my best and still not finding that inner satisfaction. The only option that could help me with my first three priorities was choosing something I would have loved to do, something that I enjoyed doing. I had to find something that I could do for the rest of my life maintaining the balance in life and Live life for what it is meant to be. For me it was the need that I had recognised for a balanced way of living life. Then the opportunities started to show up, as you strongly desire them. I saw people who were living better and balanced life. When you get closer to some such people you start to realise within that you are capable of probably more than what they are. The only difference being they've conquered the fear and taken action that gets them there. I took decisions just to dare myself to try something different, just to throw me out of the comfort of routines that I was living with.

I had to find balance to give myself opportunity to work on the purpose I had realised for my life. The book that I read by John Assaraf, just added some energy I needed to push myself further across the line to dare and act to introduce change and the laws of Karma, the Action and Reaction looks after the rest.

The insight into opportunities, that I was introduced to by certain people have influenced my decision. The passion, my natural abilities and love for technology have influenced my decision. And I must confess – forced by a close friend, I did visit this lovely psychic lady who asked me if I write, I replied - No. She said to me that I should write and also said that I will be doing something in IT industry. Now if that subconsciously influenced me, I don't think so; But I do now see those words unfolding what she saw for my future and were said sometime in the year 2000. It only raises more credibility for the existence of human capabilities to use their eternal powers.

5. Beliefs That Played a Part
1. Belief in the passion that drives my inner self for the rest of my life. I am much better than what I am living as.
2. Belief in the ability of being able to achieve anything with the right mindset and Love from the bottom of my heart. I must believe in my own self and bring the best of what I am out in the world.
3. Belief in the higher self of human beings. Life has a much greater purpose than most people realise, I must help them recognise their eternal precious value.
4. Belief in the power of thoughts and Karma. My belief that, I can learn what is needed to pursue my goals. I must empower myself to be able to help and inspire others.

Revival Action Plan (RAP)
1. I must continue to believe in the purpose of my life. I must continue to pursue my projects with good for humanity embedded in them and eliminate anything that hinders those beliefs.
2. _____

Old Beliefs that need to be killed
None, I feel energised as well as peace and contentment with these beliefs and will keep practicing to strengthen my state of mind. All beliefs that held me back have been killed; such as, Fear of change, I cannot change careers; Job is the only way of survival.

New Beliefs to Accomplish New Goal
1. **I can** devote more time and concentration to advance my skills in financial and investment strategies.

6. People who Influenced Decision

People: When I look closer to me I don't find any inspirations within my family members. They all are stuck in traditional beliefs of only working hard to earn not smart. Stories of many achieved or successful people and knowing most of them started from their garages actually inspire me and feed the deeper desires within me. I only have come in contact with couple of similar minded people who had not achieved a lot yet but believed in their dreams and continue to pursue them. I must build connections and surround myself with more such people. So far I have mostly been fighting against the norms and pushing ahead.

Revival Action Plan (RAP) –

Build more connections and surround myself with like-minded people. I am currently finding the links on a professional networking site – LinkedIn.

To achieve financial freedom associated with my goals, I must learn better financial strategies for better investment outcomes to achieve the level of passive income I desire or find a financial advisor who may help with that.

Association Assessment – Find and network with like minds.

7. Identify Your Weaknesses

Weaknesses – Not devoting as much of time as I would love to for learning about financial markets to invest better. Obviously I am more of a technology enthusiast than finance industry.

Revival Action Plan (RAP) –

At-least spend one hour a day learning about investment opportunities possibly in IT sector companies and products.

8. Identify Your Strengths

My Strengths –

1. Efficiency is my keyword. I love to achieve maximum output fairly from minimum resources and investment.
2. Writing is my love and technology is my passion.

Revival Action Plan (RAP) –

Combine my financial interest with technology investment opportunities. Find a source of financial advise in technology market.

Behavioural Strengths –

Not spending money on things for which the benefits last only for short periods. I hold on to my savings than throwing away to momentarily temptations. I would rather save and donate.

Revival Action Plan (RAP) –

Find some high risk but low investment opportunities that may not cause any real damage to basics that have been covered financially.

9. YOUR GOAL – with Clear vision

Goal – Learn more about financial investment opportunities in Information Technology industry.

Target Completion Timeframe

Achieve By Date - 31 / 12 / 2018   By _ _ _ _ am/pm

Notes: Review on achievement date. _ _ _ _ _ _ _ _ _ _ _ _ _ _ _ _ _ _ _

RELIVE – stage

10. Comprehensive Action Plan (CAP)-

Goal – Learn more about financial investment opportunities in Information Technology industry.

Target Completion Timeframe

Achieve By Date - 31 / 12 / 2018   By _ _ _ _ am/pm

Notes: Review based on results on 31/03/2018. _ _ _ _ _ _ _ _ _ _ _ _

Revival Action Plans (RAP) or New Action Plans (NLPs) to be aware of –

RAP/NAP – Beliefs (Impress Positive and New Beliefs in Mind)

1. Belief in the passion that drives my inner self for the rest of my life. I am much better than what I am living as now.
2. Belief in ability of being able to achieve anything with the right mindset and Love from the bottom of my heart. I must believe in my own self and bring the best of what I am out in the world.
3. Belief in a higher self of human beings. Life has a much greater purpose than most people realise, I must help them recognise their eternal precious value.
4. Belief in the power of thoughts and Karma. My belief that, I can learn what is needed to pursue my goals. I must empower myself to be able to help and inspire others.

RAP/NAP – People and Social Associations (Keep or Avoid)

1. Build more connections and surround myself with like-minded people. Connect with appropriate links professionally on networking site LinkedIn.
2. I must learn better financial strategies for better investment outcomes to achieve passive income.
3. Find a financial advisor who may help with that.
4. _____

RAP/NAP – Weaknesses (Remove or Convert to Strengths)

1. At-least spend one hour per day learning about investment opportunities possibly in IT sector companies and products.
2. _____
3. _____

RAP/NAP – Strengths and Behaviours (Build and Strengthen)

1. Combine my financial interest with technology investment opportunities.
2. Find a source of financial advise in technology market.
3. Find some high risk but low investment opportunities that may not cause any damage to basics that have been covered financially.
4. _____

STEPS TO SUCCESS – using Walk your Thoughts technique

1. I will read this CAP for 5 minutes every day._ _ _ _ _ _ _ _ _
2. I must find a source to learn about financial markets. _ _ _ _ _ _ _ _
3. I must spend one hour every day to read about investment strategies.
4. I must find opportunities of interest in IT sector to combine my interests with investment opportunities. _ _ _ _ _ _ _ _ _ _ _ _ _ _ _
5. I must find a financial advisor for consultation as needed. _ _ _ _ _ _
6. Find small amounts to invest in high-risk opportunities. _ _ _ _ _ _ _
7. Review the investment capacity every three months. _ _ _ _ _ _ _ _ _
8. When reviewing, look for funds to invest in own online projects. _ _
9. _
10. _

11. Sync with Master and Aspect Action Plan (MAP/AAP)-

The last and final step of this process is to transfer this Goal, Target Completion Timeframe and insert this CAP to the **AAP of your Spiritual life**. Place it as a Goal under the Spirituality Aspect of life.

Link this CAP using a **Plan Number** - "Financial Goal 1".

Act to Manifest – REWIND, REVIVE, RE-LIVE

These were the examples from main areas of priority in my life. You will have your own. The above will give you a quick feel of what and how you need to look at and assess, how you can reason the outcomes in life so far. Perform that Karmic Rewind and note down the areas of your strength, weaknesses, beliefs, and faiths that you have, and what areas you can improve on. Remember, the Idea is to **Rewind, Revive and Re-Live.** *Rewind* to identify, why you are where you are? *Revive* yourself by knowing more about your own self and empowering yourself by identifying the changes and modifications that will help you succeed. *Re-Live* the life and live the way you want to, Live the way It was Meant to be.

Finally we need to start acting to help manifesting what we have identified as our goals. Remember, No Action means No Karma Creation to reap the rewards. So, get going to Act and Create. First be charged up with the positivity and happiness around you, create that positive feel around you. I will suggest playing your favourite music, picking up a pencil and paper, and start drawing your favourites from the times when you were a child. You will be amazed with the happiness it will inject into your heart, which could be either because you drew it so perfectly even after many years or you didn't and it turned out to be a dog and not the cow you originally intended to draw.

To start manifesting the MAP of your life, you will be using the Walk Your Thoughts technique as explained previously. Though this is more of an **Emphasised Practicality Realisation (EPR)** method of visualisation, there are other helpful methods we may also use from the widely used and spoken about visualisation methods.

Visualisation is creating a picture or scenario in your mind to have a feel for something as in reality. Visualisation is to be used as a tool, which also makes use of the principals of Law of Attraction in changing the outer world with the influence and power of thoughts. The more you think about something in particular, the more you get closer to the physical aspect of those thoughts. So visualising in your mind about what you want to see as your future is very impressive method to assess your options as well as to see the thoughts coming into reality. You will need to see what you want to achieve very clearly though. The path you may choose can be decided upon through Walk Your Thoughts technique and then the chosen path can be visualised again and again until you have things manifested in reality. The quality and the intensity of your visualisation does matter a lot. The more you visualise clearly, the more you will start seeing the guidance that will lead you to realise that goal. It can be something emotional or materialistic in this world and it can also be spiritual advancement out of this world. You choose, you visualise and you will realise it through the power of Karma, the action. There are various techniques available for visualisation. Below are three of the methods to realise your dreams with the power of visual impressions on the mind.

1. **Visual Board** – This is very convenient for those who struggle to concentrate with closed eyes. Put up a small pin board with the pictures of what you want in life and see them, notice them, look at them deliberately for at-least five minutes every morning. Also try to have similar impressions in the areas where you move around mostly. You will be surprised with the changes you will start to notice in your life. You will see the Magic of Law of Attraction, so surround yourself with the visuals of what you love.

2. **Visualise with Closed Eyes** – Close your eyes, sit in peace and imagine enjoying yourself in the environment and atmosphere you want to have around you. To cut the interference, plug in your headphones with your favourite music that gets you in touch with the environment you are trying to imagine. Visualise yourself in the business you want to develop, the car you want to drive, the Job or career that you always wanted, the kind of life partner you want. Imagine yourself being where you want and going through those moments in your mind as if you were really there. It's kind of creating a dream in your mind while awake. Make your conscious mind aware of what you want. Do this for at-least 5 minutes every day or as long as it takes to visualise with clarity until you find yourself fully immersed in how you want to see yourself in the future. More immersed experience comes with more practice.

3. **Everyday Compliment** – When you get ready everyday, stand in front of the mirror and compliment yourself. Take pride in your looks, the personality you wear. Compliment your soul, your self and start behaving in

the manner of future you, behave as you would once you have realised your dream. I once attended this seminar where the guy told us that he had started to see himself as a millionaire before he actually had the money in his bank account. Visualise and compliment yourself in your future.

Train Thy Brain

With all the above knowledge and techniques to start manifesting what we want is not going to be without challenges from our brain. Our brain is so use to behaving in certain ways and changing that behaviour will take some serious commitment. You must not just be interested in making the change but You must be Committed. **With that commitment, you must Train your Brain.** The way to train your brain is to realise your own behaviour as someone else's and treat it as the knowledge and insight you have received into someone else's brain. Most people are better at advising others than implementing it on our own selves aren't we. Let's make use of that behaviour of ours to trick us for good.

You can look at the knowledge and inside secrets you have gained about yourself with this tool as someone else's behaviour, and use your intelligence to manipulate or transform that behaviour as if you would help someone else. In this case you will actually end up designing a strategy to tackle your own self for better outcomes and that too using your own ways. You must train your brain to do that and then use the strategy developed as a solution with the help of The Karmic Rewind Tool. This is what I call, **Train Thy Brain** by realising how the brain of the person you see in the mirror works and start manipulating it, start transforming it to bring out the desired results.

If you have children, you see them all the time, you learn almost each and everything about them and sometimes use that knowledge to manipulate their behaviour to get them to do one thing or another. Sometimes you will also get them to do certain things against their will because you know it is better for them. The idea here is the same. Equipped with the knowledge and tactics you have developed in the Revival Action Plans, you must treat yourself in similar manner as if you are to transform that child in you and create a better future for that child.

Let's take a look at some research to see how our brain works. Researchers advise that our brain, our conscious mind is processing close to eleven million pieces of information and we are in actual, only aware of about 40 to 2000 of those millions of pieces received. The rest are being processed as lower priority by our brain so we consciously are unaware of those. That is because we do not need that information at the time we receive it. It goes into the sub-conscious mind and is dug through by our Reticular Activation System when need arises. There is a lot of feed that goes into the brain whether consciously or unconsciously. So what our brain does is that it is adding some new impressions into our mind. And whenever in future we encounter a similar or related situation, our mind will always dig into our memory, our subconscious mind and pull that information out to deal with the situation faced. It is amazing the way it works.

The brain is what controls the body in all its functional aspects. The best bit I like about it is, that it wakes us up from the sleep mode while we do not even know or at-least not conscious about whether we were even alive or not. It keeps the body functioning and revives it overnight. It's as if we are given even shorter flickering episodes of our existence in this world in the form of us operating within the day and night mechanism not just our over all age; no one can go on for very long without having some sleep. **Could it be true** that we are hallucinated forms of existence in this world of illusion if we compare us with the way we have made TV or computer screens; visuals are displayed at a very high speed flickering of light. After all, we are made of atoms.

In computer terms I will say that **we are a computer programmed to shut down not based on time alone** but with day and night mechanism which also influences the chemical compositions in our brain to make us fall asleep. When we wake up it's a restart of our whole processing system with a given program to run basic functions of this body as well as highly intelligent programs that works with data received through various senses of our body. The world we live in is the sets of data we work with or our brain works with. In this scenario, our mind works sort of like an artificial intelligence program only that it's designed at eternal levels and unseen at our physical levels. It controls our projection in this world very powerfully and precisely based on datasets it receives, let's give it the right set of data to work with and support our brain to start working towards outcomes we want to achieve.

By learning the way your brain behaves, you can manipulate it to work in the direction of reaching your goals. Scientific proofs exist about the brain manipulation by artificial means as well. They also use something called **Transcrainial Direct Current Stimulation** technique to treat people with certain specific kind of depression, anxiety and psychological disorders. In this technique they send low levels of current constantly into the specific brain area. Why can't we do it ourselves by increasing the required energies and frequencies? Techniques for this may involve, listening to music you love, seeing things that please your heart and mind, utter the words of happiness, use positive affirmations, use the visualisation tools. You just need to identify what kind of vibrations and frequencies are right for you.

Once you have worked out how your brain works and behaves better, you can start transforming it. Sometimes you may need to trick it with the tricks and techniques just as you would to win over the strengths and weaknesses of an opponent team. You can manipulate their ways by pretending that they can predict what you are going to do but then give them a shocker by doing a surprise act out of their expectations to beat them. This is going to be the main mantra for you from this tool. You need to master the art of analysing your own personality, the way you do things, the way you behave in any given situation, the way you react, the things you would do to get something done, and how would you go about doing that task. Just be honest to yourself so you can pick on your own behaviours, weaknesses and strengths.

This is going to be the best practice for you to explore your own personality by taking it as if it is someone else you are going to help. Give your best advice and ensure you follow that up with your innermost soul's efforts along with true heart and spirit to do something for you. This is one instance where I would say that **bring out that selfish personality of yours** and sit down as a very selfish being whose motive is to help yourself in getting you out of the situation, the life and surroundings you are in, for better and help yourself in committing to that change. The change that brings positive changes in your personality, your surroundings, your friends, relationships and your possessions if the need be or if the wish be. But start living the life you want to live, spread the Love, live in Harmony, live in Peace with the Universe and everything else will work in harmony with you. Give it the Love and it will Love you back. See what you want clearly and it will materialise in clear vision to you. Just remember, that the good brings good, the bad brings bad, even though the definitions will vary for Good and Bad for all different people and communities, but again, as I said, its your life, **its your world that is around you and the ability to change it by Karma, with power of thoughts is also within you**.

You need to make the decisions about yourself, you need to decide for yourself, and ensure that you are working towards the Good with Love, Peace and towards Harmony. The more you work with it, more you will work towards it, more you will receive it. So is the Law of Attraction, So is the law of Karma, So is the Logic that flows in this universe and So is the actual Life. So make it what you want, but only by following the rules and principles of Love, Peace and Harmony. Anything opposite will only bring the opposite closer to you. So just be aware, and just follow the inner voice of your heart.

Just imagine the scientists putting their heart and soul in creating the best rockets, missiles that can fire to the other ends of the planet and destroy a large part of human community. I often wish that those brilliant brains and money were spent in the favour for better life for all human beings on earth. At the same time think of the doctors and medical practitioners. They are using their brains to help other human beings. They are helping them ease the pain they may be suffering from. Yet at times they have to give them painful treatments, but it is always for the patient's long-term health benefits.

Not that I am against any scientific discoveries and achievements. But why use those achievements towards destruction at all. We often complain about feeling threatened, so acting in self-defence makes us pursue such motives. But why do we have to feel threatened from each other when we all tend to join hands against a common threat. We all humans are similar creatures on earth. We should all be living in harmony. And once that happens, we all will not have the greedy feelings about anything at all and just behave like friends not pretend to be friends.

We all know teamwork can achieve more, then why not practice that more for making the world a better place in every aspect of life.

The only threat then left may be from the animals or other creatures. But hey, we all know treating animals with care and love can help us live along with them, at-least most of them. It's only when they are scared of us, they try to harm us. We treat a lion with love; they behave in loving manner towards us humans. The Buddhist monk temple in Thailand is a perfect example of it.

The other threat may be from nature, but we know that no matter how hard we try to control water flows in rivers and water reserves, we know when nature shows its power, there is no escape. Similar applies with Solar energy we receive, as well as the Air around us, we all know the damage hurricanes can cause and there is only so much we can do about this. End of the day, nature is also the very cause of our survival too. Don't we human beings have the same behaviour and mindset too? Don't we feel that if we are the creators of something, we have the right to destroy that as well if we wish to, especially when our creation comes back to haunt and destroy us. We have seen that in the movie, I-robot. We have also often seen a large amount of honour killings in other parts of the world. Well, **why do we think that nature should not be able to do so?** After all, Nature is actually the very cause of survival of us human beings.

So the power the energy that exists in the world, that creates the world, which runs the world, also has the power to destroy it. And this logic flows from A to Z of the universe. Anything that has started in this world has to be ended. We see that in this mortal world. We see that in the nature, we see that in the atmosphere, and we see that in the galaxies, the universe. Some of those examples will be, starting from the smallest and tiniest creatures on earth to higher level of species, or all different kinds of species, **the age is the factor** to consider. Everything has to die one day or another. As we move into the universe, the black holes, the stars, the planet system, the age is much more, but Stars do also die. We only need to learn more of physics to know this, which also tells us the billions of years old galaxies that exists.

So I believe we can learn a lot from nature alone and what exists around us. Just need to apply the logical sense. The common-sense, as I spoke about earlier. We all learn from the books, you only need to think about **where did those books came from**. After all someone has applied their common sense and logical intelligence, and realised the facts about what exists out there. Why do we believe that we do not have that tendency at this moment, in this day and age? **We have grown into a society too much dependent on academic knowledge and not our natural intelligence.** We should learn from those experiences and learn what we can along with exercising our own natural abilities, to make our life worthy by realising its true potential. We all have the same powers within, we just need to realise and nourish them.

The **mystical powers** exist within every one of us. **Their existence is not a wonder but realising them within us is**. The black magic exists and at the same time there exists the powers that can overpower any such levels or strengths of black magic that are tend to harm people. And important thing to note is who wins all the time and time & time again. The series of Harry Potter movies should help to prove the point of 'The powers of good will'. We see that too often and in movies we see it every day, if we do watch everyday movies. I am not too much into the movies but I will enjoy any boring movie if I decided to watch it in a theatre. I appreciate the time and effort that has been put in by the people. The only time I have watched many movies is probably while traveling on the planes. Not many at home, and only a few at theatres.

I certainly do believe in those powers and mystical existences. I look back at certain things and stages in my life and wonder how I got out of some of those situations with a great help from the unknown. The incidents like when I was declared medically dead once, 26th January 1999, North Wollongong beach, NSW Australia. We only need to realise with a bit of a deep thought about the incidents in the life we are living. We should be grateful for all that we have and realise our natural abilities, which our creator has equipped us with to live in the world he created. Believe in those mystical powers and the powers within. Do not let other negative energies hurt your positive energy.

I had those feelings every now and then when I will be in full mood of getting something done, with my mind fully focused but then there will always be someone who may cause you a bit of a distraction and pull that mood right down. It's just like one of those stories in the movie I just watched on television the other day, where Bruce Lee and his companion Officers are in Paris to bust a gang, and the Taxi Driver who was helping them was so passionate about helping them or even if they talked him into it, he so wanted to be a secret agent. When he tells his wife, she gives him a slap and tells him that, he is just a taxi driver and commands to leave their company to go with her. Poor guy leaves their company and goes back to taxi driving as per his wife. Later he gives them a last ride in his car saying something along these lines; I can't remember them at the time of writing exactly, but it intended: 'I can't be driving you guys anymore; my wife says I am just a Taxi driver and can't be a secret agent'. Poor guy.

This story is just for the purpose of helping people to realise the fact about how our brain gets influenced. No matter how passionate we may be about doing certain things in life or achieving something in life, there will always be certain levels of doubt only until you have showed the courage, conquered the fear and not let negative thoughts flourish. That is what a lot of writers also try to convey as well, when trying to motivate you, because they all have their own stories of similar circumstances. There is always someone who will come in and try to punch your confidence down. Don't let your brain bogged down with such incidents; you just need to build your strength and keep getting up. Even if you can maintain the strength to keep getting up every time you fall, it is much better than falling down first time and being buried in the dust.

That is not what the life is about, that is not what a human being is about and specifically as you are reading this book, that is not what Your life is about. You need to realise your potential, and believe in yourself so you can hold yourself better in the shape and personality you want yourself to be. Every human on this planet earth is really a special being, a special form of life is what we are living. You only need to realise your true essence, and your life will change forever and be on the path that you want to follow.

We also should take more responsibility towards the planet we live on and the social environment we live in. Looking at the global warming issue, I believe **we are invading Nature**, the very reason for our existence. We need to pull ourselves back a bit, and adhere to more natural ways of living the life. Nature is designed to produce food for all of us. And we know that we all have to pay much more if we want to eat organic food in today's day and age. Yet we know that Organic foods are best for us, then why are we seeing more and more of genetically modified foods.

We know what is better for us, yet we are not moving towards it. Do we need another revolution for people adapting more to the natural ways of life? More and more people are moving away from farming too in some parts of the world to live more techno high fast paced life. **I am an advocate of finding balance in life** and living a balanced life. I myself had moved from the fast paced city of Sydney to the nation's actual capital city Canberra in 2010, which is much more relaxed. We didn't have to go miles to enjoy open space areas only on a holiday. We got the best mix of city life and natural views, beautiful sky all day. It may seem enjoyable most of the times in major cities, but as per below article, researchers have studied that country life is better and healthier option. Below is an abstract from the research by Dr. Prussner.

****

Science has already proven that life in the cities is more stressful than the rural areas. Dr Jens Pruessner of the Douglas Mental Health University Institute in Quebec carried out a recent study. Dr. Jens said: 'Previous findings have shown that the risk for anxiety disorders is 21 per cent higher for people from the city, who also have a 39 per cent increase for mood disorders. In addition, the incidence of schizophrenia is almost doubled for individuals born and brought up in cities. These values are a cause for concern.'

Dr. Pruessner and his fellow team members from the University of Heidelberg in Germany monitored the brain activity of adult volunteers while they carried out mental arithmetic puzzles under time pressure.

The functional magnetic resonance imaging scans revealed that the brains of those living in cities reacted differently to stress. The area of the brain called 'Amygdala' – involved in mood and emotion – was more active among the volunteers raised in cities, and those with an urban upbringing had a more active cingulate cortex – the area of brain involved in regulating stress – while carrying out the task.

A larger study would be needed to confirm the findings. The researchers are unsure why city life affects the regions of the brain that handle stress. And they say that pollution, toxins, crowding or noise could be the contributors. The past studies have shown that spending more time in greener places and outdoors gives a soothing feel to frayed nerves and improves well-being.

****

In 2009 another scientist's research at the Essex University showed that as little as five minutes in a greener place or such outdoors could cut down stress levels. And there are other studies that show that those with access to rural and countryside are less likely to have heart disease or strokes. Psychologists have argued that millions of years of evolution means the human brain has not developed to cope with life surrounded by thousands of strangers. Now I know why I felt so good on the days I went for a walk to nearby garden from work during my lunch breaks. That may just be the trick you can use too if you are mostly stuck indoors, specifically being stuck inside during winter, when days are short.

A balanced life is the best approach to living life as per my personal belief. There are many possibilities to the way of living life on this planet, as you can design the life you want just by abiding with the laws of the universe, keeping your ability to commit karmas in check with those laws. And as we understand our self a bit better now with The Karmic Rewind tool, we understand how we can handle ourselves better and transform our own brain, by knowing how it behaves and how it reacts. We can manipulate it to achieve the desired results and use our actual potential by setting our mind free from the ropes and chains of negative thoughts and by giving us the acceleration of positive thinking. To be able to see those results in practicality of life, it's time now to start implementing certain changes.

Adapting to even the thought of change in life runs a bit of a scare and stomach butterflies to some people. I often spoke to people about making some changes in their life every time they come across whinging about going to work on Mondays and not being happy with what they are doing. When it comes to making that change they go back into the shell. The fear of change and dis-belief in themselves grips their mind and abilities. They don't believe they can do it anymore, they are wary of walking into the changed life. They think they will be unsettled from a set state of mind, as it may not be okay as it is at the moment even if it is not great. They completely overrule the possibilities of what if it is okay after the change, what if it is better after the change, but no, that positive outcome is completely overruled to get back into the present **Uncomfortable Comfort Zone**.

I have been able to push one of my friends out of that whinging routine, but he was keen and trusted my advice and encouragement. Let alone how many times he whinged on the way to the change and almost thought of dropping back to where he was time and time again. I had to keep pushing him and now he is enjoying a successfully running business and is very happy and appreciates that support.

That is why someone said that a lot of the time people don't even realise how close they are to the success when they drop out. It's just how our brains work, it wants to run back to the comfort zone that it is familiar with. One just needs that tiny little push to see the way through but they just step back out of fear of change, fear of the unknown or failure. Let this be the risk if it is, be wise but take it. This friend of mine would have stepped back too if he did not get the encouragement and support he needed. Both of us did all the hard work from lease negotiations to setting up the shop. We spent few sleepless nights of travel together riding the truck between Sydney and Canberra, but we finally did manage it. You just need to make sure that push is from someone who is sincerely your well-wisher.

I would love to see the whole world living happily ever but I am sad about people not realising their true potential and they show their back to the actual life they are supposed to enjoy. **You don't need to wait for the judgement day, to be in heaven**. You can create one here by creating the life you want. Be open-minded as it is now Time for Four Changes. It's time to learn, how to go about making those changes and create that necessary push within, which will bring to you, the Change in Life, the change into the world you want to live in. Live your life the way life was always meant to be lived.

Part - IV

Time for Four Changes

*'To exist is to change; To change is to mature,
To mature is to go on creating oneself endlessly.'*

-Henry Bergson

Time For Four Changes

So Change – What, Why, How are some of the quick questioning responses by one's brain. As soon as the word CHANGE is heard, our brain automatically gets into these questionings to try and pull us back from that weird feeling of change. It deploys the fear sensing radars in conjunction with our mind to not let us out of the currently familiar and experienced zone of comfort even if it is not the preferred zone; but at least you have it – it says, why loose it. What do we need to Change? Why do we Need to Change? How is that Important to me, and why should I change something? Once you give it back the comfort through reasoning and convince that it is actually going to be great if we make that change, it then asks, well How Do I Do It? Most people drop out because of the fear of change which doesn't go away because of the lack of information about how to, where from, what will happen, will it even happen; and because we don't have answers and don't find someone who has been there done that, we step back comfortably and not dare to make the change. It is all about how much comfort and support is created for implementing change so you have the support to get over that line to get to the other side. Let's create that comfort and support for applying change in this part and get you over to the other side.

One term that you must understand is called 'Cybernetics' which comes from a greek word meaning 'To Steer'. A term introduced by some physicians and mathematicians together with Norbert Weiner and Arturo Rosenblueth. Cybernetics is the term for control and communication, whether in technological inventions or humans and animals. We all are fitted with this system to continuously learn, assess against a goal, make desired changes and take action to reach a goal. When we communicate with someone on a topic, we continuously try to ensure all parties are on the same page; we walk towards something, we are continuously checking to ensure we are heading in the right direction or else we assess and act to change course to move in the direction of our destination. Within our body, our brain is communicating with our balance sensors and autonomously ensuring we stay in a balanced position and don't fall off. Applying the change through action is that 'Act' part of cybernetics to continuously steer towards the goal we have determined for our life's aspects. So, by making use of The Karmic Rewind Tool and through Karma by applying the changes comfortably, **we will have created a complete Cybernetic System** to achieve your desired life. Let's get comfortable with change now.

An important **Hurdle that needs to be changed is Your Ability to Hold Yourself Back**. As we all have heard enough that God Created Human in its own Image. If he did, then how can we lack in potential to create our own world, filled with what we wish to achieve. There may be an account of Karma that may add some destiny to the life, but that Karma was also created by us with our ability to be able to Do or Create Karma.

If you can see it with your heart and soul, you can create it with the help of your mind, you can achieve it through Karma, and you can live with it on this planet. But, what you must do to get there is; implement karmic change. If you are not living the life you want, and want to change it, then Change is the first thing you will need to embrace. If you do not change anything that you are doing right now you will not see different results.

If you think your mind is simply the way it is and can not be changed, then read below article that was published on news.com.au site. There was a lot in news about people working a lot of extra hours without getting paid, and also about the managers treating their staff with attitude that they are always smarter than them. Because they act that way, this developed a real strength by stimulating their brain nerves. Read below, as it should help you understand a little more about how our body works and how you can bring about those changes by carefully selecting what decisions you make and what actions you take.

****

Office managers think they're smarter than the rest of the staff and now there is medical evidence to back it up. According to research from the UNSW, managing other people at work triggers structural changes in the brain, protecting its memory and learning centre well into old age.

Researchers have identified a link between managerial experience in a person's working life and the integrity and larger size of an individual's hippocampus - the area of the brain responsible for learning and memory - at the age of 80.

Dr Michael Valenzuela, leader of Regenerative Neuroscience in UNSW's School of Psychiatry, says the findings refine our understanding of how staying mentally active promotes brain health, potentially warding off diseases such as Alzheimer's.

The study will be presented at the Brain Sciences UNSW symposium today, which is focussing on research into 'brain plasticity', or the brain's ability to repair, rewire and regenerate itself. The findings overturn scientific dogma that the brain is 'hard-wired'.

'We found a clear relationship between the number of employees a person may have supervised or been responsible for and the size of the hippocampus,' says Dr Valenzuela.

'This could be linked to the unique mental demands of managing people, which requires continuous problem solving, short term memory and a lot of emotional intelligence, such as the ability to put yourself in another person's shoes. 'Over time this could translate into the structural brain changes we observed.'

The research comprises the doctoral work of Mr Chao Suo, supervised by Dr Valenzuela in collaboration with Scientia Professor Perminder Sachdev's Memory and Ageing Study based in Sydney.

****

Interesting discovery isn't it. Imagine if you also started thinking powerfully in your brain and back up with actions, your brain will develop into what you want to achieve with it. A little like those bodybuilding enthusiasts. You want to make your body to become stronger and muscular, they visualise the body they want to develop. They have a keen desire from the bottom of their heart. But how do they succeed? It's only when they start working out harder, and push their body out of the comfort zone. They keep doing it again and again, and slowly you start to see the results. Similarly, there are a lot of guys out there who wants to build their body stronger than it is, but they haven't given this the priority it needs and haven't taken action about it. It's all in the 'deciding with your true heart and backing it up with your actions'. If something is done about a particular goal, something is bound to happen.

We are what we repeatedly do, Excellence then, is not an act, but a habit

---Aristole

And we repeatedly do only what we love to do. So we need to assess ourselves as a whole of person that we are. Give ourselves a major life shakeup to put us on the path we want to and would love to walk for the rest of our life. Ride is a bit rough in the start but may not always be for everyone. That may depend on how aligned you are with living the life you want to live. Follow your heart. The things you are passionate about will automatically encourage you and keep you on track to reach them.

'Follow your bliss and the universe will open doors for you where there were only walls. '

- Joseph Campbell, The Power of Myth

The Four Factor

I want to discuss the 'Four' factor in my Time for Four Changes title of this chapter. Some numerologists believe this to be a number for Focus – focus on building a secure foundation for the future. The number four, I learned is also considered to be a number of Death in Chinese beliefs. It is because of it's pronunciation being same as the word "death"- "Shi". Hence I want to convey it as a symbol of Death of something that is holding us back from achieving the life of our dreams, the life, as we always wanted to live and focus on building the future through four changes. Let's call for the Death of everything that is trying to hold us from recognising the true potential we have as human beings. And those enemies are not so much outside, but they are within us and are living with us every day and every moment of our life. Let's **recognise** major four of them, **Kill them and** then **Focus** on your future **through a Four-Step approach** to Karma, the Act for Change.

> **The Comfort Zone** – Let's kill what stops us from stepping into the new atmosphere to be able to achieve more. Get uncomfortable with your comfort if that is what's holding you back.
>
> **Fear of Change**– Let's kill what stops us from moving forward towards the desired life of success.
>
> **Negative thoughts**– Let's kill what stops us from creating the positive attitude and positive atmosphere necessary to achieve our goals.
>
> **Negative Beliefs**– Let's kill what stops us from becoming who we are, from making a calculated and informed decision to achieve more in life.

We need to address these four in our life every day and challenge them to be able to change our life to what we want it to be.

Comfort zone sometimes can be a good thing but not when we are not living the life we want. So get out of it and kill it as soon as you can so you can start taking further actions to bring about the change. Comfort zone is often the result of being in the similar routines and atmosphere for a longer period of time. You get use to the similar life every day for so long that you do not even want to get out of it anymore. It's like that story of a frog – you want to boil the frog; you chuck it in boiling water and it jumps straight out. But if you drop it in warm water and slowly boil the water, it's cooked and doesn't even feel the heat to jump out of it.

It may be unpleasant, but after a while you are so used to it and hardly feel the need of a better atmosphere altogether. The stresses you may put up with every day, may not seem much because you have put up with them continuously for so long that 'Practice makes a man perfect' has proven so true already. Your mind is now so perfectly coping with it every day because you have been doing it for so long. That is exactly Why I want you to get ready to be uncomfortable through small light changes, so you can start building your new comforting life and then have that comfort zone built around you with the comforts you really need and comforts you deserve.

Fear of Change can be a major hurdle in helping you move ahead or bring about change in your life. It may be OK if you are happy and content with your life and do not want to move towards something that you have assessed to be a risk to your happiness and abundance in life. But if you are not happy with the way things are then I do not want the fear of change to be holding you back. I am not surprised that it does hold back a lot of people. It held me back until I dared myself to commit to make some low risk changes. You need to kill it ASAP. I held on to this factor for a longer while than I think I should have. But I am glad I killed it when I did. I visualised my way into starting to feel fully comfortable with not doing what I have been doing for years, the feel of stress-free life I would start to live, which I always wanted to. But, just because I had never lived my life the way I wanted to, I had to constantly counsel my own self to let go off the fear of change and implement few little but daring things to start bringing the change around.

I held myself back, for two months before deciding to train myself to start working from home as an assessor. But when I did take action to go ahead, I realised the money, the benefits and comforts I had lost over those two months that I procrastinated. And I must tell you, this was one of the two best decisions I made during my struggle to bring about change in my life. The other one was forcing my-self to join a Network Marketing Business. It opened my eyes to other opportunities that exist rather than routine jobs of hourly pay rates. I challenged myself to join and learned a lot by just joining it. I did not believe in the product as such so I did not pursue that. How could I sell if I didn't believe in it myself; my ethics don't allow for that. But the experience gave me opportunity to meet up with people who thought differently; it opened up my mind to take risk and look for better opportunities.

And due to the habits we have built over the years, '*Go with the flow and Not taking action is the thing we do best*', when we know we shouldn't. We know that the actions are the only way to bring results, and yet we quite successfully do not take action and hence fail to bring about the desired changes. So kill that habit and start taking action. All we need to do is; start taking a small action in the direction you want to go, you will surprise yourself with what you will trigger and what you can achieve. I will talk more on the triggers in the 'Automatic Effect' section a bit further but know that the journey of a mile starts with a small step, not by just standing there looking at or thinking about the milestone.

Once someone asked this saint from India; the question was that ' If one is standing in front of the sculpture of God and praying for something, would they have to do anything at all except praying with full love and devotion from the bottom of their heart? The answer was, 'If a child is running late to get to school in time, and he walks to school every day, then standing in front of the sculpture of God and preying is not going to get him to school in time. Rather if he prays with true heart and starts making the effort towards walking to the school, he may get some help or a lift to get there by God's grace but not merely by standing in front of the Temple or Sculpture and praying'. We do need results in the physical world and in physical manner. You can pray with your full love and devotion but some **Karma is to be done, action needs to be taken** in the physical aspect and then with the Grace of God, the results will be achieved. Though if we expect God's grace or the Universal Law's help in our achievements, we must abide by the rules they apply on life in this world as well. We need to take action in the direction of the goal we want to achieve. Even Lottery wins are for those who took a step in the direction of winning the Lotto, which is buying the Lottery Tickets; you have to be in it to win it.

Negativity needs to be eliminated altogether. Whether it is with-in you, or with you outside. It only takes a glimpse of a negative thought to trigger a drop out of a brilliant idea or action. Most of the times it's not just the negative thought alone but the weight and belief you put behind it that stops a wonderful journey you could experience. That weight behind the thought comes from your belief, whether you believe in it's negatives or someone has said something to feed your mind with negatives about that idea. So, stop putting negative weight to your heart's desires for your life. All you got to do is focus on what could go right, not wrong. Force yourself quickly to take a moment away to think about something else when the negative thought strikes, before it consults the belief system to add more weight and stop you from steering towards your desire. Just ignore it for a duration and come back to it when feeling positive or pumped up to do something about achieving your desire.

Eliminate the negative within, anywhere outside or around your environment. People spent a lot of time and money on Feng-Shui to create such environments. Some still failed because they did not have positive within themselves. I once visited this lady for my assessment job that I was doing. She had lots of Buddha statues and Feng-Shui way of set up, as she told me. She seemed quite calm and did tell me that she also does meditation at times. And since she had started to do that, she had started to feel much calmer and much in control of her life. She agreed that she had the Feng-Shui set up before too but it was only since she started meditation, she felt much more positive and felt positive atmosphere around her. So try some meditation techniques to calm down and create positivity within and with-out.

You must do everything to kill those negative thoughts and beliefs. You must either alter them to positives or completely replace them with positive beliefs and thoughts. Make use of The Karmic Rewind tool and your RAPs will help you achieve this. God made the man in his own image, so based on that you do have the power within, let's try to realise that power.

Realise The Power Within & Our True Essence

What I believe in is something that is stronger than creating the atmosphere around you alone. I have discussed it more in the Karmic rewind section of the book but as a quick note; we actually have the enormous power and energy within us to influence the atmosphere around us. If you can build that perfect combination of your eternal being with your physical personality, be in touch with your true essence, the spiritual being that we are and realise that power within, then negativity can not affect you, your positive influence will neutralise that negativity. So bring your physical being in harmony with your spiritual being as soon as possible and eliminate the negative aspects all together.

You need to ensure that once you have decided on a path that you want to take, keep your mind clear and focused, no negative feelings should come in between. Whether it is your own self-doubt or someone else who doesn't think your efforts will work, kill the doubts. Even if you fail initially, remember it means your **F**irst **A**ttempt **I**n **L**earnng. Just learn your lessons, improve and persist. What do you think would have been the answers of such negative people to Bill Gates, Steve Jobs, Jack Ma, Mark Zuckerberg, Elon Musk; if they had gone to see someone academically strong and spoke to them about their goals. A lot of them probably thought "A university dropout talking about doing Whatt...? There's no way he can do that".

Steve Jobs made things possible that were so out of question a decade or so ago. And what would have been the answer, if you were the space scientist wanting to design a rocket ship to launch into space and there was no such idea of even flying around in those days. After all, there was a vision and that vision was followed up by the determination, continuous improvements and required action while killing the fear of failure and breaking all the comfort zones. I saw an advertisement on a news website that people can now enjoy the flight into the space for about 98000 US dollars. So, stop seeking approval from other people, believe in the power within and pursue your vision.

When I dared myself the first time, I dared to start in Network Marketing. I was never comfortable with it at all; after all, I needed proper rest to go to my other hated job (sarcasm). But I had heard a lot of stories and read a lot of articles about people working as a networker and not only they made a lot of money but they were also Time rich. Warren Buffet has also always favoured it. Once you have money then you can always buy any sort of comforts, one would think. But, they also had the freedom of time and freedom of working at their leisure. That is what the life is really about, that is what most of us want in reality.

Being Positive

I continued to work hard in life, but as I could not break away from my routines of hard working, that was only adding more pressure on life. I was doing what I did not love to do. It was then, that one-day I just decided to take that leap of faith and say `yes' to this lady who wanted me to join her network-marketing group. Largely I did it so I could break the barrier of the fear of change, Barrier of not taking action, and since I did that, I have opened up my comfort zone horizons much more wider and started implementing actions that took me closer to my goals and also caused the death of negativity around me.

I always have been an optimistic person with positive thinking. When I met my wife for the first time before engagement, we were given some time aside to talk about anything if we wanted to discuss as we were going to spend our lives together for the rest of our life. And, yes I would agree that times have changed in India about forcing the marriages on kids, it may still be happening in remote village zones but not in urban parts of India, not any more. While talking about few things and life in general, I did discuss with her too that I do not like negative attitudes towards anything and I give my 200% to do anything I always take up as a task to do, not just the 100%.

So being positive has always been in my heart, nature and on top of my brain all the time. That's a different story that I may still want my favourite team to win cricket match even though we have more than 6 runs to win on last ball, well hey, how can you rule out the possibility of a No ball, a wide ball, and a six after that un-scored No ball. Ok, Ok, I won't bore you with my cricket commentary for long. So please read carefully and do live by the techniques provided every day. The Change you may be looking for may just be around the corner. Just DO IT WITH YOUR FULL HEART and sing – 'Change is in the air'.

Automatic Effect

Apart from being positive, I was surprised when I learnt another interesting fact. We all know that most people are right-handed people in this world. I learned that if you start to move the smallest finger called The Little finger or Pinkie, towards your hand or palm, it automatically starts to move the rest of the fingers and bend them towards the palm too. And how I want you to use this concept of Four changes is in the similar way.

The same way as you would move the smallest finger and the rest start to move in the same direction and once you have them all converted into a Punch, you know that the effect is much stronger than a Slap. A bit scenical there but what

I mean is that once you will have decided and acted upon to let the change begin, even one small step at a time, the rest of the things will start to change in favour and you will have more strength like in a punch hit rather than what a slap does. When you have coordinated all the necessary ingredients of the recipe to the life you always wanted, making the effort to cook will bring the life you wanted to live, on your platter.

So read it carefully, read it over and over again if you have to, but the most important part is the Karma, the action towards change. The change is desired for you to change the life, change it from the path it is on now to the path you want it to be on. Just do it, and as the rest of the fingers follow the smallest finger on hand, the universe and energies around you also start to move to accommodate the change to fill up the space around you with what will benefit the changed conditions the most. Believe in Yourself, believe and have faith in who and what created us all and Just do it with your full heart.

'Change is a Must and has to come from Within Your Heart.
With the True Heart You need to decide
With the True heart You should Live Your Life'

Just need to ask a question to yourself and answer it truthfully. How hard has the life been thus far? I am sure most will answer, life is hard, it has been really hard and there will be some who will say, I have had a pretty good life and have no complaints. And to all these people, I am happy for you whichever way you may have answered as long as you have answered this truthfully. The happy ones should act to do more for the humanity to bring them to their levels, and those who are feeling that it has been a bit of a struggle then let me help you realise the truth you already know but never realised.

Rewind to Fast Forward

The truth is that sometimes going back downhill for good is not only easier but beneficial too my friends. Think about reversing the journey of hard climb to gain more momentum to climb higher. You do a hard climb backwards which gives your more speed as well as force. Haven't we seen the soldiers in old days, outside the fort gate holding a tree log together, they go backwards for not running away from their stronger obstruction but to come back with more momentum and force to destruct the entry gate, the hurdle in their way to win over their enemy.

Step back to basics. Learn the truth and facts about your life using the Future Probability Sphere and The Karmic Rewind tool. Learn the kind of person you are or you have become. Learning about yourself will empower you with the knowledge about yourself that you never took out time for, otherwise you would have realised your true potential and won at the game of life already. You would have been living an empowered life exploiting your true potential to the max.

Start paving the way towards a better destination in life than the one you are heading towards now, if you are not happy with what you may have achieved or heading towards achieving. Once you are easing yourself back downhill, guess what you can do. Downhill does not mean you must stop earning through that painful job if you don't have any savings to rely on or no food to put on your and your family's plate. You will simply need to change your mindset towards it until you are getting the blueprint of your future life ready and are ready to start on that MAP of your life. The mindset will ease that pain because you will be motivated towards that better future but still putting the food on the table. Having that mindset will work as anaesthetic for your pains in life until you start on the path to your dreams.

With that mindset, you should enjoy the rewind ride as it is going to be a relief, because you are not trying painfully harder towards the journey that is going to make you sick and tired and burn you out. While you are enjoying that rewind ride, start thinking about yourself more and more.

At this stage, consider yourself like a childcare teacher. Assess yourself with the eyes of a child care teacher and treat the personality of you or the person you have been so far as that of the child you will be minding as a child care teacher.

After minding the child for some time, the teacher knows how that kid behaves. She knows the child very well and has planned certain tasks accordingly to manipulate the child's brain to not only build discipline and teach him some good skills but also to ensure the child does certain things in the way he or she should be doing.

And as she has planned according to how kid behaves and interacts, she has managed to get by the day by fulfilling her duty to the child as well as making it valuable for the child too. In the similar manner you need to start paving a way for yourself. Who else would know you the best, may be your mother or your wife does but believe me No-one knows you better than You do by now. You know the best about how you would behave in a certain situation. You can work against your fear and comfort zone at times by forcefully putting yourself in the situations where you know deep inside you that you will get the best out of you. You may not want to, but if you know that is how you get the best results, then do it.

When your destination in life is re-planned in terms of the life you want to live, how can you be not putting all the effort you need? How can you be not getting excited about taking the actions that are needed to get you to that destination every day and moreover, how can you be not excited about not having to drag yourself to work on Mondays and back home Happy on Friday's, just because you will have those two days of not going to work, not doing something you do not enjoy doing. If you do enjoy doing what you do, then you should really be excited to go to work on Mondays and looking forward to it. If that is not the case, you need to reassess your goals.

Do it, Do it for your own sake, Do it for the sake of those you love and you will teach them the right thing too, the right way of living life, enjoying the life the way it is supposed to be lived. Let me tell you another story about one of the initiatives I took that I also mentioned earlier in a quick note. This will explain how I triggered and initiated the change in my life.

Trigger & Initiate Change

This lovely lady approached me to join a networking business she was involved with. They sold these specially made Bio-Discs that are made specially designed with Nano-Technology compressed in a very specific manner. The disc is designed to enhance the positive energy of whatever it comes in contact with. I was invited to the presentation and given the examples of using the water that has been passed through the disk to be used as a spray to give you a refreshing feel. Then they used the water on one half of an orange to prove that it will get sweeter in comparison to its other half left naturally. The convincing followed by more examples where such water sprayed on a wound would help heal the wounds quicker and certain examples showed where cure was achieved with people who suffered from Life threatening Gangrene. There was everything there, which makes part of the convincing someone needs to become a part of the network. I wasn't very convinced but still joined, just to do something different and break the shackle.

Until that day though, I had never been approached by someone, for any such business opportunity other than hearing stories of Amway or Tupperware. To me, selling was never my cup of tea. But, just so I could learn something about such networking environments and if they truly offered a better life style and money too; then why not? Few people had told me in the past that Network Marketing business Seminars are just the brain washers, it never works. But I wanted a change and had to be triggered for something different to happen. I said this one thing to myself –

> *'Let this be the trigger. Let this be the brain wash into a better field of thoughts than being brainwashed to live in the manner I am living in now.'*

I had to fork out about One Thousand dollars at that point in time, and it was hard for me to spare that kind of money. But, I did it, and managed that somehow, just so I could trigger that change in my life to a different direction that was told to be better. I forced myself to initiate that change. I am just not the best sales person, but if I am convinced about something, I am a good person to convince others about the same, by trying my best to clear any doubts they may have. But I am not a good sales person. I am happy to recognise what my strengths are and am willing to work with my strengths in a better way. I took the path back downhill and realised more about myself. I have projected a better spot in my Future Probability Sphere and I am strengthening my knowledge, skills and myself to have a better shot at that spot.

I hope you can do so too sooner than later. Just imagine the feeling of the person who has been wanting to achieve something and have been putting all the effort they can, and once they have achieved it, remember that Yesss... This is a feeling that sends waves of relief and confidence in the whole body along with happiness. That is what you want to be able to do when you look back at a milestone in your life, when you look back and say, '**I am glad I did that**'.

Not living the life one wants is a dose of stress we take every day. Stress has a lot to do with our health concerns. I know that as a matter of fact as in my life, I went through such a patch of more than ten years after finishing school. I worked as much as I could. I worked in factories, bakeries, in restaurants, drove security patrol cars, and drove cab in other spare time. Then I found better jobs as I always wanted to and wished for. I started working in the office jobs, even then I would work as a security patrol officer over the weekend. And if I was not doing that then I was driving a cab to make up for the expenses for myself and to keep up with the financial expectations of me towards my family.

And if that was not enough a real life drama within family broke out and that simply accelerated the stress on my mind. No matter how hard I tried to keep my cool, it never came out of my mouth but affected my body in different manners. I went for a hair cut one day and the guy pointed out my hair loss. I told him it wasn't hereditary but when he mentioned – "It must be stress then.", that is when I realised what the stress can do. One should keep stepping towards living the life they want. I have lost some hair that I once took pride in. I triggered my diabetic condition early too by ignoring health routines over work and coping with stress. Now I realise what I did to myself, putting up with stress and adding more stress by choosing the solutions that were in agreement with others but not mine.

I learned another shocking fact about Stress and its causes, as the world celebrated World Mental Health Day, on 10th Oct 2011. In India, where second largest population of the world resides, there is a suicide attempt every hour. And reasons explained by an expert; Mr. Mittal senior consultant, psychiatry and psychotherapy at the Delhi Psychiatry Centre are - 'Suicide comes later. Before that, there is a lot playing in the head of any person with suicidal tendencies. For women, emotional reasons count more, but for men it is the financial world and dependent family that could be the reason.'

I hope that has given you a bit more insight to what you knew about effects of stress on your body. So let's take the positive steps towards the change that is necessary to get rid of all the stress in your life.

The 'What' Factor

First of all, let's discuss the 'What' factor. If not all of us, a large number of us people on planet earth are living the Life we want to get out of and live it in a better way than they are living now. Whether it's true or not is not even a question, most of us are. And yet, a very interesting factor is that when it comes to taking a step towards a direction that will lead us to where we actually want to be, we all step back as strongly as we want to step ahead.

Why? Why do we do that? And I can tell you now that, a lot of us are simply looking around shaking our head slowly and looking for all those excuses, in fact any excuse we can come up with, which will justify us not taking or being able to take that action.

Let me ask a question: Have we ever seen Sugarcanes coming out of grain seeds? Did anyone say Yes? I hope not. So answer is No.

What about another question: Have we ever seen a student studying Medical Science all through University and get qualified as a Computer Engineer or a Civil Engineer? Answer is No.

Have we not all heard that; If you keep trying the same thing or **keep repeating same action; how can you expect different results**? Have we not all heard that, 'what you sow, so shall you reap'?

We all know these facts, and heard those quotations in life frequently enough. But are we acting on those when it comes to our own lives. Most of us don't. So it is Time for Change. Time for At least FOUR Changes in your Life, which I explain next as a four step process, so you can Change Your Life for the Life You want to Live. It is the *TIME FOR FOUR CHANGES*.

Start repeating and singing these words to yourself every day– 'CHANGE IS IN THE AIR' and you will see how soon it will start to show up around you as long as you mean it from your heart. There is the Law of Attraction that will start bringing around you what you start to desire from the bottom of your heart. But for all that to happen, what needs to happen is a change; the change in Karma because we live in this world governed through our Karmas. The guide to trigger and bring change in your life and how you can get to that point where changed future is waiting for you is given below. Let's start to introduce change step by step.

Change -1: Give Yourself Time for Yourself

Most of us don't realise the importance of giving time to our own self. We are living in such a fast paced world today that we never have enough time for anything. I personally follow a stream of teachings from saints and mystics of the world, which teaches a way of living life under God's will while doing your best in life and abiding by certain noble principals. This helps me live a life of contentment; however I am not going to go too much into it as that is simply a matter of personal choices for everyone. But one very important factor I learned was that in old days human kind was living a simpler life than the way we are living these days. Then the modern technological inventions of human brain came to the world. Now we are living life with everyday tasks getting done much quicker and easier. Even then, there is still one thing we are very short of, and that is Time.

How did that start to happen? All these inventions were born to help the human kind living a convenient and easier Life; they were to free up more of our time. But have we really achieved that motive. Though, it is much easier and convenient for us to write a letter in the form of an email, which should have saved us some time in reality, but we just write too many of them too often. All these machineries and modern day Information Technology was created to help us in making tasks and jobs much easier, we just started to do too many of those tasks. So what have we transformed our lives into really?

We have come to a stage where we are living a life for these machines and technologies instead of taking their help in making our life easier. We have started living a life where we have created too much for us to deal with and we seem to be indulged in wasteful, unfulfilling activities that just revolve around our superficial needs and wants. What we do these days is we want to live a modern charming life. We hardly give this a thought that what probably would be a sensible way to achieve this? We just go out and buy stuff without assessing the practical needs and then we find ourselves in the situation where that's all we are working for and sacrificing the actual life we wanted to live. We get stuck and work hard in jobs sometime two & three of them to make up for all those needs, wants and desires. That is the life most of us seem to have on our platter.

Anytime you discuss with someone about holidays, look at the cheerful smile on their face, and imagine that feeling inside one's heart, mind and also body of not having to work for that many days and enjoying the life. That is what life is actually about. I am a firm believer in God, not saying that you should be too, but I doubt that anyone has not uttered those words at one stage or another, whether knowingly or unknowingly – 'Oh My God', 'God Help Me' or 'for God sake' or in any such contrast. So, I believe when god created the universe he ensured there was everything for everyone's needs and probably also for wants but not the greed. We just need to tap into the right channels and resources with right intentions. Tune into the universal principals of Love, Peace and Harmony and let the Law of Attraction in this Universe work for you.

To be able to get to that stage you need to have a clear and relaxed mind. This is very important for everyone; this will not only help you achieve your goal, but also help you on your way towards those goals. That is why **you need time for your own self, for self-realisation**. This will be a great help for you in calmly dealing with daily life and related stresses in a far better way. With a calm mind, you can understand better the things that are happening around you, the reason for them, and how to act or react to them.

This is the first most important factor that you need to create and adapt to as a change. All you need to do is Give Yourself Some Time. Below are the four ways you can achieve this first and effective change that will prepare you well psychologically.

Step-1: Close All The Doors –

Do I mean closing all the room doors around You? Yes I do. Do I mean something deeper or meaningful than just closing those room doors? Yes I Do.

Now, this is a powerful method to attain a calm and peaceful mind. Find yourself a place where it is peaceful and quiet, away from all the noises. For some people it may be possible at home at any time of the day. For others, only certain times of the day may be suitable when kids may not be home. However, there may be some people who get tired of a long day at work and/or with kids or whatever the reason may be. Believe me it is very important to knock off the messages your brain is sending to simply go to sleep. And you will realise this after you have given yourself that half hour or an hour of silence. You will feel that you sleep much better, and wake up in a much better state of mind. By closing the doors, what I mean is close all the room and house doors if you need to, for cutting out the external noises etc., but more importantly, you need to focus, so shut off all the thoughts that come to your mind causing unnecessary worries and tensions that come along while thinking about a chore or a task to be dealt with or any of those other important things. Start with some relaxing music, it's proven to help.

Just stop adding weight to those thoughts, close it all off and start giving yourself the feel of silence and emptiness realising there's only you. Bring your mind to a state of relaxation by taking deep breaths and telling it that *'Nothing else matters at this moment any more than You and Yourself'*. Then keep telling this to your

Brain, until it has come down to the relaxed state. Have we not seen all those techniques modern science acknowledges, where you see an exaggerated behaviour of anguish and someone standing beside keeps telling them to Calm Down, Calm Down, Calm Down, repeating this again and again until the person start dropping from the peak of their anguish behaviour. Keep telling yourself and keep repeating as below –

> *Nothing else Matters at This Moment more than Me and Myself.*
> *Nothing else Matters at This Moment more than Me and Myself.*
> *Nothing else Matters at This Moment more than Me and Myself.*
> *Nothing else Matters at This Moment more than Me and Myself.*

Keep on repeating this until you start to feel how important is your own self-existence to you. As all that exists around you is only until you exist. All you can enjoy around you is only until you are in good health. All that exists for you is only valuable, if you can make use of it and feel it with your senses or with some physical action.

If you keep burning yourself the way you have been by running around all day, and never give yourself the time and attention you need, you may never be able to achieve the true happiness and meaning of living a happy life. I do not intend to say that you should stop working hard to achieve your goals. I mean to ensure that you being the driver, get enough rest and training to enrich and empower your skills to win the race or reach the destination successfully by working smarter. I do mean to ensure that you **work hard to work smarter**. We all know that any machinery without timely service and proper maintenance can degrade itself much earlier than it would last otherwise. It is simply logical and that logic flows throughout the universe. Our mortal body though being a marvellous biological gadget, is no exception to that logic. This dialogue from the very famous but now a bit old Movie– 'Top Gun', hit me hard one day.

> *'Your ego is writing cheques your body can't cash'*

How true, I am not going into the context of the movie but, what an impressive statement. *'Stop writing cheques with ego that our body can't cash'*. That is what we are doing a lot of the time, in fact most of the time. We are doing things our body can't handle. We are putting it through the demolishing stress by the means of our actions. Actions that are contradictory to our heart and soul's desires or due to the unhelpful beliefs we have in our mind. And hence we are living with a lot more sicknesses and diseases in this world today. The body is meant to heal itself; that is how it is designed. The only reason and time it can not heal its own self is, if it does not function as it was designed to. Most of the times, we have made our body dysfunctional due to the undue stresses we are putting on ourselves without building the capabilities that are required to handle that pressure. We are most of the time working only harder for unworthy results that are causing us more pain and little relief.

This applies to not only our human bodies but equally on our brain, our minds that are responsible for our psychological health. Why are we more prone to sicknesses and illnesses these days, a large part of it is also caused by the kind of lives we live today and majorly because we don't pay attention to ourselves. If we don't feed, treat or build our body properly, of course it is going to give up sooner than later. Similarly if we don't feed our mind properly, not exercise our brains properly to build strength and capabilities, this surely will result in burn out and more prone to sicknesses related to psychological issues etc.

I personally knew this guy, a brilliant student in fact an extra ordinary super brain. There must have been some sort of mismanagement in the way he was studying or was forced to study by his parents, that one day he had a mental break down. That brilliant guy just ended up walking around on the streets, singing songs, and I remember we always stopped him while passing by and will on purpose ask him what time it was. We did this partly because we loved the way he always answered the question, making the time rhyme with some sort of poetry, and partly to ensure if he was really mentally affected as all others around would tell us. He never looked like one, because he was always dressed up very professionally and with a tie on.

So once again I am not saying that students or those who are studying should stop studying hard but should manage it well. Give yourselves the time you need to ensure you understand the importance of managing your own self.

Start taking some time-out for yourself and you will see how better you will start to control your mind, command your brain and respond better to your life around you. At the same time, you will be realising your own self. Then you will slowly start realising what you are doing, where you stand in life and how can you have more self-control over the things, so you have better control of your life back in your hands. Do not let the circumstances take control of your life. Hence it's time to apply that first CHANGE – The change in Your Daily Routine, the Change in Daily Time Management for Your OWN SELF.

I do not care whether you start with five minutes a day, ten minutes a day or half hour or an hour. As long as you start creating that time, I am sure you will soon realise the importance of it and get into this as a daily habit.

Step-2: Cannotocando Booster Plan

Think of an activity that was challenging, you loved doing or wanted to do for a long time, if it does not throw you out too far from your pocket I recommend that you do it, the energy and confidence boost this will give you is going to far exceed the expectations and fill you with all the energy you need to move ahead in life to embrace the change. This will work as a **Cannotocando** pill for you. Remember what that is from the RAPs section in The Karmic Rewind Tool. It means "**Can Not To Can Do**". You must do an activity that you've been wanting to do for so long but holding yourself back thinking I can not do this for one reason or another.

I have seen too often that people seems to always fall short on their own expectations specially when making New Year Resolution. So why not try new **weekly or even a daily resolution** if that helps. You can even do short span resolutions like **half an hour resolution or an hour resolution**. This will help you build confidence from small acts of holding attention as well as improve focusing ability. You will be surprised how you will slowly improve your attention spans and kill the wondering around habit of your mind. Believe in you, You will move your thinking **from Can Not To Can Do** with this activity. You will create within the very important abilities of Focus and Attention. You must build habit of following through, completing the tasks you set for yourself. Start up with a smaller daily goal and build confidence in your ability to accomplish. Soon you will see the seed of confidence sprouting. You can not ignore giving it the care it needs, so it shall bring you the Fruit you want to eat.

Personally, I had always believed in perfectionism and 'Do What You Love', and yet was not able to walk that path. Partly I could not due to emotional downfall I had after not being able to become a Pilot (My dream Job), secondly out of the family responsibilities I found myself in. I did not realise until late that I was wrong in holding on to the belief that 'there is no Second Best'. While sitting in the park one evening, it came to my mind that we need to also be adaptable and be able to accept certain truths of life and also be able to adjust for our own good to move ahead. Then, sitting there looking into the sky I saw a bird flying in straight line towards the ground and picked up that tiny piece of bread and flew away into the sky again. I admired the bird's accuracy of hitting the target with such precision that it did not miss the target and flew back into the sky without any stumble.

Then came to my mind about how I use to love shooting, aiming and hitting a target. Whenever I walked around during my childhood, whether it was on the way back from school to home or just a walk by the roadside, I would always pick up those little stones and started hitting them onto some sort of target on the ground, or a tree, or a pole that I passed by, and 95% of the time I always will hit it. I wanted to buy an air rifle, but my parents couldn't afford to pay for such hobby items. So, I started making those bows & arrows from whatever I could find at home and started practicing being an Archer.

When I made my first trip back to India, I remember I went and bought one of those air rifles with my own money. That desire to own one was buried down for so many years that I bought it at the first opportunity I got. I revived my love for shooting and this art of being able to hit the bulls eye. I can not even come close to explaining, how great I felt within myself after noticing I could still hit the targets very well even after those years that I just have been working and working the routines of jobs.

I thought in my mind that if I was doing well in those jobs, imagine If I started working or doing what I would Love to. Now in Australia, being the sole income earner in the house, I also couldn't afford to go out and pay for that hobby. But just the thought of the skill I had loved for so long, rejuvenated my mind. I just felt so much energy and excitement within me to do what I wanted. I was so glad and happy that day to have spent time with myself and connected with my high energies within through the memory of my shooting skills. After that day even though I continued working where I was, I never felt tired because in all my other time I had started thinking and planning towards what I would have loved to do.

So, go out there and spend some time with yourself to do something that will help you raise your spirits and raise your confidence. Do something that you have been holding yourself back from for long time, just so you could make up for the bills, mortgage, car repayments or whatever else in life. You will be surprised with yourself and with realisation of your potential within after such an activity.

Step-3: Music is the Food for Soul

Another Way you can bound yourself to spend time with yourself is with music. A way to feed your soul is by listening to some cheerful music. Music is the Food for Soul. All you need to do is start listening to some music, but remember this is to Calm Your Mind. So please choose from some of those meditational or instrumental tracks that will help your mind and body go into a calm state. Think of the kind of music that is played at the spa or some yoga or meditation music. To match with scientific researches, there is also music available that is recorded at different frequencies to raise your spirit, heal, increase positive energy or even for concentration and focus. Music therapy centres are becoming popular as a holistic healing approach as well. YouTube has become a home to all kind of music so find it there if you don't have it already. Music recorded at 432 Hertz is said to have deeper impact when it comes to changing your overall energies.

Whatever it may be, as long as it helps to get into the relaxed state of mind; it is acceptable. It will work for you; it has to be appealing to you, to bring you into a relaxed state of mind. Have that on your phone, your I-Pod or be in a small closed room with a CD-Player or I-Doc's these days. The purpose is to change the energy around you to that of peace and harmony and then start thinking of self-importance and self-realisation. Once you feel that inner peace and get relaxed, start repeating the words again as mentioned in step 1– "Nothing else matters at This Moment any more than Me and Myself". You can always follow these with some affirmations of your choice. You can also use this technique when realising your ultimate priority of Your Existence as per The Karmic Tool.

Nothing else Matters at This Moment more than Me and Myself.
Nothing else Matters at This Moment more than Me and Myself.
Nothing else Matters at This Moment more than Me and Myself.
Nothing else Matters at This Moment more than Me and Myself.

Step-4: Meditation – The Best Resource

Meditation as I believe is the technique to practice your love for God. This has been the practice used by all those spiritual Gurus, Saints, Yogis and holy men since ancient historical times. They have always taught meditation being the only way to connect within. More you meditate, more you connect with higher self, more insight you get into the eternal world, the world of peace, happiness and contentment.

Meditation is an art of stilling the mind and body by concentrating or focusing at the centre behind the eyes. So you can bring your energies in harmony with the universe and our spiritual reality. This is also used as a way of communicating with the source of the soul. In some religious scriptures we have seen the saints and mystics talk about astral, causal and physical planes etc. So meditation must be a way to bring your energies in harmony with the universe and then realise what exists as those higher planes of life and be in touch with our spiritual essence.

In general, it is the technique to be able to withdraw your senses inwards and being able to withdraw completely from the external consciousness of the world. If you want to know the energy within you, just close your ears for a minute and start listening to the deep waves of sound current within you. If you've never done this before, even one minute of this exercise will give you a large amount of sense of belonging, a belonging to a strong powerful source and help you in developing the peace within and belief in our higher self.

There are lots of ancient ways of meditation. The Hinduism in India has its own Saints and Deities, who teach us the way of meditation using yoga asana or different yoga exercise techniques. There is also Buddhism; Buddhists teach meditation in their own way. Yoga has developed and is recognised now at large in the western world as well. We now at large understand the benefits of yoga for our physical body as well as using this for meditation practice.

Meditation is the best way and best resource for spending time with our own self. It is also the best medicine. There are different ways, beliefs and books on meditation. Whichever you may use as per your liking but learn the art of meditation. Read the related books in your spare time. It may be on the way to & from work, breaks or in the evening. Once you know the art of meditation, start applying this in your daily time for your own self. You will be surprised with the potential it will develop in you and for developing the real you.

Practice the four-step guide above for at least one week without any break and more will automatically follow. I am sure that it is much easier to maintain weekly resolutions than the annual New Year Resolution. All talk No Walk will not get you to the desired results. Practicing these techniques is very important to manifest the change. Let's now look at the second change I suggest to incorporate in your life.

Change -2: Create A List of Four Desires to Fulfil

Hopefully you have been or will be practicing how to calm your mind. Continue with that practice and the next task I have for you is to work out what are the four strongest desires you would like to fulfil. You never thought about this with sincerity that is needed to achieve them, so change that, do it today. I will help you in working out what those desires should be about. Let your Thoughts, Actions and Universe Synchronise, Be True To Your Heart, Your Soul and Take Your Time, Do Not constraint your thoughts to short term thinking.

If you have been sincere in practicing the first change, then that will definitely help you step back and think deeper into the true meaning and purpose of your life. It will help you in realising what you want in your life, what you would love to achieve, what you desire in life, and what you feel is the goal of your life.

First Desire has to be something about You, Yourself and only about Your Own Self. Whether it's your health aspect, your environment at home or something about your lifestyle, it must give your heart and soul the pleasure it needs to help you energise. For some it may be that spa retreat, their favourite meal at their favourite restaurant, or get adventurous for a sky dive, bungee jumping or a safari ride. Buy that favourite dress, a sports team jersey, a trip to the parlour or whatever makes you feel that you are glad you've done something for your personal self.

I often love the example of the safety videos shown on the planes. When they tell you to wear the oxygen masks first in case of emergency before you can help kids or others travelling with you. It's a similar situation in life really, only if you understand. You need to be in a healthy state all together before you can help others. With our human instincts and emotional triggers, this may be altered at times to help others, but that again you are able to do only if you are strong enough to pull the weight of others.

As I explained earlier, all that is around you exists and is useful only if you are around. Keeping yourself physically and mentally fit is an important aspect for your own-self first and then for the others around you. Think of something that will give you that boost.

A person with week body strength may not be able to help someone out there in the need of such physically demanding help. However, only if you are mentally strong, you may be able to use your intelligence to find some alternative help. A pulley can make the job to shift the weight easier. At the same time somebody who is suffering from some mental stress may not be able to help someone, whether for physical or for moral support.

That's why, when you decide on these four desires, bear in mind, It's all about transforming yourself and your life for good, for your own good first and then others. If you are in good health & with strong wealth, others around you will also benefit automatically. **The purpose of the first desire is to rejuvenate you**.

So, desire something that will lift your spirits high, something that will trigger that switch to get you into the mode of becoming strong from inside and outside, something that will make your self-belief as solid and strong as a pure diamond. We all know what diamonds are worth. Just imagine the person you will become when you have realised your True Self, your power and strengths within. Then polish your strengths with these desires that will bring energised you out to the world. With this desire, you can start on the right foot towards a better you, a better Life for You, & that will automatically better the life of others around you.

This was one step I realised and took in my life. I realised that I was working hard and really hard to keep up with the expectations from my loved ones. But, not realising that I was draining out my own self and not empowering myself to be able to keep up. The responsibilities were only going to get heavier. I am glad I had realised it soon enough, and **started investing in my own self**, empowering my own self to make it easier for me in the long run. I did not want to say to myself; '**I wish, I had done that**'. So, I thank God for helping me with courage to take action to bring the change I wanted in my life.

'I am grateful for all that exists for our existence.'

You can think of minor changes in the house you live in to give it a much better feel than the way you have them now. Hang that inspiring frame of your role model or a piece of artwork on that wall. Just make some time and do those changes, you may be surprised with how this can lift your spirit as well as the energy in the house. You don't really have to spend much money on this.

Sometimes it's just shifting and shuffling the things around the house, and the look and feel will change to inspire you.

'A house without emotions is just a building, not a Home.'

My personal belief is you as a soul have the strongest possible source of energy within yourself, to be able to change it all for positive experience all around you and for the better of everyone. So invest in your self, pick something that will personally lift up your heart and soul.

Second Desire should consider someone Close to Your Heart. This is so important that you must think about it deeply. What you need to consider is something that gives you personal satisfaction by fulfilling a **desire of someone most important in your life**. As this may very well connect you with a very strong Why, the reason to decide some aspects about the kind of life you would love to spend with your Love of the life, or your Parents, or your Children. Do you want to see yourself and all of them enjoying life better than they are now? If you do, then you do need to pick a desire that will make you feel connected with them and also give them confidence that whatever you are doing is for the family as a whole unit. Family as a collective unit works wonders.

Think of that person or your child. How much time would you love to spend with them, all those places you would like to go and visit with them, all those experiences which make the most important part of our life, the memories. What sort of memories you would like to create for everyone? Who does not deserve the best of the life? Yet we limit our own selves by just the imaginations within our mind that create a cage around our potentials.

In one of those meetings I attended when I started with the network-marketing group, the presenter really emphasized on the WHY factor. And that is so true; in the world we live in today, we tend to be derived by the reasons. A strong reason is what we have to have before we would break our cage and do something exceptional. Who else can be the best reason for you than the ones that are close to your heart, the ones you are working so hard for? One may not quit smoking for their own health but will if their child suffered lung cancer due to that smoke. Do something to make them feel you love them, you care about them and their energies will come together to help you bring and embrace that change together. It doesn't have to be big, things as little as a bunch of flowers, a chocolate or an ice-cream is a huge source of happiness and sign of care for a loved one.

We all have someone in life that meant a lot to us, but they may not be with us today, regardless of how much we would love to have them back with us. Some of those would probably need to be forgiven to come back to us. Some of them may just not be able to come back to us due to the very natural reason of this mortal body - the Death. So, think of the loved ones, and think about how much more you could do for them, if you could empower your own self to embrace that change.

Third Desire is about Deciding the Goals. Now you need to decide on what you desire to achieve in life. Go for the biggest and highest you can think of that are fit for the purpose you have identified for your life. Think of what you always wanted to become, who was your childhood hero, what did you want to do in life either as a child's dream job or as a creator of something that may be a new innovative idea. Do you have dreams left unachieved from your childhood, most people do; all those big things that you wanted to achieve, and the hero you always wanted to become. Well revive and create that desire again and decide on what you want. Dig out those deep buried dreams, assess them against the purpose and dream you have identified for your life and if still valid then you must have a Go at them.

You learned in the concept of FPS – Future Probability Sphere that the FPS is based on the belief and facts backed by Quantum Physics. It simply means that life can exist in any way possible and limited by only the vision you may have for your life. Hence, You can project the journey of your life towards any goal and in any possibility you may desire.

So, sit down alone in silence to assess your life. Assess what your personality is and how beautifully would you like to present yourself at all time. Don't worry about how you will achieve them as yet. As they say, if you say yes with your true heart and mind, the How will happen one way or the other. Just imagine doing something where you are always up really early to get onto work and waiting anxiously to get started instead. You will only do that if you are working towards your heart felt dreams. Think hard in the relaxed state of mind, as you are trying to create your future, not just another bucket load to dump in the washing machine. Even though you have heard about 'seeing is believing.' Now you will change that during your daily 'Time for Your Own Self' sessions. Start telling yourself *Believing is Seeing'*. You must believe in your dream of your career or business life and build that strong desire within to achieve it with the help of the FPS and The Karmic Rewind tools.

And only in the case of you still not knowing what those dreams are for you, I want to put this question to you – Have you worked on your self existence truthfully? You should start assessing what skills you have naturally and how you can improve on those to build better career or business. Assess what you would love to do for the rest of your life without worrying about dragging yourself to work. Something that comes as your natural passion and talent, and it will not take you too long to enhance that further.

To embrace change and create some movement towards exploring what your dream and purpose may be, you can create a smaller goal in mind to even just start researching about what you would love to do. You will be surprised how that will lead you further and further towards clarity to pin that specific final goal.

If you are cooking dinner at home, you know you have to decide in your mind, what you will cook, and how you will cook, and then a follow up with actions will put the meal on your plate. It's as simple as that once you have clarity and only made hard because of the beliefs we have in our mind. If we start cooking the meal and do all the steps that need to be done one after the other as is required, we will have the meal ready in time. If we cut some vegies, and then wait an hour, before we start heating up the fry-pan and again wait an hour with the pan being heated before we put the oil in and whatever else has to follow is given delays. The feel and love you put when cooking itself adds a great texture to the food. But if we don't care about it, how are we going to have the meal on plate in time let alone it being delicious? Ask a mother how she cooks for her child; you need to **mother your dreams** with same love and mindfulness.

Similar applies to the life when we want to do something and then take no action with the concentration and effort it needs, how do we expect to see the results. It's all about how much you love those goals and whether you've made them your priority yet. I agree that magic do happen in the universe, but that even occurs if you have a strong desire for something and have been taking required action. For most part, nothing may seem to work and all of a sudden something from somewhere has resolved it all for you. You are unable to believe that it actually happened, it is all like a magic to you because of the desperation you had towards achieving that particular goal or whatever it may be that you had thought of doing. But it is still the action taken, the Karma committed that has brought that fruit that result.

You will need to start believing in yourself, you will start seeing the results in your daily routine, and that will be like magic. Once you have taken that first step to explore, you will start seeing the rest of the steps that will lead you to that goal.

So think carefully and decide what you want to be, where you want to be, how you want to see yourself living your life in the future, in a week, a month, a year and two or five years later. You will start creating the life you want to live. The Karmic Rewind tool will help you in finding clarity and designing that pathway to your goal. But you must be committed and devoted to achieve, which can only happen when it becomes that strong desire, comes from the bottom of your heart. It is only then that you will follow it with full love and devotion it needs to be accomplished.

<u>Fourth Desire</u> should relate to Deciding Your Transport. Now that you have given some thought to or decided upon the desired goals, you need to decide on the vehicle to get you there, the transport to get there. Now this is about the How, how to achieve that goal. If you need to get to the top floor of a high-rise building, you may have two to three options to get there. You could take the steps or take lift, the elevator or escalator if it's available. That choice is what I am talking about; which method you would desire the most to get to the top, in your life it's the method to achieve your goal.

Once decided on your destination, you need to decide on the vehicle and the rout you will use to get there. This will primarily depend on decision you made for your desired goal and the destination you've decided for your life. Now that you have learned The Karmic Rewind tool, that is what you should use to design the best possible vehicle for you to get to the destination you want to reach in life. You know which strings to pull, when to pull and how to pull for you to perform the best to achieve the best results. Now is the time to make the change and start putting together the vehicle you need in the form of your skills leading to either your profession or business. The rout will consist of the time you take and the choices you make to pursue towards your goals based on the use of your skills you select to develop against the options available.

If you can, quit that job which you are not satisfied with or if you think you can survive somehow while you dedicate full devotion to build your career and get into the industry of your choice; even if it means a bit of a sacrifice, it is worthwhile as following your passion will always see you achieving much faster than you will ever do in a profession that is chosen by force. I know people who managed to do that while still working in a job that did not put much stress on them. They managed to up-skill themselves to start a new career. I may also suggest to go on part-time employment and cut back on some expenses while empowering yourself for better.

I always believe that if you want to achieve something '**Don't just give your 100%, pump it up to 200%**'. If you love it so much how can you go wrong? You love to do one thing, why do you want to sacrifice the fun from your life doing something else, which you don't like. So, do whatever it takes to get to your goal with the medium you would enjoy the most. The journey will be so much pleasure and fun. Just follow your passion. If it is related to the job you are in already and want to do more and achieve higher. It will be worthwhile to talk to your employer to see if they are happy to pay for that extra training you may need, if you cannot take up the related studies in your spare time. I decided to train and up skill myself.

I had to rely on my savings and some government support while I went to study the medium I chose and desired to use from the bottom of my heart.

I loved computers and technology so I took a step to learn more. One of the tutors I had during my course of study, he went on and achieved a PHD as well. However he tells us that, he hated to read huge books. Once he was sitting with his sister and spoke about what they could become in future. He was told that being the small built guy; he could not work in a factory or such hard task jobs. His sister suggested he would be somewhere in an office or administration kind of work. But he did not want to study and hated learning by reading books. The Idea of sitting in front of the computer and tickling the keyboard was something he liked. He thought he would enjoy sitting in front of the computer all day just playing with computer. He loved that idea so much that he went and bought a book that was quite a big book to him but when he started reading, he got more interested. He was surprised how soon he had finished that book. He went on to tell his mum to support him in his computer studies because of his newly developed love for computers. He had even started reading those thick books that he never wanted to even touch at one stage. And, he now has a PHD degree too.

We all know all these people on the Master Chef TV series that proves that there are people who were not even professional Chefs and had gone to the show, just because they loved cooking. A lot of them realised that cooking was their passion and a profession they could take up and live with for the rest of their lives. If you are one of those too, then just do it. A lot of people just love the artistic works; they have gone ahead and become interior designers. These are just some quick hints as to what you can be in life. You can be anything that you want to be, if you would love to be. So, find a trade, find a career that you would love to build and live with for the rest of your life. But just find something that you will love.

If you love computers, then get in and be part of the Internet Revolution. A lot of people are making money online. There are also a lot of multi-level marketing and networking businesses available. Now, a lot of people just have some wrong impression about these words, which I don't understand why? I do understand that most of the time, hype is created to get you in the business, as that is what happened with me in couple of the opportunities as well, but I was not really going with them for money, as I always knew that selling is not my strong point. I learned a lot from there, I learned to dream big, I learned how things could be changed in life, and I have implemented in my life what I learned. About selling, I still think I can convince but not sell.

I personally feel that we as people should be helping people in business and support each other. A business that is established at large is benefitting from your shopping anyways, then, if you find similar products from someone you know, is it a bad idea to buy from someone you know and help them make money that would otherwise be used as a marketing campaign. I don't mind and I will be more than happy knowing my friends are making money which otherwise would be in a big retail giant business's pocket anyway. Well again this is just an idea. You need to look at what seems relevant to you, what you are happy with and what you can use as a vehicle to start travelling towards the goal you want to achieve.

Please choose the vehicle you would love to ride on, while travelling towards your destination, your goal, and your dream life. That will surely **make the journey of life much more enjoyable, much more meaningful, much more achieved** and you will feel that you lived a lot more of your life than you probably would have otherwise.

Since you are shifting gears and changing directions, do not expect that it is going to be the joy ride from day one. Every time you start the car or any other vehicle to go somewhere, it is coping a bit of rough work to get the vehicle rolling on the smoother side of the road. However you will still enjoy as you are heading in the direction of the mountains that you would love to conquer.

Find that desire buried somewhere in your heart about how you wish to travel in the journey of your life. So you can start living a rich life, a life with abundance that is rich with Time, Money, Love, and Happiness. After all, these are the things we are working hard to achieve, but I will suggest - **'work hard towards working smart'.**

Change -3: Decision Making with True Heart

It's time that you started making some decisions that will impact your life for positive outcomes. With the use of techniques mentioned above, I would urge you to start making the decisions now. It may involve some tough decisions but with the love and passion you will have to the outcomes you want to achieve, you will overcome the initial rough moments and **conquer the challenges to change**.

A lot of the time we just delay making decisions. We know we want to do something. We know where we need to go, so we can get that information. The information that will get us started on the path of life we want to live. Yet we fail to take action. The biggest reason behind that behaviour is our lack of commitment. As John Assaraf mentioned that one of his mentor asked him a question before he will help John. The question was –

"Are you Interested or Are you Committed?"

First decision you must make is to **become a Committer, Commit** to the decisions you will make. **Once you know you are interested, don't just stay interested; take charge and commit to take action.** We all know what's causing the procrastination. We are just trapped in the mindset of staying stuck in our comfort zone regardless of the discomfort it may have. Our brain has been trained that way for years. Our mind has been filled with impressions of "its' okay". Let me ask you this question – *"If everything is ok, then why is implementing something for change not ok?"* How do you believe that your life is going to change all of a sudden? Sometimes we keep looking for that help and support from sources that haven't been fruitful for years. Well it's time you take a blunt call and forget about those pretend supports, cut those strings that are holding you in limbo instead and move ahead with your very own internal and eternal strength. If you have been reliant on others, then let me suggest the hard fact; know that it is you who will need to get out of your comfort zone. You must be **Committed to change** and not just interested in change. Get a bit uncomfortable, so you can achieve what you want to. Road to success is actually some beautiful and enjoyable hard work as advised by most successful people.

So, that is what you have to do, get out of the comfort zone of your brain that may have been causing you all the other grief in life for years. Do not let it continue, for you may regret at a later stage in life. Think about having a feel of 'I wish I had done that, I wish I had decided this at that point of time & it would have been much easier or much better today'. Imagine that feeling, I have mentioned before too that, what do you think your reaction would have been? If someone came to you back in Nineteen Seventies and the person's name was Bill Gates, who asked you to Join him while he is going to make Microsoft the biggest IT company in the world'.

Think hard, put all your passion and energy behind that positive thought about your dreams, give yourself that opportunity now. How often have we let some opportunities pass by, how often have you let the negative mind take full control over your life, it's time to stop that and stop the holding back attitude which is giving you the life you can live far better than how you may be living now? Let me help you understand that, just think about this - *'How has your brain been trained about risk taking ability for years?'* Were we taught that risk is dangerous, frightening, harmful or anything bad to keep us back in our safe and comfortable zone of mind and life. Why? Could people around us have overthought to keep us safe and denied us the right to learn risk taking abilities? Or maybe there was no need to take risks because people around us never took risks or did something abnormally different, hence we were naturally trained to stay away from risk taking.

It's like in old days, it was commonly believed that a Butcher's kids will become butchers, an engineer's kids will be trained to be more of an engineer, a scientist, a baker, a farmer's kids were more prone to take over the same trades. In all sorts of trades and services it was a common trend. The reason behind was that because those kids grew up in that environment, their brains were either trained to do those types of work or they unconsciously gained the knowledge and skills just by being in that environment. So, gradually and naturally, they developed and remained comfortable in those environments and naturally they were more likely to take up the family business as their means of living too.

However that may not seem to be the case these days anymore. But that again is due to the very same old reason my friends. The reason is how you train your brain or how the brain gets naturally trained, what kind of thoughts and feels are fed into the brain. If a doctor's or some other trade expert's kids did in fact chose another career, that is also because they went into the surroundings or environment where they got influenced. Some different circumstances that they encountered, which they were influenced and impressed with; their brain have adapted to liking those circumstances or may even be that something happened somewhere that made them dislike the career option their parents had either inherited or chosen due to the very fact we are discussing here.

Hence, what one believes in through influence in any shape and form is playing an important part in triggering the change that guides them throughout their life; it's their mind to the largest extent that is not only being affected but is also affecting our lives based on what it sees and absorbs. *Our mind is being influenced and then influencing our physical life.* It's their brain, which has then received message of the choice made by the mind during that particular stage of life, and it has started functioning to act towards that direction. In the end they have turned out to become what they chose to be and about which they made a decision in consultation with their mind. Luckily, we now know that our mind is an influenced influencer, so we'll now use that quality of it to create the influence in our life that we desire. Let's now *commit to not let our minds take in things by chance any more but be fed deliberately for what we want to achieve.* This is how things work at deeper level, nothing is impossible but you must decide and take a committed action.

So, commit to deliberately create relevant influences for your mind and do not hold back from the change that needs to be made to your work, your career or business choice. It might be the relationship as well as the change to achieve a better spiritual life, an abundant life with all that you would ever love to have. So, make that change, not entirely for the satisfaction of the others, but primarily yours. Whatever you may decide; it has to come from the bottom of your heart, that is when you will be able to commit to take each moment to plan towards it, plan towards the goal you want to achieve, plan every moment to arrive at the other end.

Each of those steps will take you inch by inch closer to the life you want to live. Just decide with your heart, make that promise and make that commitment. Then not only you will do whatever it takes to keep your heart happy, and spread the happiness all around you. You will also spread it in the life of all those who are around you, as you will love every moment of living on this planet. Do not let your past habits hold you back any more. Do it for the Life you would Love to have, Life you would love to teach your Kids to live as. **Leave your legacy to the world**; let the world remember you for love.

Here's a bit of my poetic side for you to now make that **Second Decision** to **spread the positive** change to the world around you. I hope you can sing it in your heart and grow the love not just in the life of yours, but let it grow so much, so the whole galaxy will glow. The whole world around you should feel the **power of heart, mind and love** that you have within. The universe will help you with that, as Love is in the very foundation of the universe. **Do what you love; the universe will help you grow with that love**.

"Your Mind, Love and Heart, Together They Are Smart,

Together If They Live, Together They Will Grow,

Not Just Your Life but, Let The Whole Galaxy Glow."

We can not only change our own life by implementing that change for the love of living the life we want, we are also known to spread around the essence of us, wherever we may go. We all know if someone with a mean personality passes by a happy cheerful group of people, the environment surely changes, even if it is for a fraction of a minute, but it does. It will depend on the personality of these happy go lucky people, that how strongly or mildly they react to that intervention. The opposite works similarly, the aura of happiness by someone who passed by and gave the group something to cheer about. But, what I mean to say is, regardless of what personality you may carry, we do influence our surroundings, consciously or unconsciously, it does happen.

There has been a recent study, which also explains the kind of social animal we are and how much the social environment influences and affects us. Read the extracts below from the news article published by news.com.au.

***

The study has revealed that the human brain gives more value to winning of an individual when one is in a social environment as opposed to, when one is winning in loneliness or without any social elements around them. Georgio Coricelli of the USC Dornsife College of Letters, Arts and Sciences led a multinational team of researchers that measured activity in the regions of the brain associated with rewards and social reasoning while participants in the study participated in trying their luck in attempt of winning lotteries.

Researchers found that the striatum, which is a part of the brain associated with rewards, showed higher activity when a participant beat a peer in the lottery, as opposed to when the participant won while alone and the medial prefrontal cortex which is a part of the brain associated with social reasoning, was more activated as well. The researchers also saw that the participants who won in a social environment also tended to engage in more risky and competitive behaviour in subsequent lotteries.

'This research's findings suggest that the brain is equipped with the ability to detect and encode social signals, make social signals salient, and then, use these signals to optimise future behaviour,' Coricelli said. He also explained that losing without social support network, a bad gamble could spell doom, whereas rewards tend to be winner-takes-all in group environments.

'Among animals, there are strong incentives for wanting to be at the top of the social ranking,' Coricelli stated. 'Animals in the dominant position use their status to secure privileged access to resources, such as food and mates.' Coricelli concluded.

***

How true it is even in logical sense, but as most of us do not use our logical sense and rely on only qualified professionals of our society to come up with some sort of studies to put some evidence in bulk, in front of our eyes. It is only then that we tend to start believing a fact. No matter how much of the same concept of logic we may see around us on daily basis in our own lives and surroundings, we tend to ignore that completely and wait until someone is able to present to us with some sort of thick evidence, the evidence that simply cannot be ignored.

We seem to be living life like the pigeons. I heard this story during my school times that when a cat is approaching to attack a pigeon, to kill him, the pigeon closes its eyes and expects the cat would disappear. We need to stop that approach and realise that we are only killing ourselves by living the stressful life, when we could simply change a lot by a simple shift in our mindset, the way we think, simply by recognising the common sense and the logic of life, finding and connecting with the purpose of our life.

Simply ask yourself whether you have recognised the purpose of your life yet. And if you have not yet, then consider this my humble request and do yourself that favour, recognise your true self and the life you want to live. **Third decision** I want you to make with your true heart is this – "**Connect with the purpose of your life**". Your heart and soul will guide you to your purpose and that purpose should become your guide for your life. Connecting with the purpose of your life through the techniques given in this book will bring your life in harmony with what the Universe also may have in plans for you. By bringing yourself in sync with your universal purpose is only bound to see you succeed. We must do everything to lift ourself up, step-by-step, one step at a time even making use of anything we find around us in a positive manner. Start with what's on hand and slowly you'll build towards more of what will support you ahead.

We must start putting our own self together, our self-belief, our self-confidence together and you will be amazed with what you will start to see in what you otherwise ignored to see around you just because of the dominance of negativity over positivity. We need to start believing in our own self more, lift our own confidence and assess things with a wise attitude to make the most of what we have around us, make the most of resources we have available. Efficiency is my key since early childhood. I often tried to make the most of what I had, rather than what I could have achieved if I had this best tool, that better equipment or better education from the top university in the world, No.

The schools and universities were also part of the inventions of human mind. Certain knowledge was regarded as credible and then that was used to educate others to be able to learn from those better brains. Those brains initially were just some wise people who gave more thought into the existence of life and everything around us. When we are born, we start life the same way as they did, when they were born but probably different circumstances that may have been more thought provoking. But, now we regard those books alone to be the guide in life and most of us have stopped thinking outside what's taught at schools and universities. We should learn from them, but also use the amazing, sort of walnut shaped mass given to us naturally called the Brain. After all God must have thought of its functions before those books were written to educate it. Education has become one of the biggest businesses in the world today. Learning from the books should always be supplemented with the ways that help us explore our own personal aura, our purpose in life. This is where I really liked a quote that I once read on someone's T-Shirt which said '*I was born intelligent, Education ruined me*'. Think about it deeply, humanity didn't become intelligent today because there were always books to teach, but also because we faced a lot naturally and tackled with our brain's capabilities. Someone decided to push boundaries and break the norms to discover and realise more than what most saw as life. And they did that, because they must have realised their purpose in life, so should you.

The only difference I believe is that, they had less stress of learning from someone else's books and used their own brains more to explore the endless possibilities life has to offer on this planet. But now when we are taking our education, we are taught too much into guided learning alone and mostly for becoming the employees. We are told that we cannot get a good job if we don't study hard. In the schools there is the race to achieve the highest marks and scores than others, rather than helping promote the natural talent that may exist within already that could flourish into something much better.

It's only recently that ideas about alternative schooling are coming into existence. We've relied too heavily on these guided studies path for too long that we are now loosing touch with creative and innovative thinking. They're now adding these as subjects under the traditional education pathways. I like the idea but you must use your brain in naturally intelligent ways too as it is capable of much more than what we learn through traditional education system. To do that, we must enhance our self-confidence by being in touch within, finding our qualities, attributes and knowing thy self to connect with the purpose of our life. Make good use of The Karmic Rewind tool to help you with that.

At times there may be a little mismatch between what we think our purpose is and the universe has for us, and that's why there may be results that will need to be recognised as destiny which may still cause some things to happen out of your control. But, that will only be because of your past karmas that you may need to bear. The world is governed by the universal laws and that of Karma is strongly unbreakable and is to be abided by. Remember what I said earlier – 'If you've given your best, how does the result matter. You could only do what you could for any given task on hand'. And if you've done that with your full heart, don't hold on to the results, learn better and improvise on all aspects to keep pushing ahead, as life goes on. If one of those results through destiny is not to your liking, then know that your positive attitude and energy will not let that negative effect last for long and help you move on because you are enlightened about the approach to move on in life.

We do have the ability to change but we must be strong at our core, understand who we are and **connect with the purpose of our life with our true heart**. If it needs giving your self the environment that will help you succeed, then by any means possible, create it. You will be surprised how soon that will start to affect the way you think about your own self. This will build your confidence, your self-belief and you will start to pave the way in the direction you want to go. Realise your potential, empower your soul, empower your life to live your purpose and empower the world.

The Power of Mind, Love and Heart

We know that nothing in this universe is stationary. It appears stationary in comparison to other objects. Our planet Earth, moves at about 1600 km/hr. on it's own axis. The **fastest moving thing ever** noted and mentioned by mystics is **your mind**. It does not take any time for your mind to travel to a distance, which is oceans away. You can be sitting in a closed room, where you as a body may not be able to escape, but you know that your mind will hardly be within those limitations; it's the brain that's bored not the mind. You may start thinking about things that are miles away, oceans away; you just need to think about it and such is the speed of the mind that it gets you having real like experiences of those places or of any kind at any distance with the fuel of just that thought.

Nothing is made and meant to be stationery. It may seem to us at times, but it is stationery only relatively, only when compared with something else but in actual it is moving. The planet earth is moving all the time. The air is moving all the time at whatever speed it may be. The table or chair, or a book on it appears to be stationery. But, Newton's third law (To every action, there is an equal and opposite reaction) explains they are pushing against each other relatively with the gravitational force. And our mind and body aren't stationery either. We may say I am standing or lying still, but there is still so much motion within our body. The blood stream, our heart beat and other continuous processes are on all the time so the body is alive; the blood stream is moving all the time. No one and nothing is ever still. We know what will happen if our body really went still outside and inside. These are the real facts of life. So I say; learn to appreciate what we have, show gratitude and live life to the full in the same manner of the energy which flows and controls the whole universe keeping it intact, the energy of love and harmony.

When it comes to the **power of Love**, just imagine the Romeo-Juliet or any other love story. Even your own if you have one, or an example around you or a friend that you had who had a crush on someone. Just imagine about the sportsman, who has achieved the topmost ranking in their sport. What do you think is common between them; it's the power of love. When you love someone or something you want it from the bottom of your heart, what does that trigger? It triggers such a need of urgency that they start creating the circumstances and start taking action, that will always be taking them closer to their beloved or their goal.

If someone is in love, their mind is set on one thing, they will always be thinking about their beloved. They will do whatever it takes to be closer to him or her all the time. Do you believe that they don't come across any hurdles, which would prevent them from getting closer to their goal? Do you think they don't feel sleepy or tired of work after a long day? But, when it comes to their love or work on their goal, their mind isn't telling them all that negative information; instead the mind is controlled with love and helps one by making that extra effort and go to see their love, just to spend some time with them or at times going the extra mile just to have a glimpse of their beloved.

Similar is the mindset of the sportsperson under love for reaching their goal. They will do all those extra hours of training schedule and repeat the task so often that it just becomes natural for them to perform at that extra level. They create that edge of peak performance to beat whoever else may be the competitor. They will create environment to help by finding the coach who can get the most out of them and teach them certain techniques to enhance their performance. Do you think they don't like their sleep; they don't get tempted to those cravings of foods and sweets that may easily get them off the track from their goal. But no, because they love their goals so much, their mind doesn't let those distractions take over, and help them to keep pushing for what they love and what they want to achieve instead. The mighty mind can push you for anything if you use it with and towards your love.

Such is the power of mind and love, but where does it all originate from? The answer is your Heart. **Your Mind, Love and Heart, together these three make up for the lethal combination to destroy any hurdles** that may come in the way of your goals. Imagine the goal itself when arising from your heart, you are bound to develop that love for it and you can then make best friends with your mind. Your mind is what plays big role in either holding you back or pushing ahead. Once mind comes together to the purpose from your heart, it will help you create everything you need so you are then bound to succeed.

It's the mind to the largest extent that is not only being affected but is also affecting our lives based on what it sees and absorbs. *Our mind is being influenced and then influencing our physical life.* It's our brain that receives messages for the choices made by the mind and it starts functioning to act towards that direction. In the end one will have turned out to become what they chose to be and about which they made a decision in conjunction with their mind. We know that our **mind is an influenced influencer,** so we must now use that quality of it to create the influence in our life that we desire. Let's now **commit whole heartedly to not let our minds take in things by chance any more but be fed deliberately for what we want to achieve**. This is how things work at deeper level, nothing is impossible but you must decide and take a committed action. Shift your paradigm with the power of your mind.

So, **fourth decision** you must now make with your true heart is to **conquer your mind**. With your heart and love, slowly moderate your mindset through right feed and you will achieve what target you set in front of you. You must start making decisions from the bottom of your heart and commit to them to see the change; spread the positive energy once you start implementing change with the purpose of your life in mind; then conquer the mind with the power of love for what your heart desires.

Change -4: Take Action in Steps

It's time to now apply the final Karma Strategy to implement change with all that we have learnt so far. It's time to start shooting the Arrows of Karma towards our goals; it's time to take action. All Talk No Walk Never gets anyone anywhere. We can all agree to that. Let me suggest that you take a firm decision and commitment to create and embrace the change through action, through Karma. Please spend more time if you need to with The Karmic Rewind Tool, creating the MAP of your life and clearly decide your goals with the best intentions and commit from the bottom of your heart to taking action and manifest the life you always wanted to live.

Now it's time to change your mind frame from just "I know it all" to start taking action; tell yourself – **"I know it all, I know what I want and I am living the actions to get me there"**. It's time to get the ball rolling, step by step to get closer to what you want to achieve. It's time to start implementing the little steps that will start manifesting the big dreams, start creating the life of your dreams, the life you want to live. I would like you to imagine your goal as the target circle for an archer. You are the archer and must now start shooting the Arrows of Karma, the Arrows of Action towards that target goal.

> *"Start by doing what's necessary; then do what's possible;*
> *and suddenly you are doing the impossible."*
> -----Francis of Assissi

Hit the Road

Let's rock, it's time to shoot that first arrow of karma to hit and break that lock to open gateway to success. Now that you know believing can be turned into seeing; it's time to hit the road. Remember that the ride may be rough in the start, but it is not going to stay like that forever. Just don't step backwards if you feel the ride is a little bumpy, keep pushing forward until you reach the success. When you start the engine of a car, you change a gear, is it always the smooth rolling transition, does the engine not work hard to bring everything that composes the car in rhythm with the road. It's also a little like walking into a room with funny or a bit weird and different smell, but after a while it all becomes normal and your reaction changes to 'what funny smell'. So, every time something new and different happens; there's always those butterflies in the stomach, one will be a little worried and anxious or a little afraid and uncomfortable. After some time you'll get comfortable with the new and positive discomfort that soon disappears to transform into comfort. That feeling of fear will slowly transition itself to the newer, happier and comfortable feel. You will gradually develop comfort and confidence and will feel proud of being able to achieve what did not seem possible to you a little while ago.

What about starting school, starting college, starting university, or starting training of any kind; was it all a smooth ride to start and then getting to the end of the qualification you wanted to achieve; but you made it to the end, scored your qualifications. Scholars were the ones who loved what they learned and just pass marks were for those who never showed interest or did not love what they were learning. Perhaps it was just not their natural abilities that they did not want to learn what they were made to or some other influences got heavier on them and they did not receive the support to keep on that track.

Just understand that starting up is always a bit rough, but who succeeds is the one who persists. And who does persist is the one who loves their goal in front of them and loves to take up the challenges in their way head on. Since you have decided on the life you would love to live, you will persist on achieving that goal and hence you will succeed. Just do whatever it takes with your heart, love and mind and persist on achieving what you want.

Those are the success stories, the ones where they did not give up just because a hurdle came along. Those are the ones who were declared the winners in their trade. In fact they made those hurdles look like a tiny bump against their persistence and effort. So shoot that **first arrow of karma** even if it is investigation into what you believe you love, or gathering information about how to get into the field of your choice that synchronises well with your love, your passion and natural abilities. This will eliminate many doubts from your mind and create further questions for you to assess. Find someone who knows about what you want to move towards, build a network of people with similar mindset to create the support around you. Do whatever is needed to trigger and initiate the move towards change, but do start and hit the road with that first little step and the rest will follow.

Action needs to be taken for an event to occur. Even if the first step is to gather information it is ok as the further actions will be of higher value and reward. It's like collect information for the start of a journey but you must also travel. If you want to travel to a destination, just by buying the map and having a look at the path or road plan is not going to get you there. It's the start of walking or sitting in a train, bus or flight to that destination which will get you there. Mere reading of medicine books is not going to heal you, you need to take its advice and practically adhere to it for you to get better.

Nurture Your Mind

This is the reminder about why it's important to be and keep in the company of like-minded people. It's important so that you have the omnipresent support from your mind for what you want to do and achieve. The **second arrow of karma** to shoot is towards the goal to **Nurture the mind**. Being the social animal that we humans are; we always pick up the habits of and learn from people we associate with. It's easier for our mind to wander off and miss the target if it doesn't have the relevant feed in it. For that reason we must continuously tap our mind to keep in the direction and mind frame it should stay in, to reach the target destination. The right mindset and support for it is required constantly to hit the bulls eye, remember we read about Cybernetics earlier; that's why it's very important to keep nurturing our mind with the right feed which works as constant reminder signals to keep us on the path.

We all know the story of Tarzan. That story is a perfect example of human behaviour being influenced with the surrounding atmosphere, or the capability of human brain to learn from surroundings and start behaving in a way which proves the implementation of those learnings in our behaviour, which eventually becomes an integral part of our life. So hopefully by now, you have learned about the behaviour of your brain, mould it the way you want to live your life and your life will become what you want it to be.

Right now your heart and mind are guiding you towards what you need to do to be able to achieve a goal. You must nurture that momentum in mind and feed it more of what it needs to steer ahead and help you create the change you desire. What you do need to ensure is that you are not accompanying the opposition bench for what you are trying to achieve. We need the supportive environment to achieve our goals. So once you have got the ball rolling, **ensure you nurture your mind** so it doesn't let your heart hit against the fear wall and talk it down. Learn deliberately more and more about people who succeeded in doing what you are trying to, to nurture the mind to believe in success and keep pushing ahead towards your goal.

Whether your goal is about Love, Money, Health, Spirituality, Business, Jobs or any other goal you may want to achieve, supportive environment to maintain focus is very important. If we want to learn computers we go and study with like-minded people, do we go and sit with a bricklayer so we can learn some computer tips with or from him, if anything; we are more likely to pick up some bricklaying tips, and same applies vice versa. A bricklayer will not be sitting with a hairdresser or an accountant to learn bricklaying. Talk about any trade, same rule applies.

We need the company of like-minded people to be able to achieve more. Accompanying other trades may still give us some extra tips but that we can leave for later times when we are done with all we need primarily to achieve our primary goal. Right now focus is very important with the help of supportive environment. With that support around you, keep learning to improve your next steps of action, take new training if the need be. The emphasis is to be on to continuously learn, improve and have that support around to keep our mind continuously looking to achieve.

It's like ensuring the fuel is there and burning to continuously push the engines of the rocket to reach the given coordinates in the orbit. The fuel I am talking about here is the supportive environment to continuously push the engine called Mind for the rocket of your life. If the mind keeps pushing with all else in synch, target will be hit, the purpose of your life will be achieved.

Persist and Practice

' Life's battles don't always go to the stronger or faster man.
Sooner or later the man who wins is the man who, thinks he can.'

-Vince Lombardi

After you've taken that initial action and built the support needed, Persistence and Practice are the keys to success for you to see the results of your dreams in reality. Let's **shoot that third arrow of karma** with the sharpened **head of persistence** and supported with **tail end of practice**.

Just imagine yourself playing merry-go-round or spinning around while young, or with your kids; you start going round and round and keep spinning. After a few spins you stop, but the world around you continue to appear spinning for few more moments. Why? It's because of the motion that is set for your senses after doing a few rounds continuously in the same direction. By deciding to take action and then by persisting and continuously practicing, you will have set that similar motion for your actions in your life. They will become habits and push you to achieve your goal in a natural manner.

As that motion is in a positive direction, the world around you will also move in the positive direction only. Follow this with true heart and devotion; the future will be moulded in that direction as well. Even if you hit a little bumpy ride, that motion set around you will help to get you out of those down times to propel your journey again. Do not stop acting towards achieving your goals. Once you practice hard and over and over again, you are bound in the direction to succeed in achieving the goal you have set for yourself.

So keep taking action and keep practicing what you may need for moving towards your goals with persistence. How can you end up somewhere else, if you follow your dream with full devotion? This applies regardless of the goal you are after, whether it is Spirituality, Money, Business, Health, Relationships, Sports, Contentment or Personal life. Take any area of life.

There will be times when you will encounter certain circumstances and the days when the morale is not high. I found hard too at times to keep up the full faith. But, **this is what I said to myself** – "If I were to live my whole life working for someone while not doing what I want to do, then I can always do it anyway at any stage of my life. Chances of me not getting a job at a Service station, a grocery store, a factory, an office administration job, a customer service job, a car yard salesman, a bus driver, a taxi driver, a delivery driver, a postman, a computer programmer, an IT guy and a web developer in my case are not so dark in the coming years; these jobs are always going to be there."

You just need to realise what you want to do; what your inner conscious hints you to do at times. That is when you will be following up with full heart and nothing can become a hurdle in your way to stop you from achieving what you want to. That is when every action you will take; will help you achieve that goal of life.

Persistence is a very important key factor, and if you are scared of the failure, then let me ask you why? What makes you think that you must succeed the very first time around; if you do that's great but if you don't then prepare well to take another shot. Do you believe you are an expert already who is not allowed to fail? And if you know you are not, why worry about failure? Let's be like that baby who falls many times in attempt to learn to walk. Does he or she feel discouraged when they fall and never get up again to walk? Be like the baby in your mind who is learning and is so desperately wanting to walk, ignore the 'what will they say' question in your mind like that careless baby, don't let 'what the world will say if you don't succeed the first time' question bother you.

Not all of us always scored hundred per cent in our schools, that did not stop us from studying. Also, it's not as if you will not score anything at all when you would be doing what you feel you can do best. You may not score 100% success the first time around but would you be not better prepared to succeed the second time around? That is a common approach taken by all those successful sports people the businessmen, engineers, scientists, artists, you name it. They constantly strive to learn more, learn from mistakes, learn from their failures and apply the learnings next time around and get further. They may have to repeat that process numerous times until they succeed, Why? Because they stop not till the goal is reached. That is why we love to learn from successful people because they've most likely seen and conquered what we are scared of. They've been there done that. So it's time now for you to know that you can also be there and say 'Done that' too. Just commit that karma with persistence and practice, take that action, learn, practice and persist and you will build confidence in your journey towards success and finally will achieve success; just don't give yourself another option.

Feel the Happiness

The **final arrow of karma** is that of the **happiness**. Feel the happiness you will have surrounding you once you are confidently moving towards your goal and see it getting closer to being achieved. The decision was made about what you want to do for the rest of your life, the change was initiated through small steps and you are now continuously improving and persisting on the journey to success. You have successfully initiated and embraced the changes in your life. I am so glad for you and wish you all the luck and success in living as what you truly are.

And if not, then let me assure you that there is nothing so wonderful which can substitute for the life you desire to live. The very reason we are here is because we have life. If we were not alive, what's there to be bothered about then? You are in this world to live your life, the time is now, and the decision should be taken now. There is really no age limits on this, you just need to sit down with a relaxed mind and listen to the inner voice of your soul and then start implementing things around you to start following the life of your dreams.

That is what will make you happy, and that is what you always wanted to achieve, Happiness. Being rich does not necessarily mean that you will be Happy. You have to work out what is it that you want in life that will make you happy. Let me tell you this story I often heard while I was learning to control my senses. Am I a master in that yet, No, but I have learned the techniques to ensure I am not carried away with every single thought that may come into my brain to disturb peace. I have learned to accept and keep my mind content most of the time while keeping my desires in line with the principals of Love, Peace and Harmony.

The story is of that fisherman, I am sure some of you may have heard it but it is just so relevant to what I am trying to convey. One day, this fisherman was sitting under the shadow of his boat on the beach. Just wearing the minimal clothing you may expect a fisherman to wear. Then a businessman, who bought fish from the fishermen and sold it further for business profits, passes by. He saw this fisherman sitting there while a lot of others simply kept bringing in more fish. He walks up to this fisherman and tapped on his shoulder. Asked him, why are you sitting here my friend and not working to catch some more fish? This guy replied, sir I am just enjoying this beautiful weather and time now. I only catch fish for as much is needed for me to earn enough money for what we need in our family.

The businessman said, well you know you can go and catch more fish rather than sitting here and make more money. The fisherman said, 'OK, but then what would I do with all that money?' The businessman replies: 'then you can save some money and buy a bigger boat'. The fisherman looked at him and asked him yet again; 'OK and then what would I do with bigger boat'. The businessman said, 'Then you can catch a lot more fish and earn more money'? The fisherman again asked, 'Then what would I do', the businessman said, 'then you can buy even bigger boat and start a business like me'. The fisherman looked at him again and asked, 'OK, and then what would I do'. The businessman said, 'Then you can relax and Enjoy Life'. The fisherman, looked at him with a little smile on his face and said, 'you mean exactly what I am doing now, Sir'. The businessman looked at him with wondering eyes and walked off.

What I am trying to intend here is that, it is not necessary that you need money alone to live happily. You just need to decide on what you want from your life that will make you happy. It may be worldly achievements or it may be achieving inner peace. It may be finding the love of your life, it may be doing the business that you feel the best about, which you can do well in or it may simply be working in a job, but you need to decide whether the job you are doing suits you the best, not for the sake of the business or the company you are working for, but for your own sake. Just so you don't have to push yourself to work on Monday mornings and run back home happy when it hits Friday. That is not how it should be.

All it takes is deciding with your true heart being fair to your own self. And that is what I intend to say, 'BE FAIR TO YOURSELF'. If you are looking after yourself, then you can look after others around you the best too. If you are stronger there is a better chance you can pull along the weight of others around you much better, but not if you are weak yourself. This does not apply physically alone, but mentally as well. So do not take long to start that action and trigger that change, you may have been procrastinating for long time. Now is the time, decide and go for it with your full heart. The actions you take today will play a large and important part in where you may end up in your life at a later stage.

You must know about Angry Birds mobile phone game application or Facebook or even Amazon, which started up as selling books online. Just imagine where an idea can lead you. The results would be all happy and happy. The developers of Angry Birds had developed about fifty or so games but almost went into bankruptcy. But he surely kept his focus on as he should have and believed in himself. He carried on towards the goal and achieved it in time to avoid the bankruptcy and it has earned him in billions now. Success may be a coincidence for some, but there is a good absolute chance that you can earn it too with the True Love, Devotion and Action.

Read more on the web world or Google it. You will find more on this and many such inspirational success stories. You just need to look for the right feed for your mind and start learning what those stories have to tell about being successful. Take action, move forward and keep persisting. How many people would have given up when facing bankruptcy after producing 51 games? I believe most. Just consider the advice they would have been getting from majority of people to quit doing what they were and get a real job to avoid the financial trouble. The ones who will make success the end result are the ones who love what they do and follow it with passion similar to the 'Angry Birds' game developer.

We all want happiness; it doesn't have to be attached to worldly possessions but the state of mind. We are the only creation in the known world around us that looses happiness by being just worried about what exists too far into the future and not even do anything to address those worries. The rest of all creatures seem to have faith in the creator and the nature to provide for them. That is why many preach about living and enjoying the present moment and feel the happiness. But Humans are and will remain humans, so we will remain worried about the future and that must be tackled for feeling the Happiness. And now, you have this book to tackle that worry and handhold you towards happiness. Here is what I say –

"Live in the present, with the best you can plan for the future and enjoy life. Be happy in the moment knowing you've done all you can for the future."

I cannot stress enough for you to start implementing the changes in life to live a happier life. This brings us to the close of the book, and I would like all readers to consider this as a humble request to start implementing the change in life for something different to happen. The direction of change can never go anywhere else, if you have decided with your full heart and given the full devotion and love to decide the goals, the love and devotional effort that it deserves. After all, it's your life and for most believers, you only get it once. So why not make the most of it. May I suggest?

'If you ever said, Who has seen the Next Life; then NOW is the time to Say it Again and Achieve the Best you can in your life.'

Throw away the thought that has been dragging you for years in the same old style, which is causing you to live the unsatisfactory life. Go on and satisfy your soul by putting it in touch with its spiritual truth, the spiritual being. If you can do that, you will never feel pain in life, you will have a satisfaction level and contentment that is much higher than feeling the need for all those worldly desires. The spiritual truth of our soul is so engaging and beautiful that you may still enjoy all that you desire in this world, the materialistic gains but you will never be affected by what you have and what you do not have as a materialistic possession because the spiritual world will have something for you of the value that can never be matched with anything that is and can be created in this physical world.

So, be grateful for what we have as life, go on and initiate that change, follow that trajectory you have planned to reach your destination, which you have decided on, in your Future Probability Sphere. Empower yourself by making use of the Karmic Rewind tool and all other techniques I have provided in this book. Do not hold yourself back from taking that slightly bold step. You will see through that change; the life you want to live.

That small step may be, taking a new business initiative or talking to your boss for providing that support and training you may require. You may want to speak clearly to people in your relationship about mutual understanding and expectations. You may want to start looking for a better coach to help you in achieving your goal in sports. You may want to start retraining yourself for the career path you have thought about following for the rest of your life. Just do it and my well wishes are with you. Good luck and God bless you.

Now that you have a fair idea of how to pen down the way of changing your life and circumstances to move towards the way you want to live life, I am sure you have the urge to get started. Go ahead and start writing the blueprint to an abundant life you want to live and Re-define it the way you want with your Karma.

A copy of The Karmic Rewind Tool is provided on the next page. Because there's only so much we can pack in this book, please be advised that as a buyer of this book, for personal use only, you can use photocopies to build your personal 'Book of My Life' or purchase a "Book of My Life' workbook manual from our website. I would love to hear back from you. On my website, you may ask any questions you wish to and discuss any issues if you want to get some help. Please do post me any feedbacks you may have. It will be nice to know that I have been able to serve someone for the purpose of finding the truth and live life for what it was meant to be. Wish you all the best and may the cause of our creation shine the Grace upon all. Live Life.

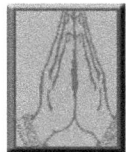

Website – www.TheKarmicRewind.com

The Karmic Rewind Tool

Book of My Life

_____

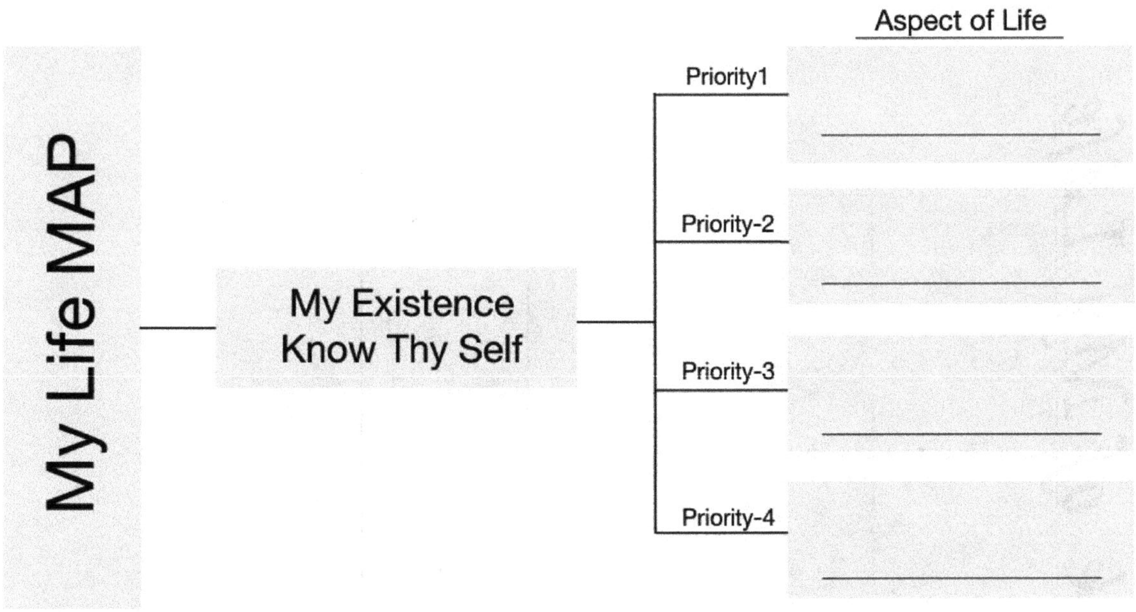

Figure 7 – Workbook – Overview of Priorities of life

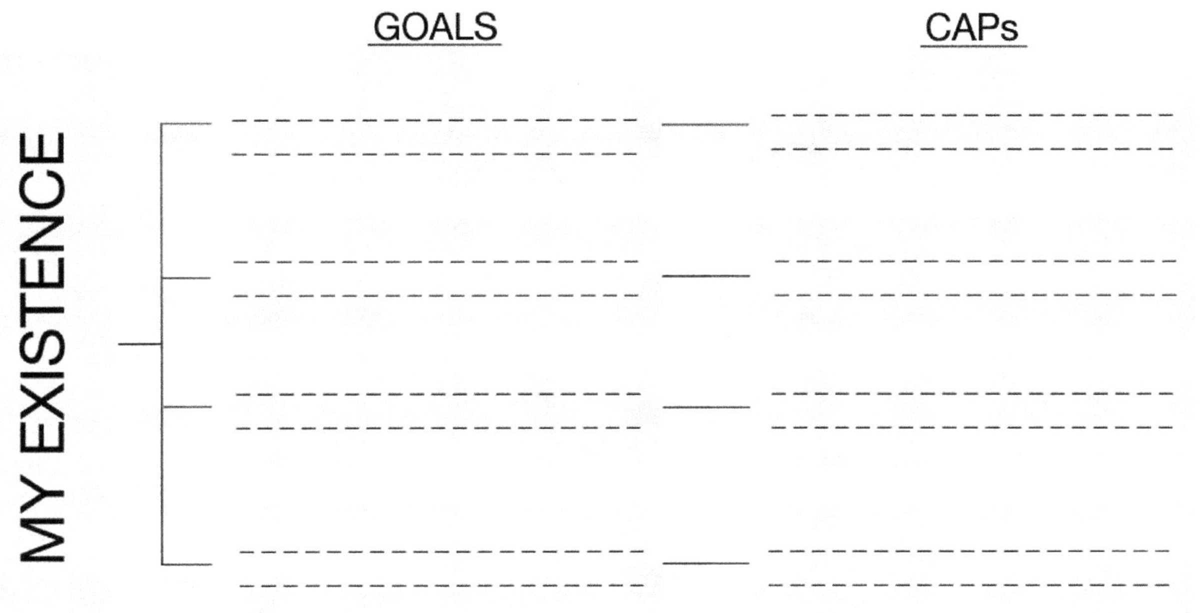

Figure 8 - Workbook My Existence Overview

Figure 9 - Workbook Overview of a Life Aspect

****
"I Am" Statement
****

I am _

I believe in my heart and soul to be my eternal guide on this planet.

I am born with natural skills of _

_ _

_ _

_ _

_ _

_ _

_ _

My Heart and Soul desire to _

_ _

_ _

_ _

_ _

_ so I can fulfil the purpose of my life.

I believe in my purpose of life and will do everything it takes to fulfil that Purpose and spread Love, Peace and Harmony that Supreme God intended.

I will pursue and take every action to achieve my goals to achieve my purpose of life.

****

Create Your Own Affirmations

Once you have created your set of affirmations, transfer them to your MAP along with Your 'I Am' Statement.

1. _____
2. _____
3. _____
4. _____
5. _____
6. _____
7. _____
8. _____
9. _____
10. _____
11. _____
12. _____
13. _____
14. _____
15. _____
16. _____
17. _____
18. _____
19. _____
20. _____

****

ASPECT – _____

****

_____ **Story**

ASPECT ACTION PLAN

5. **My Aspect** – (write the Name of aspect of life you choose to work on.)

6. **Aspect Priority Rank** (__)

7. **Happiness Statement** – (this helps you identify happiness within)

   My (aspect name, e.g. -Spiritual) Happiness is in _ _ _ _ _ _ _ _ _ _ _ _ _ _ _ _ _ _

   _

8. **Goals** (Add as many as needed but keep them together in one section. Keep The Karmic Rewind Tool plans in next section identified by the plan number and page number mentioned with the goal.)

   It is now time to identify the goals that will help you achieve your happiness. Remember that initially you may not be very clear about the goal. You must use The Karmic Rewind Tool (in next section) now and establish all that is needed to be transferred here in the AAP section.

Goal – 1   **Priority** (___)

Refreshed or New Goal - _

_ _

Target Completion Timeframe –

Achieve By Date - ___ /____ /_____   By _ _ am/pm

Notes: _

_ _

Plan Number – Priority 1 Goal 1 | Created - ☐ Page No. ____

Note: Mark your Plan number at the top of The Karmic Rewind Tool to keep proper references.

Happiness Score on achievement -

♡ ♡ ♡ ♡ ♡ ♡ ♡ ♡ ♡

Goal – 2   **Priority (___)**

Refreshed or New Goal - _
_ _

Target Completion Timeframe –

Achieve By Date - ___ / ___ / _____   By _ _ am/pm

Notes: _

Plan Number – Priority 1 Goal 1 | Created - ☐ Page No. ___

Note: Mark your Plan number at the top of The Karmic Rewind Tool to keep proper references.

Happiness Score on achievement -

♡ ♡ ♡ ♡ ♡ ♡ ♡ ♡ ♡ ♡

Goal – 3   **Priority (___)**

Refreshed or New Goal - _
_ _

Target Completion Timeframe –

Achieve By Date - ___ / ___ / _____   By _ _ am/pm

Notes: _

Plan Number – Priority 1 Goal 1 | Created - ☐ Page No. ___

Note: Mark your Plan number at the top of The Karmic Rewind Tool to keep proper references.

Happiness Score on achievement -

♡ ♡ ♡ ♡ ♡ ♡ ♡ ♡ ♡ ♡

THE KARMIC REWIND TOOL

REWIND | REVIVE | RELIVE

Plan Number – _____

Area of Priority- _____ Goal Priority (__)

I would love it if _____

_____

_____

_____

REWIND stage

1. <u>Where</u> Am I currently in this area of life or on the path to achieve this goal

Currently in this aspect of my life I am/have _____

_____

_____

_____

_____

_____

_____

_____

_____

_____

_____

2. How did I reach here? What decisions played a role?

_____
_____
_____
_____
_____
_____
_____
_____
_____
_____ _____
_____

3. Why I made the choice?

Note down the one and only Actual Compelling Reason for every decision that you made for you to be where you are. Note those here.

Decision	Reason
1.	
2.	
3.	
4.	

4. **What** caused me to think or convince into making that choice?

_____
_____
_____
_____
_____
_____
_____
_____

REVIVE stage

5. **Beliefs** That Played a Part

    1. _____
    2. _____
    3. _____
    4. _____
    5. _____

Revival Action Plan (RAP)

Old Beliefs that need to be killed

    1. _____
    2. _____
    3. _____
    4. _____
    5. _____

New Beliefs to Accomplish Desired Goal

1. _____
2. _____
3. _____
4. _____
5. _____

6. **People** who Influenced Decision

1. _____
2. _____
3. _____
4. _____
5. _____

Revival Action Plan (RAP)

1. _____
2. _____
3. _____
4. _____
5. _____

Association Assessment

1. Name - _____   Supportive – Yes ___ No ___

Association context - _____
_____
_____

    Associate More: Yes/No   _____
    Disassociate: Yes/No   _____
    Selective Isolation: Yes/No   _____

2. Name - _ _ _ _ _ _ _ _ _ _ _ _ _   Supportive – Yes _ _ _ No _ _ _

Association context - _
_ _
_ _

    Associate More: Yes/No   _ _ _ _ _ _ _ _ _ _ _ _ _ _ _ _ _

    Disassociate: Yes/No   _ _ _ _ _ _ _ _ _ _ _ _ _ _ _ _ _

    Selective Isolation: Yes/No _ _ _ _ _ _ _ _ _ _ _ _ _ _ _ _ _

7. Identify Your Weaknesses

Weaknesses –

1. _
2. _
3. _
4. _
5. _
6. _

Revival Action Plan (RAP) –

1. _
2. _
3. _
4. _
5. _
6. _

8. Identify Your Strengths

Strengths –

1. _____
2. _____
3. _____
4. _____
5. _____

Revival Action Plan (RAP)

1. _____
2. _____
3. _____
4. _____
5. _____

Behavioural Strengths –

1. _____
2. _____
3. _____
4. _____

Revival Action Plan (RAP) –

1. _____
2. _____
3. _____
4. _____

9. YOUR GOAL – with Clear vision

Refreshed or New Goal - _____
_____
_____
_____
_____

Target Completion Timeframe -

Achieve By Date - ___ / ___ / _____   By _ _ _ _ am/pm

Notes: _____
_____

RELIVE – stage

10. Comprehensive Action Plan (CAP)-

Refreshed or New Goal - _____
_____
_____
_____

Happiness Score on achievement - ♡ ♡ ♡ ♡ ♡ ♡ ♡ ♡ ♡

Target Completion Timeframe –

Achieve By Date - ___ / ___ / _____   By _ _ _ _ am/pm

Notes: _____
_____

Revival Action Plans (RAP) or New Action Plans (NLPs) to be aware of –

RAP/NAP – Beliefs (Impress Positive and New Beliefs in Mind)

1. _____
2. _____
3. _____
4. _____
5. _____

RAP/NAP – People and Social Associations (Keep or Avoid)

1. _____
2. _____
3. _____
4. _____
5. _____

RAP/NAP – Weaknesses (Remove or Convert to Strengths)

1. _____
2. _____
3. _____
4. _____
5. _____

RAP/NAP – Strengths and Behaviours (Build and Strengthen)

1. _____
2. _____
3. _____
4. _____
5. _____

Steps to Success – using Walk your Thoughts technique

1. I will read this CAP for 5 minutes every day. _____
2. _____ ☐
3. _____ ☐
4. _____ ☐
5. _____ ☐
6. _____ ☐
7. _____ ☐
8. _____ ☐
9. _____ ☐
10. _____ ☐
11. _____ ☐
12. _____ ☐

11. Sync with Master and Aspect Action Plan (MAP/AAP)-

The last and final step of this process is to **transfer** this clarified **Goal, Target Completion Timeframe** and place it as a Goal under the Aspect Action Plan of the identified Aspect of life.

Link this CAP using a **Plan Number** - "_____".

www.ingramcontent.com/pod-product-compliance
Lightning Source LLC
Chambersburg PA
CBHW060105170426
43198CB00010B/771